Stability, Justice, and Clarity

How to Restore Social Sanity

Dennis Haugh

Stability, Justice, and Clarity

(Defiance Press & Publishing, LLC)

First Edition: 2021

Printed in the United States of America

10 9 8 7 6 5 4 3 2 1

ISBN-13: 978-1-7372522-3-8 (Paperback)
ISBN-13: 978-1-7372522-4-5 (eBook)

Published by Defiance Press and Publishing, LLC

Bulk orders of this book may be obtained by contacting Defiance Press and Publishing, LLC at: www.defiancepress.com.

Defiance Press & Publishing, LLC
281-581-9300
info@defiancepress.com

"I know no safe depository of the ultimate powers of the society but the people themselves; and if we think them not enlightened enough to exercise their control with a wholesome discretion, the remedy is not to take it from them, but to inform their discretion by education. This is the true corrective of abuses of constitutional power."

Thomas Jefferson to William Jarvis
28 Sept 1820

Dedication

To seekers of truth from all generations. The founding generation of the United States had many, and they changed the world for the better. May we emulate their inspiration and virtue, so that we might avoid Franklin's fear that our government would end in despotism due to corruption of the people. His speech at the closing of the Constitutional Convention where he expressed his fear can be found in the appendix to this publication.

Contents

Foreword

Dennis Haugh is an American patriot, experienced master computer scientist, and very concerned citizen who, like many other American citizens today, is concerned about the political structure and enduring safety and future of the United States. In this book, he reviews the classic beginnings of our republic and some of the great political and philosophical forbears whose influence forged our Constitution and ultimate way of life. He proposes that some of the foresight and wisdom of our constitutional founders has been neglected or diminished in modern times. He finds the current American political climate dangerous and neglectful of the early wisdom of our philosophical and political forbears and regrets the negative influences of the current educational structure in America. He attempts to utilize the best of our classical and constitutional heritage with suggestions for revitalizing our educational and political structures based on the wisdom of our greatest thinkers and motivated by a sophisticated and concerned love of country. If you are struggling with concerns for the current political life of our country, you may find some helpful reflections and ways forward presented here in his version of *Political Vertigo*.[1]

Dr. Malham M. Wakin (USAF Brig Gen retired)

Malham M Wakin

Colorado Springs, CO
July 2016

1 This was the original title of the first edition of this book.

Preface

As an Air Force cadet and, later, an Air Force officer, I swore an oath to protect and defend the Constitution of the United States. Being the son of a Marine gunnery sergeant who served on Guadalcanal, I would not swear such an oath unless I understood what it meant. In addition to my rigorous cadet training, I had paid attention in high school civics class. In particular, I had wondered why an Article V Convention of States had never been called. That curiosity would take me on an intense search in the National Archives that would lead to the day the Bill of Rights was introduced to the First Congress by James Madison. Along the way, I gained a lot of knowledge about the founding period and the development of the Constitution.

Like most people, I believed we had won the Cold War when the Berlin Wall came down. The exuberance of the time is captured by the song "Right Here, Right Now," by Jesus Jones. It seemed that the country hadn't a care in the world. Events would unfold that show how wrong we were.

After the Wall came down in June 1990, the first crisis to unfold was the Dot Com bubble. It had burst in March of 2000, but economic forces kept its impact at bay until 9/11. Corporate executives used 9/11 as a trigger for layoffs. The production side of the US economy was about to change forever. The age of offshoring was about to take off. Middle America would begin a downhill slide that has yet to be corrected.

At this point, many decision makers in corporate America and government looked to China as a trading partner that could help economic recovery. As a Cold-War warrior, I was always leery of this perspective, but even I wound up working with the Chinese at one point. The reality has been an exodus of opportunity from the United States. What is a new generation to do when it sees no opportunity? It looks for answers to correct the system. Unfortunately, one of the answers in contention among the latest generations has been to throw out our existing economic system and replace it with socialism.

When I realized that socialism had become cool in America, I knew I had a lot to learn about what was happening in my country. After leaving the Air Force, I had lived in the world of computer science while building muscle cars and playing guitar in heavy-metal rock bands. I was having fun sending satellites to interplanetary bodies (like Mars and Jupiter), driving in the fast lane, and playing guitar on 11. I had no idea of the world outside of those stovepipes. It was time to learn.

In addition to reading a long list of books, I listened to audiobooks during my long daily commutes to Lockheed Martin. The Article V Convention of States project seemed interesting. I was puzzled by the vehement positions that many had against the idea of the people exercising our constitutional power to counter-balance government power. So, I started writing white papers in an attempt to better explain the process and why the framers thought it was imperative to include it in the Constitution.

Over time, it became apparent that the nation was not ready for a Convention of States, but that didn't mean it wasn't ready for a better understanding of the foundations of civics. The result was the first version of this book, entitled *Political Vertigo*. The title came about because I firmly believe that the left-right political spectrum is horribly flawed and a source of many misunderstandings and division. (I was definitely not the first person to have this view. Although I didn't know this while writing the first version, Ronald Reagan took the same position in his speech "A Time for Choosing" at the 1964 GOP Convention.) As a result, the initial working title for the book was *Vertical Politics*. Fighter pilots tend to lose their hearing. When I told my classmate, Ron Scott, he misheard "Vertigo Politics." As I continued working on the book, he continued to press the title. Finally, I gave up, and said "how about *Political Vertigo*?" It's a snappy title, but sadly it doesn't really explain what the book is about. Worse, having "political" in the title tends to suggest a partisan work—which it is not. In the process of writing, it became apparent that I was making good on my military oath to defend the Constitution.

This book evolved from the concept that there must be equilibrium between the governed and the government. Using the principles in the Constitution, Part 2 was written first to explain how to achieve that equilibrium. Part 1 was written next to guide through the fundamentals that the founding generation understood implicitly. But the book would have been incomplete by assuming that the tether of the Constitution will remain intact. Part 3 explores the potential impacts of a nation divorcing itself from a limiting, written Constitution. Throughout the book, I kept coming back to Madison's mortal diseases of instability, injustice and confusion. Equilibrium is stability within a dynamic environment. As Aristotle wrote, a common sense of justice is necessary for civil society to bond and maintain its bond. Confusing society's common sense of values destroys equilibrium. The choice has always been up to the living generations. Prior generations understood the wisdom of the constitutional tether. To all those who desire untethering, I can only say, "be careful what you wish for." Do you really think the US will remain stable without it? Do you really believe justice is served by *social justice*? Do you believe that clarity is enhanced by "one-party democracy?"

Acknowledgments

I would not have been able to complete this book had it not been for my lovely, long-suffering wife, Ginny. She has had to endure countless discussions about the topics herein. Not only has she tolerated me and plunked food in front of me while I sat at the computer in a vegetative state, but she has also been the primary reviewer of this entire book. Through years of Checkered Past rehearsal ("at 11") and gigs in dive bars (and some halfway decent ones), after twenty-three years of bleeding expenses restoring a 1969 Pontiac GTO Judge convertible, and now after a year of writing this book, she still talks to me. She is truly a saint. Her patience is legend.

My good friend, USAFA class president, retired Air Force Colonel, combat veteran, and all-around great guy, Dr. Ron Scott was my prime sounding board on many ideas in this publication. I became one of his informal doctorate students while writing this manuscript. It took Ron some time, but he convinced me of the book's original title and of the throwback to Alfred Hitchcock's *Vertigo*. Hopefully the new title is an improvement.

Dave Morgan is a peer software architect at Harris. In a previous life, he delivered pizzas to my house—setting land-speed records in the process. He's a polymath, who provided many hours of discussion that improved ideas contained within this work. Being more than a drummer who beats his instrument, he inspired many ideas, including details on the book cover. In fact, he taught me a lot about graphic design in the process.

My older brother, Jim, endured reading the initial Internet electrons of this publication despite being a Luddite. His brutally honest assessments were always valuable. As a sibling-rival, he has no peer.

My good friend and USAFA classmate, Col Sam Grier, PhD, provided more brutal honesty in reviewing this work while working at The Hague for MITRE. Sam has been the Dean of the NATO War College and writes spy thriller fiction.

Special thanks to Dr. Malham Wakin, (USAF Brig Gen retired). Like many from the first fifty years of "The Long Blue Line,"[2] he has long been my philosophical mentor. I am indebted to him for the time he took in reviewing and improving this book. He is one of the most inspirational and intelligent men that any cadet at the Air Force Academy could have had for a role model and mentor.

2 USAF Academy graduates. See glossary.

Part 1

The Fundamentals

Introduction

It has been said that the definition of insanity is expecting a different outcome from the same actions. In a country that is ruled by self-governance, we should consider that perhaps "We the People" are the problem. No small segment of the population can cure what ails the United States. It will take an alliance of freethinking individuals working together.

Most people know what they want, but do they know what's good for them? At its core, the theory behind democratic rule is that they do. History begs to differ. Of course, history is also replete with examples of other forms of government that are even worse. As Winston Churchill put it, "Indeed, it has been said that democracy is the worst form of government except all those other forms that have been tried from time to time."[3]

The founders of the United States struggled with a number of foundational issues that would make the modern-day American's eyes roll back into his or her head. Bluntly, we are the victims of our own success. To be more accurate, we are the victims of our predecessors' success. We shouldn't take credit for their success, but we *should* take responsibility for our failures.

Today's technology is wondrous, and we profit mightily from it. Men like Ben Franklin and Thomas Jefferson would be fascinated but probably not all that astounded by our achievements. They would also be pleased to see how tech-savvy most people have become. And they would probably take to our devices like ducks to water. On the other hand, they would be distraught over the lack of critical thinking and the devolution of society's cohesion.

---

3 Winston Churchill, "Speech about Parliament Bill NC Deb 11" (speech, Parliament Bill NC Deb 11, London, November 11, 1947). In *The Official Report, House of Commons*. 5th series. Vol. 444, 207.

Consider that wonder of ingenuity that coupled high mobility with independence—the car. There really aren't many people who could *build* a car from scratch, but almost everyone knows how to *drive* one. Self-reliant Americans of previous generations also knew how to properly *maintain* and *repair* these vehicles themselves. Today the extent of maintenance knowledge most people have is the mileage at which to take the car back to the dealership for required maintenance—if that. If the car breaks down, they only know to use their cell phones to call for a tow. This complacence is technological dependence. Even worse than the lack of knowledge about maintaining the things we own is our throwaway society. We can update the analogy of the car with the smartphone, which has a life expectancy of a couple of years. Youth today are lauded for their technical prowess, but they really only know how to *use* smartphones efficiently. How many of them know how to *make* a smartphone? Using a device is consumption. Knowing just how to consume is not only technological dependence but also economic dependence.

We are guilty of the same dependence with respect to self-governance. We have forgotten how to *maintain* and *repair* our system of governance. It took five millennia for mankind to put together the understanding of how to effectively and efficiently elevate the human condition to the standards (both technological and governmental) we saw at the end of the twentieth century. Even as our technology advances, our governments degenerate. The ancient Greeks observed this degeneration of self-rule to tyranny as a "cycle" (κύκλος).[4] The founders were well educated about government and history. They knew that only a properly educated electorate would avoid the demagoguery that deteriorates democracy.[5]

To avoid demagoguery, every thought should stand on its own merit—independent of who voices it.[6] We disrespect one another as

---

4 "Kyklos," digplanet, accessed July 06, 2016, http://www.digplanet.com/wiki/Kyklos.

5 Aristotle, *Politics*, Book 5, section 1310a. Accessed July 27, 2016. http://www.perseus.tufts.edu/hopper/text?doc=Perseus:text:1999.01.0058:book=5:section=1310a.

6 Ibid.

human beings when we evaluate the person instead of the thought. Our goal in this manuscript is to address the foundational knowledge necessary to repair and maintain our system of government in today's fast-paced world.

The political landscape is typically viewed horizontally, with a left-right axis as shown below in figure 1.[7] This particular figure shows much more than the typical view of left and right.[8] Of particular interest is that it shows totalitarian dictatorships as common to both the extreme left and extreme right. This really exposes that the typical view of the political spectrum is better viewed as a ring rather than a simple horizontal axis. There is no beginning or end to a ring, so left and right should be clockwise and counterclockwise.

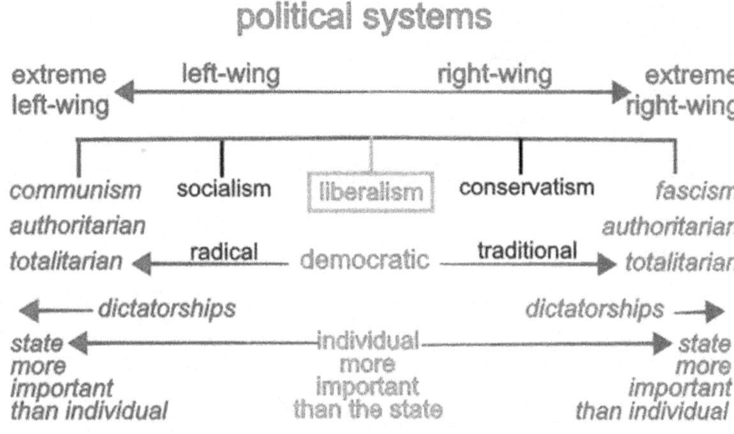

Figure 1 Left-Right Political Spectrum

7 "Politics: What Is the Difference Between Conservative, Liberal, Centrist, Leftist, Right Wing Parties in the Modern World?" Amit Sinha, Quora, accessed July 9, 2016, https://www.quora.com/Politics-What-is-the-difference-between-Conservative-Liberal-Centrist-Leftist-Right-Wing-Parties-in-the-modern-world.

8 This is not to ignore the existence of models like the Political Compass, the Nolan Chart, or the Pournelle Chart.

Is there a real difference between the extreme right and left? Once we start down the path of answering that question, we start to see that the left-right dichotomy totally breaks down. What we are really doing with the various labels (communism, socialism, liberalism, conservatism, and fascism) is best represented by a Venn diagram because it really represents sets of like-minded people on an assortment of unrelated issues. There is no legitimate ordering of the issues or the people. The left-right model tries to simplify a more complicated landscape. This leads to disorientation in our understanding of politics—like *vertigo.*

We can alleviate confusion by simplifying the model to one all-important issue and rotating the axis ninety degrees to vertical. The issue to consider is whether the faction is promoting governance that is top-down or bottom-up. The results may be surprising once the currently perceived ordering is removed. Tyranny, oligarchy, and totalitarianism are top-down governments. Republics and democracies are bottom-up governments. This simple change of perspective clarifies the true nature of each political faction. Doing so changes the first question from which side wins on any of the contentious issues to whether the issue should be decided on a national level or a local level—or by law or social norm. This forces us to approach issues from the perspective of the founders. We may indeed have different answers from theirs, but the results will be more stable for society.

About This Book

This book is divided into three parts. The target audience is any American who wants to repair and maintain our government "of, by, and for the people,"[9] so that it "shall not perish from the earth."

Part 1 is a *CliffsNotes* compilation of building blocks for any governing system. Each chapter introduces a topic that is foundational to political thought. The chapters are short but introduce key concepts while avoiding deep theory. They can be read independently, because

9 Borrowed from Abraham Lincoln's Gettysburg Address.

they provide different perspectives, like the fable of the blind men and the elephant.[10] Taken together, they provide a more complete picture of objective political thought that can be used as a tool by any citizen.

Part 2 focuses solely on the US Constitution. The Constitution was designed to protect "We the People" from a strong central government while correcting some flaws in the Articles of Confederation. The history of the United States is riddled with attempts to weaken or remove protections provided by the Constitution. Some have been successful. If the Constitution is to fulfill its role of protecting citizens' rights against a central government, it must be repaired and maintained.

Part 3 addresses current problems in need of repair, independent of the Constitution. Older theories are still applicable, but some newer tools from Part 1 are incorporated as well. The scientific method is a great problem-solving technique, but human behavior can mess up the process. Society is a complex system composed of individuals who do not always react rationally. They have emotions that can cause instability. William Strauss and Neil Howe developed a generational theory that recognizes "mood eras" that result cyclically from crises.[11] There can be no doubt that reason must prevail in order to maintain or restore stability. Solutions need to consider 1) avoiding harm to individuals in the short term, 2) avoiding systemic collapse in the intermediate-term, and 3) establishing equilibrium in the long term.

---

10 "Elephant and the Blind Men," Jainworld, accessed July 06, 2016, http://www.jainworld.com/literature/story25.htm.

11 William Strauss and Neil Howe, *The Fourth Turning: An American Prophecy* (New York: Broadway Books, 1997), 1–6.

1

Foundations

Maintenance and repair require a rudimentary knowledge of how something works. A building requires a solid foundation on which to stand. The same is true for a nation. Civil society is an important concept that goes back to Aristotle.[12] It is the foundation of any nation.

Civil Society

The term "civil society" will be used to refer to the cooperative association of a people independent of the government. With this view in mind, government has no existence on its own. It requires the existence of a civil society. If society fractures, the government cannot endure. It may impose force to keep society under its control for a time, but it will eventually fail. On the other hand, civil society can rid itself of the government or replace it at any time.[13] Society has static and dynamic components. These components interact with certain characteristics.

Cohesion

Common interests bind society from the bottom up. These common interests can be viewed as starting with the second level of Maslow's hierarchy of needs: safety. When the members of society no longer believe they are benefiting from the relationship, society disintegrates. In *Currency Wars*, the economist James Rickards[14] repeats the findings of historian Joseph Tainter. Tainter's study revealed that the true reason the Roman Empire collapsed was because of a fracture in society. The farmers in the outlying areas felt they got a better deal from the invading

12 Aristotle, *Politics*, Book 2, section 1272b. Aristotle uses "τὴν πολιτικὴν κοινωνίαν" (literally, "the social community").

13 I like to envision peasants with pitchforks and torches at night attacking the keep.

14 James Rickards, *Currency Wars: The Making of the Next Global Crisis* (New York: Penguin Group, 2012), 142–143.

barbarians.[15] Ravenna (the capital at the time) was overtaxing them with little or no benefit in return.

Aristotle compares civil society to a stream.[16] At any point in time, the actual water molecules are different from the ones that flowed through it earlier. As he notes, the same is true of the members of a civil society. At any instant, there are fundamentally four generations that comprise a society. Three may participate in governance; the fourth is not fully educated. As time proceeds, experiences and education affect the composition. Strauss and Howe have laid out this phenomenon in their generational theory.[17]

Civil society is a complex system in which its cohesion can be challenged from within as well as from the outside. The coming of age of a new generation may challenge cohesion just because that generation despises the foundational principles that bind the society. The role of education is to avoid this scenario.[18] As Abraham Lincoln put it, "A house divided against itself cannot stand."[19]

Security

As mentioned above, safety is the primal motivation for society to form. First, the family works together for the basic needs of food and shelter. Societies themselves then form by a bottom-up process where families unite to assist one another in gaining a better standard of living, starting with better security.

---

15 Joseph A. Tainter, *The Collapse of Complex Societies* (Cambridge, MA: University of Cambridge Press, 1988), 128–152.

16 Aristotle, *Politics*, Book 3, section 1276a.

17 William Strauss and Neil Howe, *Generations: The History of America's Future, 1584 to 2069* (New York: William Morrow & Company, 1991).

18 Aristotle, *Politics*, Book 5 section 1310a.

19 Abraham Lincoln, "Speech to the Republican State Convention" (speech, Springfield, Illinois, June 16, 1858).

Justice

A common sense of justice is widely acknowledged to be an essential ingredient of any civil society. Most political thinkers, from Socrates to contemporaries like Thomas Sowell, start with this essential element as a cornerstone of society.[20]

Fracturing the common sense of justice is—in a very real sense—a compromise of the very foundation of society. It is therefore a primary goal of education to instill in the next generation a consistent sense of justice. [21]

Economy

Some form of trade and economic interaction that results in mutual benefit is necessary to sustain mutual advantage. At its core, an economy has producers and consumers. Each member of society is both a producer and a consumer. Each gains the advantage of more available products than he or she could produce individually. As a producer, he or she is rewarded based on the merit of those products. The key to a good economy is a balance between production and consumption.

This is the most dynamic element of civil society. Orderly economic activity requires rules of exchange and property ownership. Execution of these rules is a key element of a sense of justice.

Institutions

Civil society is analogous to an anthill where there is nonstop activity. The dynamic nature of society cannot help but stress its cohesion by repeatedly testing justice and economic activity. In order to stabilize the activity and bolster cohesion, civil societies create institutions. Institutions include an educational system, some form of banking, and a legal system. Rising out of the legal system is the ultimate institution of civil society—government.

---

20 Sowell, Thomas. *The Quest for Cosmic Justice*. New York: Simon & Schuster, 2002.
21 Aristotle, *Politics*, Book 8, section 1337a.

Government

Thinkers have long pondered how to improve government. The foundation of government in the Western world traces its roots to ancient Greece and the Roman Republic. The founders of the United States studied these sources, as well as their own Anglo-Saxon heritage. The distance in time since these systems existed makes them ideal for objective study. By studying these systems without personal bias, we can better understand cause and effect with respect to governance. This is what the founders did.

Aristotle's Insights

As stated in the introduction, every thought should stand on its own merit. The sheer number of concepts and thoughts we inherited from the ancient Greeks is astounding and should not be overlooked. None was as prolific as Aristotle. His genius dominated the world of thought up to the Age of Enlightenment as both a blessing and a curse. He was wrong about a lot, but he was right about even more.[22] Thanks to his keen insights into human nature, the foundation he laid for political thought endures. Even more astounding is his implicit understanding of the nature of complex systems (which is covered later) millennia before the theory was developed. He innately understood that complex systems produce nonlinear results and that the whole system is greater than the sum of the parts.[23] If we look abstractly at his general promotion of the golden mean, it is a strategy to avoid instability in a complex system.

Most political writers promote an agenda. According to Plato, Socrates believed that the only good government could be one that is run entirely by philosophers. In Plato's *Republic,* Kallipolis (Καλλίπολις)

---

22 Paul Strathern, *Aristotle in 90 Minutes* (Lanham, MD: Ivan R. Dee, 1996).

23 Aristotle, *Politics*, Book 1, section 1253a. He uses the whole body versus parts of the body in a number of places.

resembled a communist state run by philosopher-kings.[24] Plato's student Aristotle took a different perspective. Aristotle studied every government in the known world at the time. Rather than develop a theory out of thin air, he dissected these governments and developed a unified theory of good and bad government based on empirical results.

It is important to take note of a key element in Aristotle's thinking that is not normally emphasized. He sees a difference between theoretical perfection and what is humanly attainable—in all matters. He talks often about the "perfect constitution" as a reference only. He spends much more time talking about human approximations in practice.

Aristotle starts his analysis by considering the household and the relationships among the various members. The core element is the relative "virtues"[25] of the various occupants and their relationships with respect to "household management."[26] His fundamental conclusion is that a well-run household will fit the characteristics of all members and promote the common good. He then extrapolates this to the nature of the relationship between government and civil society.[27] In short, a well-run government fits the society.

---

24 "Plato's Ethics and Politics in *The Republic*," Eric Brown, Stanford Encyclopedia of Philosophy, accessed June 30, 2016.

25 Aristotle, *Politics*, Book 1, section 1259b. The word "virtue" is perhaps a little too vague in its meaning. ἀρετή ('arete') definitely implies unselfishness and a commitment to excellence. Carmen Sánchez-Mañas has done an extensive analysis. See Carmen Sánchez-Mañas. "Excellence: Tyrtaeus' Own View. A Literary Analysis of Fragment 9 | Sánchez-Mañas | Erga-Logoi. Rivista Di Storia, Letteratura, Diritto E Culture Dell'antichità." Excellence: Tyrtaeus' Own View. A Literary Analysis of Fragment 9 | Sánchez-Mañas | Erga-Logoi. Rivista Di Storia, Letteratura, Diritto E Culture Dell'antichità. Accessed July 27, 2016. http://www.ledonline.it/index.php/Erga-Logoi/article/view/448/0.

26 Aristotle, Politics, Book 1, section 1259b. Accessed July 27, 2016. http://www.perseus.tufts.edu/hopper/text?doc=Perseus:text:1999.01.0058:book. (οἰκονομίας)

27 This is intentionally condensed to skip to the conclusion.

In Book 3, he first divides governments into two categories: 1) congruent[28] with the good of society and 2) incongruent[29] with the good of society. The incongruent forms cater to specific segments rather than society as a whole. He then creates a six-way classification of governments by considering the number of people who rule, whether one, some, or many. The following table represents his categories.

Table 1 Aristotle's Taxonomy

	One Rules	**Some Rule**	**Many Rule**
Congruent	monarchy	aristocracy	republic
Incongruent	tyranny	oligarchy	democracy

The forms of government in the first row are differentiated by the fact that they assist in the cohesion of civil society by looking after the interests of the entire society. They enhance cohesion by a consistent application of justice and a positive approach to economy.[30] They fit a good society. Those in the second row, on the other hand, may be inconsistent in their application of justice and may suppress the economy. Laws may be improper. Tyranny and oligarchy tend to favor the rich. Democracies tend to favor the indigent (and potentially the rich) at the expense of the

28 The usual translation of ὀρθάς is "good." The Perseus Project uses "right constitution" instead of "congruent." For the original Greek, see the Perseus Project, http://www.perseus.tufts.edu/hopper/text?doc=Perseus:text:1999.01.0058:book=3:section=1282b&highlight=right.

29 The usual translation of παρεκβεβηκυίας is "perverted," but this is not an entirely accurate translation. The Perseus project uses "divergent" as opposed to "incongruent." For the original Greek, see the Perseus Project, http://www.perseus.tufts.edu/hopper/text?doc=Perseus:text:1999.01.0058:book=3:section=1282b&highlight=divergent.

30 Note the similarity to Adam Smith in *Wealth of Nations*: "Little else is requisite to carry a state to the highest degree of opulence from the lowest barbarism, but peace, easy taxes, and a tolerable administration of justice; all the rest being brought about by the natural course of things." From the class notes of Dugald Stuart in 1755. "Online Library of Liberty." Adam Smith on the Need for "peace, Easy Taxes, and a Tolerable Administration of Justice" (1755) -. Accessed July 28, 2016. http://oll.libertyfund.org/quote/436.

middle class. Where there is a lack of fit, these governments threaten the society's cohesion.

Aristotle goes on to consider the nature of these classes vertically as well. In general, the fewer virtuous members of society, the more to the left of the table the government needs to be to fit that society. The greater the number of virtuous members, the greater the number of people within society that are able to rule. This, then, is the source of the adage that "the people get the government they deserve." Naturally, with Aristotle being a Greek, he concludes that only Greeks are virtuous enough for self-governance (the right-hand column). Another point of view on this is that: 1) monarchy depends on the virtue of the single ruler, 2) oligarchy depends on the virtue of the ruling class, and 3) democracies depend on the virtue of the whole of society. This last point was up front in the minds of the United States' founders. Aristotle considers tyranny to be the worst form of government and democracy to be the least bad of those in the second row.[31] He considers what we now call a republic the best form of government.

Complete coverage of Aristotle's *Politics* is beyond our scope here, but we need to mention that he does not just consider these pure forms of government. In Book 4, he describes a continuum where the systems mix these pure forms. In particular, he does a case study of three political systems that are considered good throughout the Greek world. It should be pointed out that he studies every known system from Africa to Europe to Persia to India. The three he chooses to expound on are 1) Sparta, 2) Crete, and 3) Carthage. In his analysis, he ruthlessly points out their weaknesses but also their strengths. He stresses that all three of these "good" systems have elements of monarchy, oligarchy, and democracy.[32] We would recognize these in two of the three branches of the US government—the executive (monarchy), the Senate (oligarchic), and the House of Representatives (democratic). The US system of

31 Aristotle, *Politics*, Book 4, section 1289b.

32 Outside of defining the pure forms of government, Aristotle tends to use "oligarchy" generically for "rule by some" and "democracy" for "rule of many," without the value judgment of congruence or incongruence.

government is built on these principles. Our judicial branch evolved out of later Anglo-Saxon tradition. Courts in ancient Greece were entirely different from ours.

Book 5 discusses why governments fail and how to preserve them. As stated previously, Aristotle sees the distinction between perfection that is theoretical and that which is achievable by man. His concept of justice is consistent with this. He recognizes that no man-made government could ever achieve what he calls "absolute justice." The perception of injustice is the primary cause of collapse. He relates the difficulty with comparing the qualitative concept of justice to the quantitative concept of equality. He uses the *linear* example that three exceeds two and that two exceeds one equally (by one). His *proportional* example is that four divided by two and two divided by one are both two.[33] He explains that the difficulty of selecting either can be a source of instability and collapse. This is the innate understanding of complex systems shown in his reasoning. He sees that stability is best achieved by avoiding the extremes of avarice or envy (the golden mean). The rich are prone to avarice and the poor to envy. He calls the middle class "the best" for being prone to neither.

Aristotle identifies the following keys to a stable society:

- **Justice:** The smallest transgression can lead to collapse. Flatterers in an oligarchy promote division and instability for self-gain. Demagogues do the same by flattering the people in a democracy.[34] Where the rule of law does not apply, demagogues rise.[35]
- **The middle class:** He recognizes the middle class as "the best."[36] They are neither envious like the poor nor avaricious like the rich. They blunt the enmity between the rich and the poor. In addition, they do not shrink from duty. He believes that

33 Aristotle, *Politics*, Book 5 section 1301b.
34 Ibid., Book 5, section 1310a and 1313b.
35 Ibid., Book 4, section 1292a.
36 Ibid., Book 4, section 1295b.

they should be as large as either of the other two but preferably larger than both combined.

- **Education:** Aristotle innately knows the importance of handling generational turns properly. The first goal of the educational system should be perpetuating the cohesion of civil society[37]—the sense of justice being the most important.
- **Rotation of office:** That's right. The founders of the United States did not invent this concept. Aristotle recognizes it as promoting a sense of justice and community. He advocates six-month terms.[38]
- **No profit from office:** We hear about campaign finance reform all the time. Aristotle states that allowing officials to profit should not be permitted.[39]

John Locke's Influence

The cornerstone theory behind the United States is the concept of "natural law," a product of the Age of Enlightenment. Thomas Hobbes and John Locke were two of the more influential writers of the Enlightenment. The founders definitely preferred Locke's optimistic view, but they frequently referred to Hobbes's leviathan[40] as an ever-present threat.

Locke's position was that we all have three natural rights: 1) life, 2) liberty,[41] and 3) property.[42] They are unique in that we have them without the involvement of anyone else. Liberty is a right, and freedom is a state. Both are constrained by the legitimate contextual laws—whether in a state of nature or civil society. This is a foundational meaning used by the

37 Ibid., Book 5, section 1301a and Book 8, section 1337a.

38 Ibid., Book 5, section 1308a.

39 Ibid., Book 5, section 1308b.

40 Thomas Hobbes. *Leviathan: Or the Matter, Forme and Power of a Commonwealth Ecclasiasticall and Civil* (Mineola, NY: Dover Publications, 2009). Originally published by Andrew Crooke in 1651.

41 Aristotle has a different view, believing that some men are slaves by nature. See *Politics*, Book 1, section 1255b.

42 John Locke, *Two Treatises of Government*, (New Haven, CT: Yale University Press, 2003). pp. 100-121.

framers of the Declaration of Independence. One was free to do as he or she wished within the confines of just law.

The foundation of Locke's thinking about property is that every individual *owns* himself or herself. Therefore, each owns his or her own labor. Man must eat to sustain life. In a state of nature, where everyone is free and equal, an apple on a tree is sustenance. His conclusion is that the apple becomes the person's property when it is picked because his or her labor is mixed with the fruit. The key factors in his right to property are that 1) he or she does not have to get permission from everyone in the world to take from "the common" and 2) that he or she leaves "at least where there is enough, and as good, left in common for others."[43]

Locke's influence on the founders shows through in their position on revolution. Madison's position on secession highlights that the generation held revolution in high regard. Unlike Aristotle, Locke's agenda was to justify overthrowing the English king. He is often quoted as stating that the people have a "right, if not an outright obligation"[44] to resist the authority of a tyrant. Madison believed that secession was appropriate for a state if it was responding to tyranny. The founding generation was concerned about the "tyranny of the majority."[45]

Defense

The most essential role of government is to protect society. There is no society or government without defense. Aristotle considers the

---

43 Ibid. See the second treatise, chapter 5, section 27.

44 Friend, Celeste. "Internet Encyclopedia of Philosophy." Internet Encyclopedia of Philosophy. Accessed July 28, 2016. http://www.iep.utm.edu/soc-cont/#SH2b.

45 John Adams. "A Defence of the Constitutions of Government of the United States of America: Against the Attack of M. Turgot in His Letter to Dr. Price, Dated the Twenty-second Day of March, 1778." A Defence of the Constitutions of Government of the United States of America: Against the Attack of M. Turgot in His Letter to Dr. Price, Dated the Twenty-second Day of March, 1778." pg. 291. Accessed July 28, 2016. https://archive.org/stream/defenceofconstit03adamrich#page/290/mode/2up/search/majority.

military to be essential if a nation is not to be "the slave of every invader."[46] John Locke considers not just national defense but also self-defense and society's defense against tyranny:

> Must men alone be debarred the common privilege of opposing force with force, which Nature allows so freely to all other creatures for their preservation from injury? I answer: Self-defence is a part of the law of Nature; nor can it be denied the community, even against the king himself; but to revenge themselves upon him must, by no means, be allowed them, it being not agreeable to that law. Wherefore, if the king shall show an hatred, not only to some particular persons, but sets himself against the body of the commonwealth, whereof he is the head, and shall, with intolerable ill-usage, cruelly tyrannise over the whole, or a considerable part of the people; in this case the people have a right to resist and defend themselves from injury; but it must be with this caution, that they only defend themselves, but do not attack their prince.[47]

This is why the US military swears an oath to protect and defend the Constitution against "all enemies, foreign and *domestic*." (italics added)[48] The oath is not to the presidency or to the national government, if either disobeys the Constitution.

Justice

Government's secondary role as an institution of society is to administer justice. The alignment of this administration with the common sense of justice is crucial to whether a government is congruent or incongruent. A government that violates the society's sense of justice is incongruent and subject to overthrow. Government can only strive for Aristotle's perfect justice because man is imperfect.

---

46 Aristotle, *Politics*, Book 4, section 1291a.

47 Locke, *Two Treatises of Government.* See the second treatise, chapter 19, section 233.

48 "ARMY.MIL Features." Oath of Enlistment. Accessed July 28, 2016. https://www.army.mil/values/oath.html.

Economy

The economy is the most dynamic element of society. Government is not an economic producer, but it can be a consumer. Two intersections of government with economy are unavoidable.

First, government's role in administering justice requires ensuring that trade is fair. By necessity, the government must reactively respond to unfair trade practices. On the other hand, regulation is the proactive administration of justice in trade. Regulation is unnecessary if society is well behaved. The less the government trusts its citizens, the more it will regulate. Congruence is determined by how well its laws and regulations match society's sense of justice.

The second means by which government affects the economy is in taxation. Taxation is an unavoidable overhead on the economy. Taxation can be made on either the producer or the consumer side of the economy. If taxation is balanced between production and consumption, it can be transparent in terms of influence. Emphasis on either will discourage that side of the economic model.

2

Importance of Language

Languages are how we express thoughts and concepts. They are dynamic. The use or meaning of a word can change in less than a generation, and the cumulative change can be dramatic over the course of several generations. This is true of all languages. Analysis of the language's original meaning is important to understand the author's true meaning.

As a simple example, consider the date within a month. Today we say "the fifteenth of the month." In 1787, they would have stated "the fifteenth instant."[49] In 44 BC, Julius Caesar was warned about "the Ides of March."[50]

Significance of English Dynamics

An American who reads the Constitution literally in good faith will understand a large percentage of it without further reference. However, sometimes this is not enough to avoid misinterpretation of founding documents because English has moved in two centuries. The website http://www.usconstitution.net/ does an excellent job of hypertexting key word differences between today and 1787.

Unfortunately, there are people who purposefully misinterpret the language. Worse, some of these misinterpretations come from the courts. Responsible citizenship should not abide misinterpretations.

49 George H. Smith and Wendy McIlroy, *The Federalist Papers*, Audible (unabridged) (Nashville, TN: Carmichael & Carmichael, 1986).

50 Plutarch. "P443 The Life of Julius Caesar." Plutarch • Life of Caesar. 1919. Accessed July 28, 2016. http://penelope.uchicago.edu/Thayer/E/Roman/Texts/Plutarch/Lives/Caesar*.html#63.

"Life, liberty, and the pursuit of happiness" implies specific meanings that elude most Americans. I covered the specific meaning of "liberty" in the section on John Locke. Likewise, "pursuit of happiness"[51] meant something very specific when Jefferson penned it. I cover this in my discussion of the Declaration of Independence in the chapter on the founding.

The term "direct tax" in the Constitution actually dates back to Thucydides' coverage of the Peloponnesian War. In *The Original Constitution: What It Actually Said and Meant*, Robert G. Natelson has a concise discussion of direct taxation.[52] It is fundamentally a tax on productive elements of society or a capitation tax (e.g., income tax). An indirect tax is essentially a tax on consumption.

Interpretation of the Constitution is not only subject to our understanding of specific words. It is also subject to abstraction. As Aristotle puts it, "It is impossible to frame a constitution in detail. It must be general, but our actions are specific."[53] This has given rise to two schools of interpretation: 1) strict construction and 2) Woodrow Wilson's "living Constitution."[54] The former faithfully attempts to understand the intent of the founders. It requires research into original source material from private letters, the Convention, and ratification debates. Natelson's research provides solid coverage of the topic. The latter has its roots in Hamilton's doctrine of discretionary powers. The intent of discretionary powers is to bypass the main goal of the Constitution—limited government. Aristotle would recognize the danger of this latter doctrine

51 "Lexical Investigations: Happiness," Dictionary.com, accessed July 06, 2016, http://blog.dictionary.com/happiness.

52 R. G. Natelson, *The Original Constitution: What It Actually Said and Meant* (Los Angeles, CA.: Tenth Amendment Center, 2011). 116, 159–161.

53 Aristotle, *Politics*, Book 2, section 1269a.

54 Ronald J. Pestritto, *Woodrow Wilson and the Roots of Modern Liberalism* (Lanham, MD: Rowman & Littlefield Publishers, 2005), 12.

to the core principles of limiting the national government.[55] It opens the door to instability.[56]

Significant Meanings from Ancient Greek

Lawyers stress the importance of understanding Latin in understanding our legal system. There are two very good reasons for this. The first is that our legal system has its roots in Roman law. Terms like "sub-rosa" (Latin for "under the rose") come from the Roman convention that nothing was to be repeated outside of a room where a rose had been put above the doorway. Second, Latin is a dead language, meaning it has not moved as described above. That is not true of Greek. A full understanding of Aristotle requires understanding some nuances in Greek as opposed to the words' English translations. These terms are translated as "virtue", "right", and "deviant."

Democracy

Aristotle does not use a special label for what we call a "republic." He uses the word that is sometimes translated as "polity" or "constitutional government."[57] Aristotle's republic differs from Plato's philosopher-kings in that he disagrees that the rulers have to be philosophers. He considers the middle class the best of the three classes and the one that would govern most wisely. A republic depends on a large middle class.[58] In his view, the term "democracy" was used in earlier times when the middle class was not big enough to balance the rich and poor. As the middle class grew, it was better able to balance between oligarchy (the rich) and democracy (the poor), enabling a new constitutional form of government.[59] The founders of the United States embraced this philosophy and developed a system that encouraged the growth of the middle class.

---

55 Aristotle, *Politics*, Book 2, section 1269a. Aristotle encourages great caution in modifying a constitution.

56 See my discussion of complexity theory in the next chapter.

57 Aristotle, *Politics*, Book 4, section 1289b. The actual Greek used is πολιτεία. He also refers to this as the "best."

58 Ibid., Book 4, section 1297b.

59 Ibid., Book 4, section 1293b.

A century and a half after Aristotle, Polybius[60] used the term "ochlocracy" where Aristotle used "democracy."[61] "Ochlo" translates literally to "mob." This term probably expresses the classification more accurately. Unfortunately, Polybius then uses "democracy" where Aristotle uses "polity" (republic). Why the difference? A few possible answers relate to the Greek language itself. First, the meaning of terms in a language can change a lot in 150 years. Second, Polybius was an Achaean born in Arcadia and spoke Doric Greek. Aristotle was born in Stagira, Chalcidice, and was an Ionic Greek. The Academy and Lyceum were near Athens, where the Attic version of Ionic Greek was spoken. The difference could have merely been in dialectic idiom.

Another reason why Aristotle considers "democracy" incongruent is that the Athenians referred to their form of government as democracy. Aristotle sees Athenian government as unstable. It had yielded to tyranny and oligarchy. In particular, he does not approve of their practice of what the English-speaking world calls the "tall poppy syndrome,"[62] which is an oligarchic policy whereby the government eliminates the best people from society. Aristotle relates the story of Thrasybulus of Corinth sending a herald to Periander of Miletus for advice. Periander says nothing but proceeds to a cornfield where he hacks all the stalks to level. Thrasybulus knows that the advice means to eliminate the best citizens.[63] Athens had a policy of ostracizing at least one citizen yearly. As human nature would have it, the most prominent citizens were usually the ones ostracized. Themistocles, the victor at Salamis, was ostracized, and he spent his last years in the court of his archenemy, King Xerxes of Persia.[64] The Athenians even ostracized the historian Thucydides.

---

60 Greek who served as a Roman historian during the second century BC.

61 "Polybius, *Histories*: The Rotation of Polities," Perseus Project, accessed March 29, 2008, http://www.perseus.tufts.edu/hopper/text?doc=Perseus%3Atext%3A1999.01.0234%3Abook%3D6%3Achapter%3D4.

62 "Tall Poppy Syndrome," *Wikipedia*, https://en.wikipedia.org/wiki/Tall_poppy_syndrome.

63 Aristotle, *Politics*, Book 3, section 1284a.

64 Sara Forsdyke, *Exile, Ostracism, and Democracy: The Politics of Expulsion in Ancient Greece* (Princeton, NJ: Princeton University Press, 2005), 11.

Virtue

The Greek word ἀρετή is conceptually somewhat different from our understanding of the English word "virtue." English thinking considers the *absolute* moral issue of virtue or vice. The Greek term is *relative.* From Aristotle's *Nicomachean Ethics*, "At the right times, about the right things, toward the right people, for the right end, and in the right way, is the intermediate and best condition, and this is proper to virtue."[65] Most of Book 1 of *Politics* echoes the same golden mean concept where virtue is *relative* to the *role*. That is, it is virtuous to be the best human being for one's role in life.

As an example of how this thinking diverges from our own, consider courage. A real event in history is the story of Aristodemus. He was the only one of the three hundred Spartiatai at Thermopylai who actually survived because he was ordered home by Leonidas before the end came. Upon returning to Sparta, he was shunned as a coward. No one would "give him fire"—a uniquely Spartan standard. One year later, he broke ranks, charged the Persians at Plataia in front of the phalanx, and was summarily killed. He was not considered a hero. To Greek (not just Spartan) thinking, he was guilty of excess (recklessness), not courage. He took a useful shield from the phalanx. Most Americans today would probably consider his actions the virtue of courage.

Carmen Sánchez-Mañas does a deep analysis of ἀρετή in *Excellence: Tyrtaeus' Own View. A Literary Analysis of Fragment 9.* The subject of the investigation is Tyrtaeus' Spartan poem where the author actually defines the word. Her conclusion is that the term (in Laconic Doric) implies military excellence, oriented to the common good with courage and honor. Of course, Tyrtaeus was a Spartan, so the relative meaning is consistent with Aristotle's use. The US Air Force's core values of

65 It is interesting to note that Aristotle has hit on two key differentiators between "leader" and "manager" in today's thinking on the subject. A leader is concerned about doing the right thing. Managers are concerned about doing the thing right. An "excellent man" (or woman), then, needs to be capable of leadership and management.

"Integrity First, Service before Self, Excellence in All We Do" captures the Doric meaning quite well.[66]

An indication of how well-read the founders were is that they had a very good phrase to capture Aristotle's meaning. The term was "public virtue." Whereas Aristotle's ideal was the golden mean, the founders' ideal was the golden rule. The golden mean is quantitatively limiting. The golden rule is qualitatively limiting. The founders would allow for excess, but behavior was regulated by what one might accept as reciprocation. Reciprocation is an important element of social cohesion. It is important to note that the founders well understood that self-governance depended on the virtue of the public, not that of a monarch or oligarchy.

Congruent and Incongruent

ὀρθάς and παρεκβεβηκυίας are somewhat elusive. ὀρθάς has almost a geometric meaning of straight or aligned. It's usually translated as "right" or "good." παρεκβεβηκυίας does mean "deviant" or "abnormal." Luckily, the overall meaning behind these terms is clear in Aristotle's text, but it is challenging to find a suitable English label for the generalizations. Some translations use "perverted." As the Perseus Project at Tufts University notes, this latter translation is too strong. They use "right" and "divergent." This translation is good, but I have a different personal preference. In mathematics, functions converge or diverge. In geometry, objects (like triangles) are congruent or incongruent. Functions imply activity (dynamics). Objects are static in nature. Given that government is an institution whose purpose is to stabilize society, it seems more appropriate to use terms that are more static in nature. This book will use the convention of "congruent" and "incongruent."

66 This motto was adapted first by the US Air Force Academy before the US Air Force at large.

3

Modern Tools

Both Aristotle and the US founders understood human nature instinctively, and they understood it well. Both studied the interaction between government and society and came up with similar conclusions. A government "by the people" depended on a well-executed form of virtue that would last. Aristotle advocated the golden mean. The founders advocated the golden rule ("Do unto others as you would have them do unto you.").[67]

Today we have progressed in our formal understanding of human nature even as our instincts on the subject have deteriorated. This chapter presents some modern tools that work together for better understanding ourselves and our interactions with the institution of government.

Recognizing Cognitive Traps

Perception is the most important human process for understanding the world around us. In recent years, the intelligence community has become very aware of the pitfalls of cognitive traps. Cognitive traps (also called "personality traps") keep an analyst from clear thinking.[68] We might refer to these traps as "blind spots" in everyday speech. It is the nature of personal bias, and intelligence analysts are not the only ones prone to them. We all are. That has repercussions for self-governance because the government is a part of the world around us. One of the cornerstones of this book is that self-governance works best if personality traps are overcome.

---

67 Puka, Bill. "Internet Encyclopedia of Philosophy." Internet Encyclopedia of Philosophy. Accessed July 28, 2016. http://www.iep.utm.edu/goldrule/.

68 *Richard J. Heuer, Jr.*, "Perception: Why Can't We See What Is There to Be Seen?" chap. 2 in *Psychology of Intelligence Analysis (Langley, VA: Center for the Study of Intelligence, 1999).*

Overcoming a personality trap requires self-discipline, open-mindedness, and a desire for the truth. It can mean overcoming peer pressure. One must view an issue from several perspectives. It is not just the intelligence community that should be educated on this subject. It should be a part of core curriculum in the educational system. James Payne's *Six Political Illusions* is a cornerstone book that directly addresses the most common cognitive traps with respect to government.

Psychology professionals have abstract categories for the many cognitive traps.[69] As mentioned in the introduction, determining the merit of a thought based on who came up with it, rather than evaluating its absolute merit, is a cognitive trap. It can lead to groupthink. Here we are concerned about specific traps that impact our ability to govern ourselves.

Pleasant versus Nice

One of the more insidious cognitive traps that has increased in our society is the inability to distinguish between *pleasant* and *nice*. Pleasant is superficial and merely reflects the ability to carry on casual conversation with an individual. It has nothing to do with actions. On the other hand, a person is *nice* if he or she *acts* kindly or protectively toward other people. It is quite possible—even likely—that someone who is pleasant is not nice. In fact, being pleasant is a way that devious people can get what they want. It is indeed possible that someone can be both pleasant and nice, but we have socially lost sight of the fact that an unpleasant person can actually be one of the *nicest* people on the planet. It is common to assume someone who is pleasant is nice. This is dangerous.

Although this trap is no doubt part of human nature's desire to trust, earlier generations of Americans were not as prone to this cognitive trap. One possible explanation for the shift is that the US has shifted from

69 See "Fifteen Common Cognitive Distortions," John M. Grohol, Psych Central, http://psychcentral.com/lib/15-common-cognitive-distortions/. While this source enumerates fifteen common personality traps, there are many more.

emphasizing production to emphasizing consumption. Someone who is accustomed to making things relates to action and the associated result. A consumer relates to gratification, not action. Earlier generations looked more closely at actions because they constantly relied on their own judgment about those actions. We now value pleasant intercourse much more than results. Political correctness reinforces this trap.

Incumbents condition the electorate to ignore results, and the prevalence of incumbency is indicative of their success. There is a symbiotic trap that government can legislate good behavior, leading to overregulation.

Mirror Imaging

One of the most common traps is mirror imaging.[70] Mirror imaging is a perception problem where we assume that others think as we do. Individuals who fall prey to this trap tend to examine differences from a personal frame of reference. A person who is suffering from mirror imaging may regard legitimate objections as personal attacks rather than examine the merits of the question.[71] It should be apparent that this trap can lead to justifying tyranny because of the belief that everyone thinks the same way. Overcoming mirror imaging requires internalizing the different perspectives of others.

James L. Payne—*Six Political Illusions*

The French political thinker and historian Alexis de Tocqueville was deeply concerned about what he saw as a future "benevolent state" enervating the citizens.[72] What he describes in *Democracy in America* is the modern welfare state. He considers it a form of bondage worse than any slavery in ancient societies. In this state, the people only periodically go to the polls and then go back to a lackluster existence. The lack of

70 *Lauren Witlin, "Of Note: Mirror-Imaging and Its Dangers," SAIS Review of International Affairs 28, no. 1 (2008): 89–90.*

71 Ibid.

72 Alexis de Tocqueville, *Democracy in America*, trans. Stephen D. Grant (Indianapolis, IN: Hackett, 2000), 304–308.

independence is very much like the *Star Trek: The Next Generation*'s Borg ("you *will* assimilate").

It is important that the founders spoke of society as being vigorous during the "critical period."[73] Vigor is a form of excellence extracted from the meaning of the Greek term ἀρετή. A vigorous people are capable of self-governance. The modern welfare state does not trust the people to care for themselves. People tend to respond to the level of confidence placed in them. Dependency leads to a meek people that must be led. We have heard the term "wussification of America" from such notables as former Pennsylvania Governor Ed Rendell. Payne's *Six Political Illusions: A Primer on Government for Idealists Fed Up with History Repeating Itself* is a clarion call to reverse that trend and restore the vigor of America. It is a short, well-written book of 126 pages.

James Payne spent his career as a professor of political science. After retiring to a new community, he had his eyes opened to what he calls "political illusions" about government when he wound up repeatedly in conflict with it. Listening to the perceptions of his young daughter solidified his understanding of these illusions.[74] His book is a quick and easy read. It should be essential reading in the educational system.

These illusions are seductive and hypnotic. They lead to a Pavlovian response and an inability to perceive the real nature of government. It takes little focus on each subject to realize the truth of Payne's thesis. The section on Myers-Briggs below briefly covers how we perceive input for decision-making. What Payne exposes is how we bias our inputs in the political arena.

---

73 Specifically, John Fiske identified this period to be from 1783 to 1789. John Fiske. The Critical Period of American History . . . Illustrated, Etc. Boston: Houghton, Mifflin &, 1898.

74 James L. Payne, *Six Political Illusions: A Primer on Government for Idealists Fed Up with History Repeating Itself* (Sandpoint, ID: Lytton Publishing Company, 2010).

Here is a brief summary of the six illusions[75]:

- **Philanthropic illusion:** The belief that the government is actually an economic producer. In fact, it is a necessary drain on the economy.
- **Voluntary illusion:** The rationalization that government is not based on force (just because we're a democracy). Of course, all governments are based on force.
- **Illusion of the frictionless state:** The belief that government overhead is small. The section on complexity theory below augments Payne's arguments as they relate to this illusion.
- **Materialistic illusion:** The belief that money solves all problems.
- **Watchful-eye illusion:** The belief that the government has greater knowledge than the public. This leads to overregulation.
- **Illusion of government preeminence:** The belief that government is the only problem solver in society.

An awakening from these illusions by a single generation of Americans is all it would take to deconstruct de Tocqueville's unhappy vision. Of course, one who is comfortable is not inclined to action. One who is threatened is. The next section puts the nature of the threat into better focus.

Complex Systems

During the 2008 economic crisis, the term "too big to fail" became a popular catchphrase. The term itself goes back at least as far as Congressman Stewart McKinney's use of it during a congressional hearing in 1984. The theory is that certain corporations are so large and tightly coupled to the economy in general that their failure would be catastrophic to the national economy. This is why a rough understanding of complex systems is important. There has been a movement toward consolidation in the United States since the industrial revolution. Size has advantages when it comes to endeavors like sending a man to the moon. On the other hand, complexity theory warns that consolidation,

75 Ibid.

in general, is a very dangerous process. It's more than just putting all your eggs in one basket. It is putting everyone's eggs in one basket. It raises both the potential for failure and the impact of failure exponentially, not linearly.

The world around us is full of complex systems. We learn to deal with these systems from our earliest years. James Rickards gives an excellent, easy-to-understand coverage of complex systems in chapter 10 of *Currency Wars: The Making of the Next Global Crisis*. Although he gives a number of examples, his detailed coverage of how a falling snowflake triggers an avalanche is the most frequently quoted.[76] When the snow piles on a mountainside, the snow becomes unstable. The instability of the mountain snow creates a critical state. At some point, one too many flakes will fall on the mountainside and cause an avalanche. Had the flake fallen on the flat field, nothing would have happened.

A complex system[77] has the following characteristics:[78]

- It evolves on its own from the bottom up, not top down.
- The whole is greater than the sum of the parts.[79]
- It requires exponentially more energy to sustain it as it grows.
- It is prone to catastrophic collapse.
    - The size of the system is the only limit to the damage.

A complex system has a state. Examples of states are stable, unstable, solvent, insolvent, liquid, solid, gas, windy, rainy, and so forth. Systems undergo state changes, or "phase transitions." A change in the weather is a phase transition. Any transition has the potential for catastrophe. A volcanic eruption is an example of a violent phase transition. A very important point is that the catastrophe is bounded by the size of the

76 Rickards, *Currency Wars*, 133.

77 There is a difference between a complex system and a complicated system. A complex system has all these traits.

78 Rickards, *Currency Wars*, 127.

79 An apple pie is more than just its ingredients. Aristotle uses the example of the human body being more than just its components, such as a foot, a nose, and so on

system. A volcanic island can be completely obliterated, but an island halfway around the world might be unaffected. On the other hand, complex systems can interact. A catastrophe in one can trigger either no reaction or a symbiotic catastrophe in a connected system. In the opening paragraph of this section, we saw that the corporations themselves are complex systems. The too-big-to-fail theory worries about the domino effect of one complex system failure causing others to fail until the largest of all—the national economy—fails.

Remember the story of Aristodemus from earlier? The Greek phalanx was a complex system. Hoplites lining up in formation was a bottom-up activity. The whole idea behind the phalanx was to provide a force on the battlefield greater than that of individual combatants. The disadvantage of phalanx warfare was that keeping it tightly packed and orderly got exponentially more difficult as it increased in size. Phalanxes were usually limited to a depth of eight to sixteen. The collision of two phalanxes put both systems into a transition (critical state). Loss on the battlefield was a catastrophic collapse. There was no bigger offense in the Greek world than a hoplite throwing his shield so that he could run faster.[80] This act would lead to a ripple effect of losers turning their backs to the winners. That was when the worst bloodshed occurred. It is precisely why the Greeks did not consider Aristodemus' actions at Plataia courageous. The loss of a shield was a phase transition and risked collapse.

Complexity theory is a mathematical field related to chaos theory. These may be scary terms to a non-math person, but we each have an innate understanding of the important phenomena associated with these systems. To be clear, "We the People" do *not* need an understanding of the mathematical theory. It is only important to remember the general principles: complex systems do not react linearly; any phase transition risks catastrophic collapse; and the collapse is bounded by the size of the system.

---

80 Plutarch relates how Demosthenes talked boldly of war against Philip and then threw his shield at the Battle of Chaeronea. Plutarch, and Grace Voris Curl. Plutarch's Lives. Boston: D.C. Heath and Company, 1937. pg. 115.

Tainter has applied complexity theory to studying the collapse of societies. Societies are very complex systems. As societies age, the complexity of their governments increases. This causes input requirements to the government to increase exponentially. However, as government's complexity increases exponentially, at some point, services per input unit decline likewise. Taxes increase, but services decrease.[81] This is known as *diminishing returns*. Tainter's analysis reveals that civilization in Europe itself collapsed when Rome did. Society had become so centralized that there were no alternate societies. Universal social collapse did not happen later when European societies were not so tightly coupled. When one European nation declined, another rose in its place.[82] One such phase transition was in 1588, when England clearly rose while Spain declined. Unfortunately, Tainter projects that disintegration today would be worldwide, because nations are so tightly coupled. Tight coupling is a by-product of globalization—which is a form of consolidation.

The Greeks' golden mean was a rule to avoid extremes. It was a rule of thumb to avoid perturbing the complex system that is society. The founders' promotion of public virtue is another example of a social tradition to limit both the number and result of phase transitions. These are intuitive approaches to problem-solving within complex systems. The last two principles of complex systems reinforce the wisdom of the US founders for advocating a small government. By not heeding their guidance, we have exponentially increased the drain on society from government. Likewise, we have increased the risk to society from a potential collapse of the government because government has become so tightly coupled with society. It is not a question of whether or not the modern welfare states will collapse. It is a question of how large the collapse will be.

Cohesion Versus Coupling

At first, the difference between cohesion and coupling may seem difficult to distinguish, but the terms have a consistent use across multiple

81 Rickards, *Currency Wars*, 127.

82 Tainter, *Collapse of Complex Societies*, 138.

disciplines. The computer-science notions of cohesion and coupling were first introduced in June 1974, in the *IBM Journal.* The stability of software has improved greatly based on the realization that *tight cohesion* and *loose coupling* are good practices. Today's Internet is only possible because of the understanding of the relationship between cohesion and coupling in computer science. *Tight cohesion* means that the lines of code that define a module are minimal and work together. *Loose coupling* means that module interaction is minimized. It has led not only to increased capacity but also to enhanced stability. If a backbone node fails, traffic is easily rerouted through others. Tightly coupled systems could not begin to approach this kind of fault tolerance. In addition to computer software, there are parallels in chemistry, geology, and sociology. These principles can be applicable to an understanding of relationships within society and between nations as complex systems.

Cohesion is a bottom-up process that bonds members into a social unit. That unit might be a team, a military unit, or a complete society. It cannot be legislated by law, nor can it be bought. The society that formed the United States evolved from the bottom up. The individual colonies became more tightly cohesive, complex systems over time. Tighter cohesion enhances stability. Today the greatest threat to cohesion is due to technology. Rather than form cohesion among members of a local community, citizens today may bond more tightly with people virtually. This is a challenge to the very cornerstone of civil society since bonding is no longer local. Virtual cohesion leads to an absence of cohesion in the real world, because the bond becomes rooted in ideology instead of rooted in geography. This is dangerous to civil societies throughout the globe. The family is one institution of society that can balance the virtual and the real; therefore, dissolution of the family is a great threat to a society with increased technology.

Coupling is simply the interaction between (complex) systems. Unlike cohesion, coupling can be legislated by law or purchased. Loose coupling minimizes the interdependence between them. Loose coupling of nations does not mean an absence of communication or commerce. It is distinct from isolationism, which is an absence of coupling. The goal is to enable mutual benefit but minimize damage from collapse by preventing a domino effect. For example, Britain and the United States went from being *loosely* coupled trading partners to being *tightly* coupled allies leading up to World War II. The two nations weathered the Depression independently. The future of both nations became linked during World War II. After the war, they eventually once again loosened their coupling to a trading partnership.

Economics

"Too big to fail" makes the role of government in society's economy impossible to ignore. Karl Marx and Maynard Keynes both believed that government should have a large role. In the spirit of Adam Smith, the Austrian School of economics differed. Marx and Keynes promoted a top-down view of economics with central planning, although they differed in the degree of central planning. (Keynes did have great disdain for Marxism.) The Austrian School of economics has promoted the Smithian view of liberty and bottom-up economics with decentralization and minimal regulation. The underlying theory is the *mutual benefit* of Smith's "invisible hand."[83]

Prior to Adam Smith publishing *An Inquiry into the Nature and Causes of the Wealth of Nations* in 1776, mercantilism dominated world economics. Mercantilism promoted the theory that a nation could only gain economically by taking wealth from another nation. Privateering (piracy) was a common economic instrument for this conquest ethic. Smith defeated the theory by showing that "opulence" is achievable by trade rather than conquest. Smith focused on economic growth. French economists like J. B. Say took Smith's theory to the next level. Say established that production precedes (not creates) consumption and that

83 Adam Smith introduces the term "invisible hand" in *Wealth of Nations* to describe unintended benefits from self-interested, individual actions. Austrian economists, like Hayek, promoted the concept of "spontaneous order." The concept is that bottom-up, decentralized allocation of resources is more efficient than top-down, central planning. The underlying principle of distributed intelligence might be viewed as two heads are better than one. Adam Smith. The Wealth of Nations. Munich GmbH: Bookrix. pg. 598.

value is based on utility. Unfortunately, Smith's disciple David Ricardo focused on distribution rather than growth and promoted the labor theory of value.[84] This teed up the ball for Marx.

Karl Marx rejected Say's law of markets and jumped on Ricardo's labor theory of value to create rage against exploitation.[85] The labor theory of value declares that labor is the sole producer of value. As such, Marxism takes the position that the "capitalists" and landlords are stealing the "surplus value" (profit) from labor. Marx predicted the imminent failure of capitalism. His prediction is interesting with respect to complexity theory. Economies are prone to catastrophe since they are complex systems. Marx's conjecture of capitalism's demise is a prediction of human behavior that has not yet occurred. In the 1870s, the Austrian School of economics resurrected Smith's economics with new models.[86] The fact that capitalism, to this point, has not failed has eroded the viability of Marxism as an economic theory.

The Austrian School lost favor during the Depression because it viewed business cycles like the common cold, which couldn't be cured. Being a complex adaptive system, the economy would eventually rid itself of "malinvestments."[87] Keynes believed otherwise and got the ears of world leaders like FDR. Keynes believed that government intervention could get the economy going again and that its participation could avoid business cycles altogether. Paul Samuelson's textbook *Economics*, which dominated academia from 1948 with nineteen editions over fifty years, promoted Keynesian economics. Keynesian economics emphasizes the consumption side of the producer-consumer model and misinterprets Say's law of markets to be "supply creates its own demand."[88] Keynesianism's credibility took a huge hit in the 1970s. Milton Friedman's monetary theory poked holes in most of Keynes's

---

84 Mark Skousen, *The Big Three in Economics: Adam Smith, Karl Marx, and John Maynard Keynes* (New York : Routledge, 2007), 57.

85 Ibid., 83.

86 Ibid., 107.

87 Ludwig von Mises, Human Action: A Treatise on Economics, 1966.

88 Ibid., 181–185.

model and demonstrated that bad monetary policy by the Federal Reserve (Fed) was the major contributing factor to the Depression. Today schools of economics have shifted back to the neoclassical model of Austrian economics, but Keynesianism is not completely gone.[89]

At a minimum, all can agree that taxation is a necessary intersection between government and economy. Smith called for "easy taxes," and Keynes championed more government participation. Of course, Marx championed government ownership of everything.

The US political climate since 2006 indicates that the US citizenry is keenly and intuitively aware that society and the economy are both in a critical state. Human nature being what it is, this has resurrected a mood era (see Strauss-Howe below) where Marx's prediction of the demise of capitalism gains appeal. On one hand, complexity theory supports Marx's prediction. On the other hand, Marx's prediction suffers from too much abstraction. That is, capitalism is not a complex system per se. It is a theory by which people build economic systems. Just as Aristotle acknowledged that no man-made government could achieve perfection, no economic system achieves perfect capitalism. It is undeniable that implementations of capitalistic economies are going to fail, but that doesn't mean capitalism itself fails. The questions to be answered regard the scope of the damage and the resilience of the affected society. Tainter's warning about international collapse remains unheeded. Globalization has increased everyone's risk and left no safe haven.

James Rickards exposes the faulty economic assumptions of efficient markets and value at risk (VaR).[90] These theories assume that investors always react rationally and that risk is based on normal distributions. Normal distributions (a bell curve) assume that major extremes almost never happen. In a way, advocates of efficient markets and VaR are anti-Marx. Whereas Marx is somewhat like Chicken Little predicting that the sky is falling, advocates of the former are like the three monkeys seeing, hearing, or speaking no evil. Newer behavioral economics has

89 Ibid.

90 Rickards, *Currency Wars*. 126.

demonstrated that, in fact, investors react emotionally, not rationally. History and complexity theory state that major extremes will always happen. These newer theories embrace a distribution known as *the power law* that better models economic risk than does the normal distribution.

Teddy Roosevelt's trust-busting may have been well-intended, but his motivation and means were not correct. Although justice is imperative to society, the real motivation for restricting the size of corporations is limiting the damage of collapse. Growing government to shrink the size of corporations is antithetical to limiting the damage of collapse.

Hayek introduced the concept of complex systems into the field of economics to support the Austrian view of *spontaneous order*.[91] Current economists like James Rickards continue to champion this view. Rickards points out two fundamental types of crises that can afflict an economy: liquidity problems and solvency problems.

A national liquidity problem means that the nation is healthy but is suffering from a lack of liquid assets. That is, there isn't enough currency in circulation. This problem can be solved by printing money. The second problem is solvency. Just as a business can be bankrupt, a nation can. The sovereignty of a bankrupt nation is in severe jeopardy. Just as a debtor is subject to confiscation, a nation's treasures are at risk from other nations. In 1929, the United States had a liquidity problem. The Fed should have printed money. Instead, it withdrew money, which caused deflation and irritated the liquidity problem. This was one of the causes of the Depression. In 2008, the United States had a solvency problem. The Fed printed money, which made the problem much worse.[92]

91 F. A. Hayek, "The Theory of Complex Phenomena: A Precocious Play on the Epistemology of Complexity," in *Studies in Philosophy, Politics and Economics* (London: Routledge & Kegan Paul, 1967), 22–42.

92 Rickards, *Currency Wars*, 113.

Strauss-Howe Generations

While writing their 1991 book *Generations: The History of America's Future, 1584 to 2069,* William Strauss and Neil Howe noticed a four-generational cycle of what they subsequently called "mood eras" or "turnings."[93] Each is marked by a significant crisis approximately eighty to ninety years apart.

What the authors discovered is that—because no one is alive to remember the mistakes of a lifetime before—history does in fact repeat itself. Society experiences a series of *mood eras* that repeat according to where society is in the crisis cycle. These mood eras are strongly influenced by generational turns. The implications of this phenomenon with respect to the cohesion of civil society are worthy of note. Aristotle makes the point that the births and deaths within society are like the water flowing through a river.[94] His point is that the constitution of a society is subject to change. Society is a complex system constantly encountering phase transitions. The mood era is society's reaction over time to the predominant crisis. They label the turnings:

1. **High:** The post-crisis era. Institutions are strong and individualism weak.
2. **Awakening:** Individualism rises and attacks institutions.
3. **Unraveling:** The opposite of high. Individualism is strong, institutions weak.
4. **Crisis:** Institutions are destroyed and (maybe) rebuilt. (This is why their second book was titled *The Fourth Turning.*)

The mood era belongs to society as a whole, but each generation has certain predictable traits. Every fourth generation shares similar traits because they are born at the same time relative to the major crisis.

---

93 William Strauss and Neil Howe, *The Fourth Turning: An American Prophecy* (New York: Broadway Books, 1997), 4.

94 Aristotle, *Politics*, Book 3, section 1276a.

Strauss and Howe define each generation accordingly as an archetype as follows:

1. **Prophets (baby boomers):** This is the generation born at the end of the last crisis. They are spoiled when young, crusade during the awakening, and focus on principles in midlife. They die out during the subsequent crisis, for which they are largely responsible.
2. **Nomads (Gen X):** This generation is born during the awakening. They are neglected by the prophets, come of age as alienated, are midlife leaders through the crisis, and are elders during the high period.
3. **Heroes (Millennials):** They are born during the unraveling. They are protected by the nomads, come of age during the next crisis, and emerge as optimists during the next high. They are elderly during the next awakening.
4. **Artists (post-Millennials):** They are born during the crisis. They are overprotected by the heroes, are more socialized and conforming, and emphasize process in midlife.

With the start of the country in 1776, the theory projects crises between 1856 to 1866, 1936 to 1956, and 2016 to 2046. The Civil War and World War II fall within the first two windows of time. The Revolutionary War, the Civil War, and World War II did not just occur instantaneously. According to Strauss and Howe, events during prior turnings can be directly traced back to the crisis. The two World Wars were not strictly internal crises to the United States, but they did bracket an internal crisis. The wars resulted because other complex systems (nations) were also in crisis at the same time. Likewise, 9/11 was not an internal crisis; however, it was the result of crises in other nations. It also seems to have been a catalyst to the current internal crisis—another fourth turning.

The Strauss-Howe model is helpful in identifying complex phase transitions. It also identifies a higher threat of collapse during the crisis turning. But there are key trends within society that fuel the dynamic. Earlier Americans were patient and looked to a better world for future generations. This was a convergent trend that ensured a certain gravity to society that would ensure cohesion through a crisis. Modern Americans have become an impatient bunch, expecting instant gratification. This is a dangerous trend because it is divergent. Subsequent phase transitions run a higher risk of catastrophic collapse. Add patience, unselfishness, and a drive for improvement to the list of public-virtue elements.

Myers-Briggs

Myers-Briggs testing is based on the psychology of Carl Jung. There are competing theories, but the Myers-Briggs Testing Indicator (MBTI) has been around for a long time. Results gathered from the MBTI provide useful statistics. It measures four continuums: 1) introversion/extraversion, 2) intuition/sensing, 3) thinking/feeling, and 4) perceiving/judging.[95] The goal of the test is to measure one's natural decision-making inclinations. The results of the testing published by the Center for Applications of Psychological Type reveal some insights with respect to self-governance.

There is a difference between learned behavior and natural tendencies. Education and maturity enable us to overcome our natural tendencies when they could be detrimental. Reason tempers emotional overreaction. It also helps guide when a decision is truly required. Finally, reason tells us to cross-check data. This latter issue is difficult in the information age, where we're barraged by conflicting data. The sheer amount of information amplifies emotional bias. When we resist emotional bias, we follow George Washington's example. Self-discipline, courage, and reason are three of the most important elements of public virtue.

The most important continuum for decision-making is thinking versus feeling. It must be emphasized that this is not a reflection

95 "MBTI Basics," The Myers & Briggs Foundation, accessed June 30, 2016, http://www.myersbriggs.org/my-mbti-personality-type/mbti-basics/.

of intelligence. It is only a metric of how we value reason in the decision-making process. Myers-Briggs testing reveals that over 50 percent of the US population prefers to make decisions based on feeling rather than thought.[96] This one indicator reveals why democracies have failed throughout history and should make us worry. If the majority rules and the majority of people react emotionally, it amplifies the risk of the complex system (society) reacting out of rage rather than reason. One defining characteristic of a republic is that the people react out of reason.

The conjunction of our feeling side of decision-making with our innate understanding of complex systems is why Marxism continues to have an appeal. Given that the economy is a complex system, our fear of economic collapse is well-founded. On the other hand, any and every economic system is prone to collapse because of its complexity. Marx was a thinker (ENTJ[97]), but he plays to our feeling side with a theoretical remedy. He amplifies the potential for instability with a system of socialism or communism that is every bit as prone to collapse. In fact, his system promotes the ultimate in consolidation: globalized socialism. The increase in size increases risk exponentially. It also increases the damage upon collapse. (Of course, globalization today has promoted tight coupling of nations, which is equivalent to consolidation. As Tainter says, we are at risk.)

On the other side of the coin, decision-making that is based on thinking has many benefits. David Keirsey and others have used the writings and actions of historical figures to deduce the MBTIs of these individuals. This is an interesting exercise but one that shouldn't be

---

96 "Estimated Frequencies of the Types in the United States Population," Center for Applications of Psychological Type, accessed July 07, 2016, https://www.capt.org/mbti-assessment/estimated-frequencies.htm.

97 The *Fieldmarshall.* Extroverted, iNtuitive, Thinking, Judger. He was naturally an abstract thinker who tended to hurry to a decision based upon thought, not feeling. "The Myers & Briggs Foundation - The 16 MBTI® Types." The Myers & Briggs Foundation - The 16 MBTI® Types. Accessed August 02, 2016. http://www.myersbriggs.org/my-mbti-personality-type/mbti-basics/the-16-mbti-types.htm.

overvalued. It should be no surprise that a number of the US founders were thinkers by nature.[98]

The fourth continuum (perceptor versus judger) measures the need for closure. Judgers want closure. Perceptors want to gather more data and delay making a decision. The problem is that judgers tend to reach a decision prematurely and will remake decisions. Premature decisions are bad with respect to self-governance because they are prone to error and they inject instability. Remaking decisions erodes confidence and opens opportunities for enemies to exploit changes in strategy or tactics. On the other hand, a decision delayed too long invites being overrun before reacting. Testing shows that over 54 percent of the population tends to make premature decisions.

Finally, there is the issue of how we perceive the input with which to make a decision. The intuitive versus sensing continuum provides no direct perspective about political decisions, but it may provide some insight as to how demagogues can manipulate perceptions. Our perceptions are biased by the feedback of our desire for the world to be as we wish rather than the way it truly is. This is a personality trap. Testing shows that two-thirds to three-quarters of the US population are sensors. This means that they focus on trees instead of the forest. Fixation is dangerous. Openness to a wider view is the antidote. It is easier for spin doctors to focus attention on a single tree as opposed to a whole forest. This is the epitome of the single-issue voter. The consequence of leaders with a propensity toward sensing is an ability to convince the public of bad priorities. He or she can easily escalate an inconsequential issue within society to mask the existence of real threats.

Self-discipline, courage, reason, patience, and openness to a wider view are the essential elements of public virtue. As John Adams writes, "Public Virtue cannot exist in a Nation without private, and public

98 David Keirsey and CelebrityTypes.com are split on Thomas Jefferson. Keirsey pegs him as an INTP. For Keirsey's personality assessment, see keirsey.com.

Virtue is the only Foundation of Republics."[99] MBTI is an effective tool for us to improve our private and public virtue.

Pournelle's Iron Law of Bureaucracy

Jerry Pournelle had a master's degree in psychology and a PhD in political science. Being a technology enthusiast, he wrote a column called "Chaos Manor" for *BYTE* magazine. Pournelle's 1963 PhD thesis categorized political factions along psychological lines, so he had some fascinating insights into behavior and political science. He labeled his insights "laws." One such law that is of interest to us is Pournelle's iron law of bureaucracy.[100] Paraphrased and enumerated, his law is:

1) Any organization is composed of two sets of people:
   a) Those dedicated to the **goals** of the organization.
   b) Those dedicated to the organization **itself**.
      i) I would add "and **themselves.**"
2) The second group (b) will always gain and keep control of the organization. They will write the rules.

He gives some examples:

1) Education
   a) Classroom teachers who work and sacrifice to teach students.
   b) Teachers' union officials who protect any teacher, even the most incompetent.
2) NASA
   a) Technicians and scientists who work to advance human knowledge.
   b) Headquarters staff who seek a budget and protect the brand.

---

99 John Adams (Federalist) to Mercy Otis Warren, letter, April 16, 1776, https://www.masshist.org/publications/apde2/view?id=ADMS-06-04-02-0044. Warren was an anti-Federalist.

100 "The Iron Law of Bureaucracy," Jerry Pournelle, http://www.jerrypournelle.com/reports/jerryp/iron.html.

The basic goal of a teacher is to educate, and the goal of a school is to teach students. Union goals are not necessarily counter to these goals; however, they certainly can be. A similar relationship exists between NASA scientists and the staff who keep the lights on. To a degree, we can see a relationship between idealism and realism; however, the danger is the potential for corruption on behalf of the realist side. Without realism, the idealistic cannot be pursued. On the other hand, corruption can misdirect the idealistic goals. NASA was started to send a man to the moon—not to "reach out to the Muslim world."[101]

In truth, Pournelle's iron law is applicable to virtually any institution, not just bureaucracy. From here forward, it will be shortened to Pournelle's iron law. The second group tightly couples its interests to the existence and promotion of the organization, not the organization's goals. Over time the goals of the organization take a back seat to its existence. There is a natural life cycle for an institution, but the second group may prevent its natural termination. Another possible scenario is that the second group may grow the institution beyond the point of diminishing returns, just like any other complex system. In either case, the institution can inject instability rather than its societal goal of stability.

Aristotle and the republicans in the founding generation innately understood this long before Pournelle formalized it. That is one reason why they both advocated rotation of office.[102] Rotation breaks the control of the second group and checks corruption.

A very important point to be made is about the concept of what makes one an expert. A deception has arisen in society today that the second group is composed of experts. This can be true—*if* that individual is "hands-on." However, the pace of technology and the mindset in business schools has increased the likelihood that group two

---

101 "NASA Chief Bolden's Muslim Remark to Al-Jazeera Causes Stir," Michelle Spitzer, Space.com, accessed June 30, 2016, http://www.space.com/8725-nasa-chief-bolden-muslim-remark-al-jazeera-stir.html.

102 100 Aristotle, *Politics*, Book 5, section 1308a.

tends to become disconnected from the true experts, those in group one. Whereas the framers of the Constitution eschewed titles of nobility, we have substituted the title of "expert" for paper tigers.

A corollary to Pournelle's iron law is that if society does not manage an institution, that institution will manage society.[103] Such an institution is incongruent with society; however, it will expend every effort to make itself indispensable to society—even to the detriment of society. The modern welfare state is an example of an institution becoming indispensable to society.

103 Francis Fukuyama, "America in Decay, The Sources of Political Dysfunction," *Foreign Affairs,* September/October 2014.

4

The Party Systems

The founders did not want a party system in the new country. George Washington in particular loathed the idea. In fact, he was the lone president in American history who showed no party affiliation at all for his first term. He is considered a member of the Federalist Party for his second term, but the label may be an overstatement since there was no campaign as we know it today.

Political scientists are not universal in their views, but many believe that the United States has undergone five transitions in party systems.[104] As generations turn, mood eras and political demography change. If we rethink the party systems using complexity theory, what we are really looking at are phase transitions. The phase transition that led to what political scientists identify as the third-party system was a catastrophe: The Civil War. Society was able to reunite to a degree, but one side was forced to do so. Mapping the crisis-cycle timing onto history, it seems like a no-brainer that, indeed, we transitioned from a fifth- to a sixth-party system after World War II. The rise of Donald Trump for the Republicans and socialism within the Democrats strongly suggests that a new party system has already occurred. Yesterday's Democrat may well be more aligned with the Republican Party than a socialist party.

However, one issue remains constant throughout the life of the US republic: the size of government. From the beginning of the republic, the Federalists and anti-Federalists argued over the power of a centralized government. Power and size of government are related but different

104 Mark D. Brewer and Louis Sandy Maisel, *Parties and Elections in America: The Electoral Process* (Lanham: Rowman & Littlefield, 2011), 42.

issues. Earlier generations fought over the power of the national government. Today's politicians seem to take power for granted and only talk of size. Throughout our history, the national government's growth has proceeded without a significant reduction. The fight continues, but like a tug-of-war, the side for smaller or weaker national government has a 225-plus-year losing streak.

The First-Party System (1792–1816)

The first-party system was a direct result of the fight over ratification of the Constitution. On one side, Hamilton's Federalist Party pushed for more centralized power in government, national banking, and closer ties with Britain. On the other hand, Madison and Jefferson's Democratic-Republican Party favored alliance with France and opposed centralization. Hamilton was able to establish the First Bank of the United States in 1791. It was a precursor to today's Fed, but with a sunset provision that expired in 1811. The Federalist Party collapsed with the positive end of the War of 1812. The Era of Good Feelings during James Monroe's presidency (1816–1824) marked the only party-system vacancy in our history.

The Second-Party System (1828–1854)

Andrew Jackson founded the modern Democratic Party after the 1824 election went to John Quincy Adams. Jackson felt robbed when a three-way tie was resolved against him. The new party promoted the supremacy of the presidency over Congress—counter to the Constitution. It also opposed the Bank of the United States and just about any form of modernization that was viewed as costing the taxpayer. In other words, with the exception of promoting presidential supremacy, its stances were exactly the opposite of today's Democratic Party. On the other hand, the Whig party favored the supremacy of Congress over the president (per the Constitution) and industrialization. The Second Bank of the United States was created in 1816, but it met the same fate as the First Bank in 1836. Jackson would successfully veto a Third Bank of the United States.

The Third-Party System (1854–1894)

The third-party system started with the rise of the antislavery Republican Party. For the first time, social issues were front and center with a complex of factions within both parties. After the Civil War, the newly freed slaves swelled the ranks of the Republican Party. Southerners were a large component of the Democratic Party. The Democratic Party had a large component of fiscal conservatives. Throughout this period, the Republican Party was actually the party of consolidation and industrialization. The Compromise of 1877 ended Reconstruction with Rutherford B. Hayes as president and initiated the withdrawal of federal troops from the South. Détente existed for the remainder of the system.

The Fourth-Party System (1896–1932)

The fourth-party system sprang from the initial Progressive Era. The Republican Party held the upper hand throughout this period by successfully blaming the Democrats for the Panic of 1893. Since the original progressives were Republicans, the progressive agenda dominated this era.[105] Woodrow Wilson won the presidency due to a split in the Republican Party, when Teddy Roosevelt started the Bull Moose Party.

The Fifth- and/or Sixth-Party System (1933–?)

The fifth-party system was a direct result of the Great Depression. Republicans had been in power, so they bore the brunt of the blame. The Republicans had no answer for Franklin Roosevelt. The 1936 landslide victory for FDR put the Republicans on their heels. There is debate as to whether this era ended with the end of the New Deal coalition, the Reagan Coalition, the Third Way, the emergence of Donald Trump—or at all.

105 "The Progressive Era (1890–1920)," Eleanor Roosevelt Papers Project, accessed July 06, 2016, https://www.gwu.edu/~erpapers/teachinger/glossary/progressive-era.cfm.

It is undeniable that a shift did take place when high-profile figures like Ronald Reagan and Charlton Heston left the Democratic Party and became figureheads of the opposite party. As Heston put it, "I didn't change. The Democratic Party changed."[106] The early 1970s was a tumultuous time, and conservative Democrats like Heston and Reagan left the party in reaction to the sharp left turn of the party leadership.

It is worthy of note that we have been undergoing a similar tumult since 2008. It is another complex-system phase transition. It remains to be seen whether there is just a party realignment or a catastrophe of some form.

The Vertical Axis

As we can see from this quick overview, the conventional view of left-right politics fails to capture our political history. If we turn the horizontal axis ninety degrees, we can reassign our thinking to top-down, centralized power versus bottom-up, decentralized power. Hamilton's Federalist Party pushed for more centralized power. Clearly, his party belonged on the top of the axis. Madison and Jefferson led the folks on the bottom side. Their victory over the Federalists put an end to these factions until the Civil War. At that point, the Republican Party assumed the top of the axis, with the Democrats at the bottom.

Since the fourth-party system, it hasn't been a party as much as the progressive movement that has been on the top of the axis. The Republican Party has presented itself as if it is on the bottom. Other than a brief congruence with Calvin Coolidge, Ronald Reagan, and Donald Trump, Republicans have been little better than the Democratic Party at championing a smaller central government. The unrest today suggests a party realignment in which one representing the true bottom may eventually emerge.

---

106 Emilie Raymond, *From My Cold, Dead Hands: Charlton Heston and American Politics* (Lexington, KY: University Press of Kentucky, 2006), 6.

5

The Founding

The New Republic

The term "republic" is actually a fairly new word. No such word existed at the time Plato wrote what we call *Plato's Republic*, nor did it exist at the time of the Roman Republic. Aristotle simply used the general word for politics, often translated as "polity" or "constitutional government."

The founders of the United States stayed true to Aristotle's labels for governments. To them, the word "democracy" was "mob rule." The founders, being fans of Cicero, embraced the Latin-derived word "republic"[107] for the system of government they then created. Since then, the term "republic" has meant what Aristotle called the "best" government. They fully embraced Aristotle's contention that the middle class was the best. Most hoped that the people's representatives would come from this class. They would not approve of a permanent political class.

Public Virtue

The founding generation was not just concerned that the form of government would be congruent. They were keenly aware of the causes of governmental collapse outlined in Book 5 of Aristotle's *Politics*.[108] The generation as a whole was concerned about their translation of ἀρετή, *public virtue*[109] or *civic virtue*.[110] Whereas Aristotle's concept was based

107 This etymology is circa 1600. From Latin "*res republica*" ("a public affair").

108 Aristotle, *Politics*. Book 5 covers why governments fail and how to preserve them.

109 W. Cleon Skousen, *The 5000 Year Leap* (Orem, UT: National Center for Constitutional Studies, 2007), 50. The founders referenced Romans Cicero, Tacitus, Plutarch, and Livy.

110 Edward Gibbon, *Decline and Fall of the Roman Empire* (New York: Penguin Books, 2000), 17.

on the golden mean, the founders' version was based on the golden rule. The difference is subtle, but as Aristotle professes, "Nothing in excess." The founders were less restrictive. The golden rule actually allows excess but does not allow crossing a line where one's behavior negatively affects another. Everyone in the founding generation recognized and admired the public virtue of one man—George Washington.

There is one place in today's America where the concept of public virtue has been alive—the military. The core values at the US Air Force Academy have been "Integrity First, Service before Self, Excellence in All We Do." The US Air Force at large has since adopted it. The importance of this with respect to civil society cannot be underestimated. It implies that society has individuals who are willing to lay down their own lives for others—but not foolishly.

A key element of early American society was that it relied on public virtue more than law. In today's terminology, peer pressure regulated behavior. There was less need for law to do it. Today we defy Aristotle's advice that laws need to remain general and create more and more laws to cover details. Aristotle identified education as supremely important in the stability of society as generations turn. The loss of public virtue as an American principle highlights the failure of the nation's educational system to provide generational stability.

We have already identified some elements of public virtue that we can extrapolate from the thoughts of the masters, from Aristotle to the founders and on to Hayek, Rickards, and Tainter. Here is an updated list of what the founders might have considered virtuous:

- **The golden rule:** "Do unto others as you would have them do unto you." This qualitative measure encapsulates the founders' views. It is a solid litmus test for all behavior.
- **Self-discipline:** Early generations of Americans were taught this from a young age. It is an anchor to the natural world, and the closer one is to nature, the more important it is for survival. Avoiding personality traps also requires self-discipline. This is a

repudiation of today's permissiveness, but it is independent of any religious issue. It requires other virtues:

- **Courage** is required for self-discipline.
- **Honesty** requires courage—especially honesty to oneself.
- **Accountability** is the willingness to suffer the consequences for actions and deeds.
- **Reason** means "think before acting." Again, this repudiates today's permissiveness and is coupled with self-discipline.
- **Patience** comes in the old adage "patience is a virtue." Without question, rage was a motivator in the founding period, but the folks we think of as founders did not just react. They reasoned first.
    - **Open-mindedness** is important, as a single perspective is usually incorrect. There is more than one dimension to reality. Different viewpoints are important for solving problems, instead of just addressing symptoms. Likewise, it takes self-discipline to avoid personality traps. Contrary to modern perception, the founders very seriously discussed abolishing slavery.
    - **A wish for better circumstances for subsequent generations** is the best way to ensure convergence of society after a crisis. It requires
        - **Unselfishness**
        - **Drive for improving the human condition:** The founders were keenly aware that they were acting for the benefit of generations unborn.
        - **Self-sacrifice:** This is perhaps the most important ingredient of all. As we can paraphrase Aristotle, "Those who will not defend themselves are the slaves of every invader."[111] In a nutshell, this is why Rome fell.

Republican Principles

The founders spoke frequently of republican principles. These principles evolved out of the Glorious Revolution. They are based on

111 Aristotle, *Politics*, Book 4, section 1291a.

Anglo-Saxon heritage and enlightenment thinkers, with advice from Cicero and Aristotle's Book 5 of *Politics*. Here are some:

- Limited, representative government
  - That protects natural rights
  - That the people have a right or obligation to overthrow if the government (incongruent) infringes on these natural rights
  - That demonstrates distributed, decentralized government
    - Separation of powers
    - Federalism
- The rule of law
- Equality before the law
- The oath of office (dependent upon public virtue)
- Rotation of office
- A classless society (predomination of the middle class)
- Education promoting these principles

Founding Documents

The founding documents for the United States are like the cornerstone of a building. All laws are based on the principles and rules within them. The founders themselves were like the masons who carved the cornerstones. Many documents were written during the founding, but three deserve emphasis.

Declaration of Independence

Of course, there would have been no United States without the Declaration of Independence. For one thing, it was fundamentally a declaration of war. It laid out the first principles on which the nation was based. We already discussed liberty under the previous section on John Locke. The phrase "pursuit of happiness" deserves a little attention. This phrase meant significantly more at the time of the founding than what we understand it to mean today.

It was the Age of Enlightenment, and the Irish philosopher Francis Hutcheson was a mentor to Adam Smith at the University of Glasgow.

In 1725 he wrote a treatise called *An Inquiry into the Original of Our Ideas of Beauty and Virtue*.[112] His philosophy was "that action is best which accomplishes the greatest happiness for the greatest numbers."[113] The founding generation tied happiness to civic responsibility to coin the term "public virtue."

Contrary to modern thinking, life, liberty, and the pursuit of happiness are not completely self-centered. Liberty is freedom constrained by systemic law. Pursuit of happiness is not self-gratification. It really means that we have a right to dignity and self-worth as a result of accepting civic responsibility and actively doing well for the community. At the National Conference on Citizenship in 2005, Supreme Court Justice Anthony Kennedy noted that the "hedonistic component" to the definition of happiness did not match the framers' interpretation. As he put it, their interpretation was that "happiness meant that feeling of self-worth and dignity you acquire by contributing to your community and its civic life."[114]

Articles of Confederation

This was the first attempt at unifying the states. The union was more loosely coupled than it is today. Nationalists, like Alexander Hamilton, were unhappy with this arrangement and sought a tighter union. At the time, any sane person would worry about being surrounded by the European powers of France, England, and Spain. It was especially worrisome because the British refused to remove troops from the frontier. The revolution had exposed that the lack of the power of the purse made the nation weak militarily. It was dependent on the states for funding a military. As a consequence, the army was underfunded and poorly provisioned. The Federalists used Shay's Rebellion to augment the concern. This raised the additional threat from within,[115] about which Aristotle warns.

In *The Federalist Papers*, Madison argues both that the Constitution is merely an amended Articles and that it is a completely new document.

112 "Lexical Investigations: Happiness," Dictionary.com.

113 Ibid.

114 Ibid.

115 Aristotle, *Politics*, Book 5, section 1302a.

Jefferson wished that the convention had merely amended the Articles. The Articles really lack a process to amend. It only states that amendment requires unanimous consent. The results of the Annapolis Convention in September of 1786 left little doubt that unanimous consent was problematic. Only five states were represented to solve problems of interstate trade. The delegates realized that solutions to the problem required systemic changes. The inability to amend the Articles led to the Constitutional Convention in Philadelphia. Scrutiny of Madison's notes from the Convention reveals an evolution from the Articles of Confederation to the Constitution that reflects the same problem-solving techniques used by software engineers in architecting revisions of software.

Constitution

The Constitution addresses the flaws in the Articles of Confederation head-on. The national government can tax. Taxes are divided between "direct" and "indirect." Direct taxes have to be apportioned among the states. The exact meaning of direct taxation is evasive to us today, and there is debate about the founders' exact meaning. It can, however, be approximated by viewing a direct tax as tax on production[116] and an indirect tax as tax on consumption. Direct tax is required to be apportioned among the states to protect the agrarian South from economic disaster. The Sixteenth Amendment withdraws the requirement. The amendment legitimizes our current tax leviathan and the associated behemoth of a government. The documented confusion during the ratification of the Sixteenth Amendment brings the amendment's legitimacy into question.

Article V of the Constitution addresses the need for amendment, which was lacking in the Articles of Confederation. The basis for it was proposal thirteen in the Virginia Plan, fifteen proposals presented by Edmund Randolph. The original proposal states "that provision ought to be made for the amendment of the Articles of Union whensoever

116 This includes capitation tax as taxing a productive worker.

it shall seem necessary, and that the assent of the National Legislature ought not to be required thereto."[117]

The current two-thirds requirement for the call for the convention of states made its first appearance on 6 Aug 1787, presented by the Committee of Detail. At that point, it was known as Article XIX. On 10 Sep 1787, Alexander Hamilton raised a concern that the states would assume too much power unless Congress could also propose amendments without the states. Madison captured the results of the subsequent debate on the subject.

On 12 Sep 1787, the Committee of Style presented the general form of the Constitution as we know it. On 15 Sep 1787, George Mason raised the concern that both methods of proposal required approval from the national Congress and that "no amendments of the proper kind, would ever be obtained by the people, if the Government should become oppressive, as he verily believed would be the case."[118] He recognized the opposite problem of Hamilton's earlier objection. Mason's proposal was approved without dissent.

It is important to realize that an Article V convention of states is *within* the Constitution. It is a mechanism of the Constitution for its amendment. Delegates are restricted to the boundaries of the commission they are given. A constitutional convention is *outside* of the Constitution. It would intentionally bypass the Constitution and the national government. Additionally, the states would have to specifically commission delegates to replace the Constitution with a new system.

The system of government the founders constructed included the best practices in government compiled by Western history. The three branches of government are familiar to all Americans, but the role of each is not properly understood. During presidential campaigns, we pelt the candidates with questions about "What will you do?" That is the role of the president in international affairs, but it is not the role of the

117 "Madison Debates May 29," Avalon Project, accessed June 30, 2016, http://avalon.law.yale.edu/18th_century/debates_529.asp.

118 Ibid.

president internally. It is the legislature's role to determine *what* the laws are to be. The president determines *how* the laws will be enforced. This simple distinction clarifies the difference between a ruler and a president.

Key Founders

Like normal human beings, the founders didn't agree all the time, but it is surprising how much they did agree on.[119] Understanding the positions of some of the key founders is important to understanding what they intended the nation to be and why some weaknesses exist in the founding documents. The following are some *CliffsNotes* on four key founders. Three of them were among our first four presidents.

George Washington

George Washington was more of a Renaissance man than he gets credit for. He considered himself a farmer, experimenting with crop rotation and many innovative techniques. He was a general. He liked to dance. He distilled whiskey and brewed beer. He was self-conscious about his lack of advanced education, but he made up for it by reading. More to the point, he was very self-disciplined. David Keirsey pegs Washington's MBTI as ESTJ.[120] He was brave to a fault but realized his weaknesses and adopted a Fabian strategy[121] to avoid losing the army in winning the Revolution.[122]

Part of George Washington's education included copying a set of rules derived from those composed by French Jesuits in 1595. Francis Hawkin translated them to English in 1640. Washington filled ten pages at the end of a personal book with what we know as his 110 rules of civility.[123] His *Rules of Civility & Decent Behavior in Company*

---

119 Skousen, *5000 Year Leap*, 22.

120 The *Supervisor*. Extroverted, Sensing, Thinking, Judger. See glossary.

121 After Roman General Fabius, who defeated Hannibal by wearing him down.

122 Joseph J. Ellis, *His Excellency: George Washington* (New York: Vintage Books, 2004), 99–122.

123 "The Rules of Civility and Decent Behaviour," Mount Vernon, http://www.mountvernon.org/digital-encyclopedia/article/the-rules-of-civility-and-decent-behaviour/.

and Conversation can be purchased on Amazon. His rules can also be found online. A number of the tenets don't make a lot of sense in today's world; however, most of them can be updated.[124] The founding generation considered him the epitome of public virtue. It is no wonder he is considered the father of his country.

Washington was well aware of the precedents he could set as the first president. He totally respected the limitation on the presidency within the Constitution. It was his original intention to serve only one term. He agreed to the second when the divide between Hamilton and Jefferson threatened to escalate to a regional conflict. Washington was a fan of Lucius Quinctius Cincinnatus. Cincinnatus was a Roman statesman whom the Romans twice declared dictator. Cincinnatus twice took care of the existing crisis and immediately resigned and went back to plowing his fields. The Constitution had no term limits on the presidency, but Washington compensated for it by bowing out after two terms. It wasn't until FDR that the precedent was ignored. The Twenty-Second Amendment institutionalized the limit in 1951—more than 150 years later. It demonstrates how law is unnecessary if public virtue guides behavior.

Washington grew up in a slave state. The Mount Vernon website has a number of good articles that detail his involvement in, maturation with, and attitude toward slavery. It is apparent that fighting alongside blacks in the Revolution and rubbing elbows with the Marquis de Lafayette's antislavery position turned Washington against slavery.[125] He and Lafayette strategized for hours about how to eliminate it. They went so far as to plan experiments by buying plots of land for pseudo-freed slaves to work as their own. It wasn't until 1782 that Virginia law allowed manumission (freeing of slaves). Washington knew that just releasing people without means to support themselves was little better

---

124 "George Washington's *Rules of Civility and Decent Behavior in Company and Conversation*," *Foundations Magazine*, http://www.foundationsmag.com/civility.html.

125 "George Washington and Slavery," Mount Vernon, http://www.mountvernon.org/digital-encyclopedia/article/george-washington-and-slavery/.

than a death sentence in a slave state. When the Quakers asked him, as president, to free the slaves, he responded as follows:

> I hope it will not be conceived from these observations, that it is my wish to hold the unhappy people, who are the subject of this letter, in slavery. I can only say that there is not a man living who wishes more sincerely than I do, to see a plan adopted for the abolition of it; but there is only one proper and effectual mode by which it can be accomplished, and that is by Legislative authority; and this, as far as my suffrage will go, shall never be wanting.[126]

Washington always respected the boundaries of presidential power in the Constitution. Congress had the legislative power to determine what was to be done in the interior, and he was not going to undermine it.

Alexander Hamilton

Alexander Hamilton ("the Little Lion") was one of a kind in the founding generation. He was a brilliant lawyer and served closely with Washington during the Revolution. Hamilton was Washington's aide-de-camp when Benedict Arnold plotted his treason at West Point. Hamilton's MTBI is believed to have been either an ENTJ or an ENFJ.[127] His learned behavior was clearly that of a thinker.

Hamilton was the alpha nationalist. The dispute between the large and the small states at the Constitutional Convention had reached a crisis by 16 Jun 1787. On 18 Jun 1787, Hamilton felt compelled to speak up. He presented a five-hour dissertation on his plan for the new government, modeled from the British system.[128] States would all but disappear, becoming merely administrative entities. Madison's notes provide a sketch of Hamilton's eleven proposals.[129] The other members of

---

126 George Washington to Robert Morris, letter, April 12, 1786.

127 *Extroverted, intuitive, judger.* There is disagreement on thinker/feeler. See glossary.

128 "Hamilton and the US Constitution," PBS, http://www.pbs.org/wgbh/amex/duel/sfeature/hamiltonusconstituion.html.

129 "Madison Debates June 18," Avalon Project, http://avalon.law.yale.edu/18th_century/debates_618.asp.

the convention were polite but stunned. Afterward, there was only silence until someone cracked a joke, and then the convention continued.[130] However, Hamilton had his own public virtue. He called the convention together at the close and called for unity to get the Constitution ratified.

The Constitution would probably not have been ratified if it weren't for Hamilton's efforts. The plan for a central government was not popular, especially in Hamilton's home state of New York. His first attempt at defending the new Constitution against Governor George Clinton was an abysmal failure. Hamilton was haughty and signed it "Caesar." Clinton made mincemeat of him. Then Hamilton enlisted John Jay and James Madison to team up to write *The Federalist Papers.*

After ratification, Hamilton served in Washington's cabinet as secretary of the treasury. He pushed the nationalists' goal of more centralized power through the formation of institutions like the US Post Office and the First Bank of the United States.

James Madison

James Madison was only thirty-six during the Constitutional Convention, but he had a significant impact. Madison is known as the architect of the Constitution (he started enumerating the Virginia Plan). His MBTI is universally recognized as an INTP, the architect. He and Jefferson lived fewer than thirty miles apart. Keirsey believes that Jefferson was also an INTP.[131] As a consequence, Madison and Jefferson shared similar views—most of the time.

Scholars have puzzled over Madison's positions in *The Federalist Papers*. They were so apparently contrary to his later positions and definitely contrary to Jefferson's view in a number of cases. The fact that Jefferson was in France while *The Federalist Papers* were written is interesting with respect to Madison's positions.

130 Smith and McElroy, *The Federalist Papers.*

131 The *Architect.* Introverted, iNtuitive, Thinking, Perceptor. See glossary.

Historians may be overvaluing the label of "Federalist." It is not black and white. In his 1888 book of the same name, John Fiske labels the 1780s "The Critical Period of American History." Shay's Rebellion in 1786–1787 had a profound impact on the psyche of the founding generation. Edward Gibbon had published *The Decline and Fall of the Roman Empire* in 1776, and his conclusion was that the empire fell from within due to a lack of Aristotelian virtue. Coupled with the very real threat of being surrounded by European powers, there was a real concern for stability with the nascent country. It is not unreasonable for reasonable people to err on the side of safety in times of threat. Madison no doubt believed that the Articles of Confederation left the nation vulnerable, but this does not mean he was "all in" on Hamilton's plans for an American monarchy.

Thomas Jefferson

Thomas Jefferson's position on the Constitution was aligned with the anti-Federalists. He was in France from 1784 to 1789, so he didn't directly participate in the ratification debates. Initially, he didn't like the Constitution. He didn't like the fact that the convention was done behind closed doors, and he wished they had only modified the Articles of Confederation.[132] Other grievances he had were 1) government was too centralized, 2) the president resembled "the bad addition of a Polish King,"[133] and 3) he didn't believe the House had an adequate ratio of representatives.

Jefferson objected to the lack of term limits in general, but he especially worried about the lack of term limits on the president. He feared a dictator for life.[134] Jefferson also saw having the Supreme Court as "ultimate arbiter" to be a "very dangerous doctrine."[135]

---

132 Ibid.

133 Thomas Jefferson to John Adams, letter, November 13, 1787.

134 Ibid. He writes, "Once in office, and possessing the military force of the Union, without the aid or check of a council, he would not be easily dethroned, even if the people could be induced to withdraw their votes from him."

135 Jefferson to William Jarvis, letter, September 28, 1820.

For all his objections to the Constitution, Jefferson didn't hesitate to use his presidential power as commander in chief when it came to the Barbary pirates. He sent the marines to the "shores of Tripoli."[136]

It would be irresponsible not to link the modern-day issue of Islamic terror to Jefferson at this point. It is not a new problem. The Barbary pirates were actually the Islamic terrorists of their day. After the Revolution, the new United States was no longer under protection of the British Navy. The British had paid tribute (jizya) to the Barbary pirates. Without British protection, the impact of pirates seizing ships and enslaving sailors had a large negative economic impact. Franklin proposed eliminating Mediterranean trade, but Jefferson reported in 1791 that one-sixth of all wheat and flour exports were to the Mediterranean.[137] The Treaty of Tripoli (1796) left the United States paying roughly one-sixth of its annual revenues for protection against pirate seizures. John Adams became the "father of the navy" in response to the need for protecting the merchant marine in the Mediterranean. Jefferson actually used the US Navy (and US Marine Corps) to get a better deal—ultimately defeating the pirates.

The Founders' Axis

With the usual left-right model, Hamilton would be on the left, but almost the entire founding generation would be on the right, if not the hard right. Again, turning the axis ninety degrees clockwise clarifies this point. Hamilton was almost alone in wanting to create a top-down government. His five-hour dissertation at the Philadelphia convention on 18 Jun 1787 was ignored.[138] The founding generation's mood era embraced bottom-up government and rejected top-down centralization.

136 The line in the Marine Hymn refers to Jefferson sending the Navy against the Barbary Pirates.

137 Patrick N. Teye, "Barbary Pirates: Thomas Jefferson, William Eaton, the Evolution of US Diplomacy in the Mediterranean" (master's thesis, East Tennessee State University, 2013), http://dc.etsu.edu/cgi/viewcontent.cgi?article=2355&context=etd

138 "Debates in the Federal Convention of 1787," James Madison, TeachingAmericanHistory, http://teachingamericanhistory.org/convention/debates/0618-2/.

Part 2

The Constitution

6

On Constitutional Checks and Balances

This chapter provides an atypical perspective of the Constitution. Rather than the work of a constitutional scholar or lawyer, it is a blue-collar view through the eyes of a mechanic who understands how mechanisms work. One merely needs to understand a tug-of-war. Newton's third law of physics states that "for every action there is an equal and opposite reaction." The Constitution defines a political system intended to keep the political tug-of-war stalemated so that it does not infringe on the liberty of the people. This is why the military oath is to protect and defend the Constitution, not government officials.

The founders were brilliant men who created a landmark document; however, they would be the first to admit that it was imperfect as ratified in 1787. This chapter rejects the belief that we have no one among us of the stature of the founders. How could that possibly be so with the technology we have developed in just the last decade? The intelligence is there. That there are many men and women who volunteer to risk their lives by entering combat should give us hope that we also have men and women of the same character today. We have not degenerated as a species. We just need to find the character and intelligence embodied in an adequate forum. Furthermore, we need to address not just the Constitution as it was initially ratified. We need to address the Constitution as it is today. In some ways, it has been improved; in other ways, it has been weakened. We must ask ourselves if the Constitution as it is today is sufficient to protect our liberty.

Introduction

The typical view of the term "checks and balances" is that the three branches of the "federal" government keep one another in check with a balance of power.[139] This view only sees the horizontal balance of powers within our "federal" government. It ignores the strength of federalism's additional vertical checks, where the levels of government participate interactively rather than dictate from the top down. Bottom-up interaction is rule by the people. Without it, the people do not rule.

The framers well understood human nature and designed a structure of government that would limit itself—as long as human self-interest between parts of the federal system (intraconstitutional) were not corrupted by tighter allegiances to entities outside of the constitutional framework of the government (extraconstitutional). That balance has been compromised today, and the result is that government officials universally ignore their sworn responsibilities. The extraconstitutional[140] factions exerting forces are complex, but they include the two major political parties and the administrative state itself. There is less tension[141] between the constitutional branches of government than there is between political parties. The administrative state has its own self-interest, and it certainly does not include a reduction in the size of government to its constitutional boundaries. Virtually every institution

---

139 "Checks and Balances: The Constitutional Structure for Limited and Balanced Government," W. David Stedman and LaVaughn G. Lewis, National Center for Constitutional Studies. accessed July 29, 2016, https://nccs.net/online-resources/our-ageless-constitution/checks-balances-a-limited-and-balanced-government.

"Index Page—The US Constitution," USConstitution.net, accessed July 01, 2016, http://www.usconstitution.net/.

140 *Extraconstitutional* should not be confused with *unconstitutional*. It implies that the entity is not described within the text of the Constitution. *Intraconstitutional* implies that the entity is described within the Constitution.

141 The use of the word "tension" is significant. In mechanical engineering, tension and compression are opposite forces used to stabilize structures. For example, a truss is designed to keep a house up using this concept. They are designed by a method of joints. For an example of this method, see "Trusses—Method of Joints," University of Memphis Department of Civil Engineering, http://www.ce.memphis.edu/3121/notes/notes_03b.pdf. The checks and balances in the Constitution are probably better visualized as a tug-of-war, where the factions pull against each other. The government is stable as long as neither side is pulled into the mud. The term "tension" is still appropriate. The model proposed can be viewed as *extraconstitutional* forces joining in on one side of the rope to defeat the other side, where there is tension between the *intraconstitutional* parties.

in the country (inside or outside of the government) ignores Washington and Madison's warnings[142] and exerts forces that overwhelm the constitutional framework.

The difficulty in which we find ourselves cannot be fixed by only addressing the structure of government. The extent to which the current system of checks and balances reinforces the tension between branches and levels of government needs to be understood for its strengths and weaknesses. The proper balance between intraconstitutional and extraconstitutional forces must be ensured for the government to run properly. Intraconstitutional tensions need to be strengthened, and the extraconstitutional forces need to be seriously reduced. This chapter focuses on strengthening intraconstitutional tension. The next chapter will address reducing the extraconstitutional forces.

Perspective

The perspective taken in this chapter is that the US Constitution describes a mechanism of government. The framers actually described the structure and behavior of a government exactly as computer engineers do when they solve a problem with *object-oriented* techniques today.[143] A closer inspection of the Constitution and closer reading of supporting documentation from the framers reveal that they were not so naïve as to rely solely on a horizontal system of checks and balances. They did not view it as a solution to limiting the national government. That is why they instituted vertical checks.[144]

---

142 James Madison, "Federalists Nos. 9 and 10," *The Independent Journal*, 1787.

George Washington, "The Address of General Washington to the People of the United States on His Declining of the Presidency of the United States," American Daily Advertiser, 1796.

143 Object Modeling Group, "OMG Unified Modeling Language (OMG UML), Superstructure. Version 2.4.1." 2014.

Bertrand Meyer, Object-Oriented Software Construction (Cambridge, MA: Prentice Hall International Series in Computer Science, 1988), 23.

144 US Const. art. I, sect. 3, par. 1, cl. 2. It states, "chosen by the Legislature thereof."

Ibid., art. V. It states, "on the Application of the Legislatures of two thirds of the several States."

US Bill of Rights, amen. X.

Consider the following passages from *The Federalist Papers*:

> *No. 51:* The different governments will control each other, at the same time that each will be controlled by itself.
>
> *No. 39*: In its foundation it is federal, not national; in the sources from which the ordinary powers of the government are drawn, it is partly federal and partly national; in the operation of these powers, it is national, not federal; in the extent of them, again, it is federal, not national; and, finally, in the authoritative mode of introducing amendments, it is neither wholly federal nor wholly national.
>
> *No. 45*: The operations of the federal government will be most extensive and important in times of war and danger; those of the State governments, in times of peace and security. As the former periods will probably bear a small proportion to the latter, the State governments will here enjoy another advantage over the federal government.

It should be clear why we refer to it as the *federal* government rather than the *national* government. Madison was selling the Constitution to a suspicious public. A *national government* would have been a much harder sell. The public at the time well understood the true meaning of "federal" as "distributed." It is derived from the Latin term for "league." When Madison describes the function of government as *federal*, he means that it functions with the power emanating from the bottom up (with the people in control), putting liberty over security. Referring to the function as *national* implies that the people defer to a top-down power structure where direction comes from the national level, prioritizing security over liberty.

Computerized flight systems today depend on *federated* system architecture for redundancy and reliability to protect human life. These systems are loosely coupled and function independently and are distributed in nature. Madison's arguments were so persuasive that succeeding generations have lost the political context for the distinction between the words "national" and "federal." We should rightfully only refer to the government centered in Washington, DC, as *national*, not *federal*. The *system* is *federal* only if the states are included in context.

In the Constitution, the founders confine themselves to defining the relationships between the *national* government and the *states* rather than addressing governance all the way down to the local level. Their view was that the states were appropriately viewed as agents of the people and further relationship development would be antithetical to liberty. Again, there are parallels in modern computer software that promote loose coupling.[145]

Most Americans today view the "federal" government as being supreme to the states. Misinterpretation of the supremacy clause is perhaps the main reason for this. The supremacy clause establishes that the Constitution itself and all laws derived by application of the structure and behaviors of the Constitution are the "supreme law of the land." The phrase "made in Pursuance thereof" is conveniently ignored.[146] The fundamental problem is that the Tenth Amendment should be interpreted *before* the supremacy clause, not after it. This was the intent of Madison, the First Congress, and the states that ratified it. The framers viewed that the national government was granted powers from the bottom up, by the people, via the states.[147] This means that the states participate with sovereign authority to check the power of the national government, not as inferiors being held hostage by the national government withholding funds that it should probably not be collecting.[148]

---

145 In particular, the principle of data hiding makes the inner workings of a lower-level component invisible to a higher level. Likewise, the Constitution allows recursion, where states, counties, and localities can define their own detailed constitutions—so long as there is no conflict in sovereignty.

146 US Const., art. V, par. 2.

147 Declaration of Independence, par. 2. It states, "That to secure these rights, Governments are instituted among Men."

US Const., amen. X. It states, "are reserved to the States respectively, or to the people."

148 Mark R. Levin, *The Liberty Amendments: Restoring the American Republic* (New York: Threshold Editions, 2013), 6.

The Sixteenth and Seventeenth Amendments have combined to disrupt the relationship between the national and state governments, but the process actually began during the Civil War period. After the Civil War, the southern states were forced to submit to the will of the northern states through reunification. As a by-product of this process, the national government's authority over states in general grew, and the vertical checks on the national government's power diminished. With each generation, the national government became more powerful, while state power diminished.

Horizontal Checks and Balances

The first three articles of the Constitution lay out the three branches of the national government, complete with some high-level rules of behavior for each. Article I, section 7 describes the familiar *horizontal* checks and balances between the executive and legislative branches. These *horizontal* checks are the most familiar and frequently mistaken to be the complete set.

Article III, section 1 gives the legislature the power of structuring the judiciary. To a degree, this is a form of check with no balance.

Impeachment is a big hammer when it comes to checks and balances. The House of Representatives brings the charges, and the Senate tries the case. Impeachment is not confined to the presidency. The lack of its use is indicative of a government that is not policing itself due to extraconstitutional forces, like political parties. In addition, those same forces can cause unjustified use of the power.

Notice that there is no judicial branch check or balance over either of the other two branches outlined in the Constitution. The conundrum is that the framers never clearly established what entity or entities determine constitutionality.[149] The Constitution itself is silent on judicial review; however, there is actually a wealth of information on the subject in the writings of the various founders. It is important to remember that

149 US Const., art. III.

the English language has moved since the Constitution was ratified. The term *judicial review* itself was introduced in 1910 by Edwin Corwin.[150] The founders did in fact recognize the importance of an entity to determine constitutionality. The term they used was *ultimate arbiter.* As will be seen, the judiciary was specifically excluded from this power in the convention. Unfortunately, some sources of the time do occasionally promote what we call judicial review. The debate continues to this day.

Dr. Natelson argues that the founders assumed there would be agreement on judicial review because of colonial precedence.[151] Hamilton's opinion in *Federalist No. 78* supports this view. Among other sources, Jefferson's letter to William Jarvis below suggests that the agreement was not universal. Professor Natelson's view is that the Federalists believed the court would strike down unconstitutional laws; the anti-Federalists did not.

Evidence from the convention notes shows that proposed amendment number eight of the original Virginia Plan contains a provision to join the executive and members of the judicial branch into a *council of revision.*[152] Elbridge Gerry is the first to raise an objection to this proposal on 4 Jun 1787, stating that the judiciary would have the opportunity to decide if a law is unconstitutional when it is brought before the court.[153] The proposal is defeated but brought up again by James Wilson on 21 Jul 1787. In both cases, the framers seem to worry about diminishing the power of the executive. Their perspective from colonial experience is that the legislature will be the dominant branch,

---

150 Wood, Gordon S. "The Origins of Judicial Review Revisited, or How the Marshall Court Made More out of Less." Review. *Washington and Lee Law Review* 56, no. 3 (June 1, 1999): 789.

151 Natelson, *Original Constitution*, 148–149.

152 "Debates in the Federal Convention of 1787: Tuesday, May 29," TeachingAmericanHistory, accessed July 08, 2016, http://teachingamericanhistory.org/convention/debates/0529-2/. Amendment 8 of the original 15 amendments of the Virginia Plan.

153 "Debates in the Federal Convention of 1787 | Teaching American History." Teaching American History. Accessed August 02, 2016. http://teachingamericanhistory.org/convention/debates/0604-2/.

and they worry that the executive must be capable of defending itself from the legislature. The proposal subsequently becomes the presidential veto in the final document.

We *do* have direct evidence that the delegates in the Convention did not ultimately approve of Supreme Court rulings as the final word on constitutionality from Madison's Constitutional Convention notes on 27 Aug 1787. The notes read as follows:

> Doctor JOHNSON moved to insert the words, "this Constitution and the," before the word "laws."
> Mr. MADISON doubted whether it was not going too far, to extend the jurisdiction of the Court generally to cases arising under the Constitution, and whether it ought not to be limited to cases of a judiciary nature. The right of expounding the Constitution, in cases not of this nature, ought not to be given to that department.
> The motion of Doctor Johnson was agreed to, *nem. con.*, it being generally supposed, that the jurisdiction given was constructively limited to cases of a judiciary nature.[154]

The section in question here became Article III, section 2. It was ultimately altered by the Eleventh Amendment in 1795, whereby Congress and the states restricted the power of the court.[155] The use of the term *constructively limit* is important and precise in meaning. The framers are specifically telling us that the Supreme Court should not have the power to dictate what is constitutional to the other branches. These notes make it clear that all the delegates present intended that the Supreme Court would confine itself to issues within the judicial branch.[156] This is reinforced by further rejections elsewhere during the convention proceedings to allowing the court into extrajudicial functions.[157]

---

154 Dr. Johnson is William Samuel Johnson from Connecticut. "Madison's Debates August 27," Avalon Project, http://avalon.law.yale.edu/18th_century/debates_827.asp.

155 US Const., art. III, sec. 2.

156 Hamilton was not present on August 27, 1787, but he did sign the Constitution.

157 "CRS Annotated Constitution," Legal Information Institute, accessed July 08, 2016, https://www.law.cornell.edu/anncon/html/art3frag14_user.html.

The debate over the oath in amendment fourteen of the original Virginia Plan on 23 Jul 1787 shows the belief that public virtue was to determine the viability of the republic.[158] The body of evidence in the notes is that the delegates to the convention believed that the *ultimate arbiter* was not the Supreme Court. It was the people. The first limitation was to be each official's virtue and restraint. It appears the expectation was that the legislature would impeach judges as well as presidents who behaved badly. Closer reading of *Federalist 44* reveals that the framers expected the people to remove officials who refused to respect their constitutional restrictions and elect officials who would undo the damage. A subtle implication of this is that defying constitutional restrictions *is* bad behavior.

> If it be asked what is to be the consequence, in case the Congress shall misconstrue this part of the Constitution, and exercise powers not warranted by its true meaning, I answer, the same as if they should misconstrue or enlarge any other power vested in them; as if the general power had been reduced to particulars, and any one of these were to be violated; the same, in short, as if the State legislatures should violate the irrespective constitutional authorities. In the first instance, the success of the usurpation will depend on the executive and judiciary departments, which are to expound and give effect to the legislative acts; *and in the last resort a remedy must be obtained from the people who can, by the election of more faithful representatives, annul the acts of the usurpers.*[159] (italics added)

This section shows the executive has the option of vetoing or refusing to execute an *unconstitutional* act. He is obliged to execute a constitutional act. Madison does appear to reverse himself from his convention notes on the judicial role; however, his meaning is not clear since "expound and give effect" could mean that they could refuse to

158 "Debates in the Federal Convention of 1787: Monday, July 23," TeachingAmericanHistory, accessed July 08, 2016, http://teachingamericanhistory.org/convention/debates/0723-2/.

159 "The Avalon Project: Federalist No 44." The Avalon Project: Federalist No 44. Accessed August 02, 2016. http://avalon.law.yale.edu/18th_century/fed44.asp.

hear a case. He does make it clear that the people provide *the last resort remedy* (e.g., *ultimate arbiter*).

To the founders, judicial review is *not* the final word on constitutionality. The people are the *ultimate arbiter*. We should evaluate whether the Constitution sufficiently enables the people to effectively fulfill that role. It is a sensitive adjustment to diminish rage and enable thoughtful sentiment.

Postconstitutional Ratification Modifications

Judicial activism started almost immediately. The Eleventh Amendment was one result to check it.[160] Madison and Jefferson both believed that the Alien and Sedition Act was unconstitutional. They responded by writing the Virginia and Kentucky Resolutions in 1798. These resolutions have been interpreted to support the states *nullifying* unconstitutional national acts.[161] No other states adopted these *principles of '98*. Ironically, both Madison and Jefferson later denied that the resolutions amounted to more than protest.[162]

In 1820, William Jarvis published a book called *The Republican: A Series of Essays*.[163] Jarvis supports judicial review to determine constitutionality on page 84 and supports lifetime appointment on page 148. Thomas Jefferson read his book and voiced his objection to this view in a letter on 28 Sep 1820:

> You seem, in pages 84 and 148, to consider the judges as the *ultimate arbiters* of all constitutional questions; a very dangerous doctrine indeed, and one which would place us under the despotism of an oligarchy. Our judges are as honest as other men, and not

160 Natelson, *Original Constitution*, 257. The court stepped on state sovereignty in *Chisholm v. Georgia*.

161 "1. Thomas Jefferson and the Principles of '98." Mises Institute. Accessed August 02, 2016. https://mises.org/library/1-thomas-jefferson-and-principles-98.

162 "Nullification: Unlawful and Unconstitutional." The Heritage Foundation. Accessed August 02, 2016. http://www.heritage.org/research/factsheets/2012/02/nullification-unlawful-and-unconstitutional.

163 This book is available from Amazon or online at Google Books.

> more so. They have, with others, the same passions for party, for power, and the privilege of their corps . . . Their power [is] the more dangerous as they are in office for life, and not responsible, as the other functionaries are, to the elective control. The Constitution has erected no such single tribunal, knowing that to whatever hands confided, with the corruptions of time and party, its members would become despots. It has more wisely made all the departments co-equal and co-sovereign within themselves.[164] (italics added)

Jefferson's opposition to judicial review as the final word is clear above, and he was not alone. On 27 Jun 1823, Madison wrote to Jefferson as follows:

> I am not unaware that the Judiciary career has not corresponded with what was anticipated. At one period the Judges perverted the Bench of Justice into a rostrum for partizan harangues. And latterly the Court, by some of its decisions, still more by extrajudicial reasonings and dicta, has manifested a propensity to enlarge the general authority in derogation of the local, and to amplify its own jurisdiction, which has justly incurred the public censure. But the abuse of a trust does not disprove its existence. And if no remedy of the abuse be practicable under the forms of the Constitution, I should prefer a resort to the Nation for an amendment of the Tribunal itself, to continual appeals from its controverted decisions to that *Ultimate Arbiter*.[165] (italics added)

What does Madison mean by "I should prefer a resort to the Nation for an amendment of the Tribunal itself?" Perhaps he is calling for an Article V convention to address the issue of determining constitutionality. It is clear that after thirty-five years of experience with the Supreme

---

164 Thomas Jefferson to William Charles Jarvis, letter, September 28, 1820, http://founders.archives.gov/?q=Correspondent%3A%22Jefferson%2C%20Thomas%22%20Correspondent%3A%22Jarvis%2C%20William%20Charles%22&s=1111311111&r=2.

165 James Madison. "Founders Online: To Thomas Jefferson from James Madison, 27 June 1823." To Thomas Jefferson from James Madison, 27 June 1823. Accessed July 29, 2016. http://founders.archives.gov/documents/Jefferson/98-01-02-3597.

Court, he was unhappy with the result and believed the existing solution was unacceptable.

Over years the American public has accepted the view that judicial review as the final word is a part of the checks and balances. It was not intended to be that at all. Perhaps the single biggest weakness in the original Constitution is the lack of a mechanism to determine constitutionality. It is apparent that the designers of the Constitution relied on the public virtue of the legislators to confine themselves to constitutional bounds. History shows that this is insufficient for our current society. The framers and Aristotle would assess that we are not virtuous enough for self-governance since we continue to elect and reelect officials who ignore their constitutional limits.

Analysis

According to strict construction, the national government is restricted to "enumerated powers." Alexander Hamilton immediately attacked this with his doctrine of discretionary powers. Nevertheless, national law that is derived outside of the bounds of the Constitution should not be supreme. In the founders' view, it shouldn't even be a law. Each branch was expected to faithfully observe its limitations.

None of the three branches of the current national government observe their limitations, but an imbalance among the branches has developed that was not envisioned by the framers. The framers worried that the legislature would overpower the other two national branches. In point of fact, it has delegated its legislative responsibilities to the other two branches, which have willingly accepted the power. The legislative branch has delegated its power in exchange for incumbency. By avoiding key legislation, incumbents can avoid blame and get reelected. Instead of exceeding its power horizontally, the legislature has exceeded its power vertically—and the perception of judicial review enables it. *We the people* have failed to fulfill our role as the *ultimate arbiter*.

There is still a great degree of controversy over judicial review. Although Hamilton suggests judicial review in *Federalist No. 78* and although there is colonial precedence for it,[166] the issue is established by Supreme Court rulings, not the Constitution itself. Strictly speaking, that means that the judicial branch itself usurped powers it is not granted by the Constitution.[167] Thomas Jefferson well understood that and objected to the danger of oligarchy by the Supreme Court.[168] Likewise, Madison was clearly against it. Questionable decisions like *Dred Scott v. Sanford*, *Wickard v. Filburn*, and numerous others have clearly been outside the bounds of the Constitution and set the country on a dangerous path where national power grows without bound.[169] The net effect has invariably been less liberty.

Marbury v. Madison is cited as establishing judicial review as we know it. The overlooked point on the ruling is that it is actually confined to the constitutional restriction of a *judiciary nature*. The judicial branch did not invade the domain of either of the other branches. Likewise, *Federalist 39* is frequently cited as Madison's support of judicial review. In fact, his point is consistent with *Marbury* and the notes from the convention. He speaks of the national tribunal determining jurisdiction—which is *of a judiciary nature*.[170]

Robert Lowry Clinton prefers the term *judicial supremacy* to *judicial review* to describe the encroachment of the judicial branch over the other two branches (and the states). He points to *Cooper v. Aaron* in 1958 as actually establishing judicial supremacy.[171] This latter point is unsatisfying given that the Supreme Court struck down the legislature's

---

166 Natelson, *Original Constitution*, 148–149.

167 Levin, *Liberty Amendments*, 5.

168 Jefferson to Jarvis, September 28, 1820.

169 Levin, *Liberty Amendments*

170 Federalist 39. "It is true that in controversies relating to the boundary between the two jurisdictions, the tribunal which is ultimately to decide, is to be established under the general government. But this does not change the principle of the case."

171 Robert Lowry Clinton. "How the Court Became Supreme | Robert Lowry Clinton." First Things. Accessed August 02, 2016. http://www.firstthings.com/article/1999/01/001-how-the-court-became-supreme. Robert Lowry Clinton. *Marbury v. Madison and Judicial Review*. Lawrence, Kan.: University Press of Kansas, 1989.

(and FDR's) *National Industrial Recovery Act* as unconstitutional in 1935's *Schechter v. United States.*[172] Let scholars debate judicial review. The important point is that the executive branch today will enforce law based upon judicial supremacy. The national legislature and bureaucracy will continue to encroach upon state sovereignty and individual liberty, sanctioned by the Supreme Court. Instead of each branch restraining itself, the branches are reinforcing each other's bad behavior.

Since the start of the twentieth century, some of the nastiest political maneuvering has centered on composing the Supreme Court to favor a political party. This is an example of party allegiance trumping the duties of office and illuminates that judicial review is actually a weak point in intraconstitutional tension, because extraconstitutional forces converge on the Supreme Court as if it were a battlefield. Instead of enhancing the balance of power, judicial review is less a check and balance than it is a usurpation that places the Supreme Court as a parent figure settling disputes between political parties for the sake of party power. The founders never intended for the public to be concerned about Supreme Court rulings in their daily lives.[173] Today, their rulings have incredible impact.

The United States will never obey the Constitution unless the role of *ultimate arbiter* is taken from the Supreme Court and placed back in the hands of the people. It has become the epitome of a fox guarding the henhouse. In the early days of the republic, it was not the problem it is today. In those days, the extraconstitutional forces were relatively weak and the intraconstitutional forces were stronger. Government officials first viewed themselves as citizens of the several states instead of citizens of the country at large.[174] This attempted horizontal check could be better accomplished by a vertical check whereby a determinant entity

---

172 "Schechter Poultry Corp. v. United States (1935)." LII / Legal Information Institute. Accessed August 05, 2016. https://www.law.cornell.edu/wex/schechter_poultry_corp._v._united_states_1935.

173 "Madison Debates August 27," Avalon Project.

174 Joseph J. Ellis, *Founding Brothers: The Revolutionary Generation* (New York: Alfred A. Knopf, 2000), 26.

beholden to the states determines what is constitutional. This would replace a top-down establishment with a bottom-up determination, thereby restoring a semblance of self-governance to the people. It is also consistent in that the creators of the Constitution (the states) determine constitutionality henceforth.

Replacing the existing Supreme Court review with a vertical check emanating from the states may in fact move the battlefield from the Supreme Court to the states. At first, in *Federalist No. 10*,[175] this distribution appears to defy Madison's reasoning for a large republic. Madison suggests a way to avoid faction. Today the factions have indeed formed, and we need to break them up. It is a different problem from the one Madison pondered.

The recommended solution is a divide and conquer strategy familiar to anyone with a military background.[176] I cover this more in the subsequent chapter on weakening the extraconstitutional forces, but it does also strengthen the intraconstitutional tensions. The states have much more interest in adhering to the Constitution than does the national government. Moreover, this change to a state-centric review strengthens the Tenth Amendment.

Vertical Checks and Balances

Although not commonly viewed as such, there were originally two vertical checks on national power in the Constitution, with one more added with the Bill of Rights. The three vertical checks established by the Constitution and the Bill of Rights were[177]

- **Article I, Section 3:** Appointment of senators by state legislatures
- **Article V:** The convention of states

---

175 James Madison, "Federalist No. 10," *The Independent Journal*, 1787.

176 Sun Tzu, *the Art of War*, translation and commentary by Lionel Giles (Singapore: Graham Brash, 1993), 38.

177 US Const.

- **Tenth Amendment:** All powers not enumerated are reserved to the states and the people.

Senatorial Selection (the Seventeenth Amendment)

The framers believed that by having the states select senators, the upper house would be accountable to the states. Madison argues that this is a federal characteristic in *Federalist 39*. The states were to be the agents of the people. The clear implication of this is that the unique interests of the citizens in each state would be equally represented in the upper house of the national government. The balance of overall popular representation would be in the lower house.[178]

Postconstitutional Ratification Modification

The Seventeenth Amendment changed the selection of senators from state legislatures to popular vote within the state.[179] It was actually the states that wanted the selection process changed. State legislatures have just as much difficulty in agreeing as the national legislature does. As such, many Senate seats were plagued with vacancies because the states had trouble making appointments. Some states allowed governor appointment to fill the vacancy. Others did not. Leaving a vacancy was counter to the interests of the state, but it was *up to the state* to determine the best approach. The final motivation for what became the Seventeenth Amendment was the conviction of two senators for corruption and David Graham Phillips' "Treason in the Senate" articles in 1906. Teddy Roosevelt called Phillips a muckraker. Although Phillips was scorned for making things up, circulation and sentiment were high in the Progressive Era.[180]

---

178 Ibid.

Alexander Hamilton, John Jay, and James Madison, "Federalists Nos. 62–66," The Independent Journal, 1787.

Natelson, Original Constitution, 61.

179 US Const., amen, XVII.

180 "February 17, 1906: 'Treason of the Senate,'" US Senate, http://www.senate.gov/artandhistory/history/minute/Treason_of_the_Senate.htm.

Today not many know that the states came within two petitions of the required two-thirds for an Article V convention because of the outrage. The national government stepped in and changed the selection process to a popular vote. This was in keeping with the progressive agenda to "bring the government closer to the people."[181] It has had the opposite effect. It has also totally removed the vertical check and strengthened national power at the expense of state power. We cannot know if the result of a convention might have been different, but state legislators at the time may well have recognized their abdication of constitutional power and may have substituted another check rather than simply removing this check.

Analysis

In the framers' day, a person's integrity was very important. The same cannot be said for today's society. As a result, extraconstitutional forces are much stronger today than in the founders' time. As such, the original provision in the Constitution might be insufficient today. There is a need to reinstitute a check by the states on the national legislature. The founders were probably correct in putting the check on the Senate. The problems with state appointments were exaggerated during the Progressive Era.

Solving the representation issues was originally up to the states, and they could have resolved them with the original constitutional authority. The states have more motivation for being a watchdog trained on senators than does the national government—*because* the senators *are* the national government. Senators have more interest in covering up corruption than exposing it. Because of the prevalence of incumbency, there is no watchdog looking out for the states' interests in the Senate. In a system where the states are agents of people, the people's interests are being ignored. An improvement to the original mechanism would clearly be to give the states the power to recall senators. There is no doubt a spectrum of creative solutions between the absence of the check we have today and the original mechanism, but it needs to be a check

181 Robert La Follette 1913.

that is both strong enough and easily enforced—unlike the current requirement on the states for an Article V convention.[182]

Article V

Although not acknowledged as such, part of the reason for replacing the Articles of Confederation with the Constitution was the lack of a functional amendment process. We tend to forget that the very existence of a detailed amendment process was new when Article V was inserted into the Constitution. The amendment process itself was included in the Constitution for four reasons:[183]

1. Repair framer fallibility
2. Correct abuses in the system (fix corruption and fraud)
3. Settle disputes over interpretation
4. Adapt to changing conditions

There is only one fundamental way to ratify an amendment: it requires three-quarters of the existing states to approve an amendment. There are two ways that an amendment can be proposed to the states. The first way is for two-thirds of each house of the national legislature to agree on a proposal. The legislatures meet periodically. This is the only means exercised to date.

The second way to propose amendments to the Constitution is for two-thirds of the states to petition for a convention of states.[184] This aperiodic mechanism directly addresses the second reason for amendment: abuses in the system by the national government itself. The notes from the Constitutional Convention for 15 Sep 1787 suggest that the motivation for the second method is to escape tyranny peacefully:

---

182 "Homepage," Bill Walker, Friends of the Article V Convention, http://www.foavc.org/.

183 "Archive for the 'Rob Natelson' Category," John Caldara, Independence Institute, accessed July 01, 2016, http://www.joncaldara.com/category/rob-natelson-2/.

184 US Const., art. V.

> Col: MASON thought the plan of amending the Constitution exceptionable and dangerous. As the proposing of amendments is in both the modes to depend, in the first immediately, in the second, ultimately, on Congress, no amendments of the proper kind would ever be obtained by the people, if the Government should become oppressive, as he verily believed would be the case.[185]

Postconstitutional Ratification Modification

Article V has never been modified.

Analysis

Our normal view of an Article V convention of states as an emergency measure to avoid tyranny is problematic. There has never been a successful call for an Article V convention of states in over 225 years. Is it accurate to say that the national government has never been oppressive? The definition of oppression is subjective and based on perception. As the national government has steadily gained power, the states and the people have adjusted their perception of what oppression is. Each generation has accepted more intrusion by the national government than did its predecessors. The fact that the national government routinely threatens to withhold funds to states that defy it is evidence of oppression. The National Maximum Speed Law (a speed limit of fifty-five miles per hour) is just one clear example.[186] What recourse have the states (as agents of the citizenry) had? Individual citizens have also been intimidated by national power. One example is the Gold Reserve Act that made possession of gold illegal for private citizens. History is telling us that the mechanism of vertical checks is ineffective as is because abuses in the system by the national government have gone unchecked.

Although there was a unanimous consensus at the Constitutional Convention that the second method was necessary, what has been

---

185 "Madison Debates September 15," Avalon Project, http://avalon.law.yale.edu/18th_century/debates_915.asp.

186 P. Grimes, "Nixon Approves Limit of 55 MPH," *The New York Times*, January 3, 1974.

overlooked for over two centuries is that the use of the two methods of amendment proposal needs to be balanced to check power at *both* levels. Although the common fraction, two-thirds, seems consistent, it limits different functions. For Congress, it is merely a supermajority of votes on a proposal that has already been discussed by a Congress that meets periodically. For the second method, the states cannot even convene to discuss amendment proposals until a supermajority of them petition to convene an aperiodic convention under Article V. The founders did not have two centuries of empirical evidence to evaluate the performance of Article V, as we do today. Likewise, they may not have considered the consequences of the limit with fifty states (requiring thirty-four) as opposed to thirteen (requiring nine). The amendment process is intended to be used to fix flaws in the Constitution. This is a flaw.

The fact that a convention of states has never been called reinforces the perception that the intention was that this method only be employed as a last resort. What if that isn't the case? Closer inspection of George Mason's argument for inserting the second method exposes a severe flaw of omission; however, it does not assert that the method is *only* to be used to remedy oppression. In fact, the convention of states method of amendment was the only method in the first revision of the original Virginia Plan on 6 Aug 1787.[187] Mason's use of the term *oppression* ensured unanimous consensus. It is not clear how the requirement for two-thirds of the states came to be, but it appears that the framers underestimated the difficulty. Consider the profound functional change of the government if conventions were called, say, every five years. The mechanism (federal system) would work in a much more bottom-up fashion with the agents of the people (the states) more empowered.

Recently, the controversy over judicial review has been eclipsed by hysteria over the convention of states by organizations like the John Birch Society and the Eagle Forum. This hysteria is confounding. How states proposing amendments could be any more dangerous than the

187 "Debates in the Federal Convention of 1787 | Teaching American History." Teaching American History. Accessed August 03, 2016. http://teachingamericanhistory.org/convention/debates/0806-2/.

national legislature proposing them is amazing to ponder from a people who supposedly champion self-rule. The very reason the second method exists is to preserve liberty, not destroy it, as has been suggested.[188] The argument is even more preposterous when one looks at the rate of failure to propose within the national legislature. There have been more than 11,500 motions in the legislatures to amend the Constitution.[189] Only thirty-three have been sent to the states for ratification. That's a success rate of approximately one-quarter of 1 percent. That is just to get an amendment proposed. Why would we think a convention of states would have significantly higher results? The representatives in Congress meet all the time. State convention commissioners would never have even met. Is it reasonable to believe that they will be more inclined to propose amendments than Congress? The real concern should be that a convention might produce no amendments and that it would never again be possible to get another one called.

Nevertheless, the controversy doesn't stop with whether a convention should be called. There is skepticism about whether we even know what the process should be. This includes disagreement on how the two-thirds requirement is satisfied.[190] This is political atrophy because states have ceased meeting as they did during the founding period.

---

188 "Madison Debates, September 15," Avalon Project.
Levin, Liberty Amendments, 16
Robert Greenstein, "A Constitutional Convention Could Be the Single Most Dangerous Way to 'Fix' American Government," The Washington Post, October 21, 2014, http://www.washingtonpost.com/posteverything/wp/2014/10/21/a-constitutional-convention-could-be-the-single-most-dangerous-way-to-fix-american-government/.

189 "None," Xavier Becerra, PolitiFact, accessed July 06, 2016, http://www.politifact.com/truth-o-meter/statements/2011/aug/30/xavier-becerra/11000-attempts-amend-us-constitution-only-27-amend/; "List of Proposed Amendments to the United States Constitution," *Wikipedia*, last modified June 8, 2016, http://en.wikipedia.org/wiki/List_of_proposed_amendments_to_the_United_States_Constitution.

190 Robert G. Natelson, "The Article V Convention Process and the Restoration of Federalism," *Harvard Journal of Law & Public Policy* 36, accessed June 30, 2016, http://www.harvard-jlpp.com/wp-content/uploads/2013/05/36_3_955_Natelson.pdf.
"Homepage," Bill Walker.

Assume that the two-thirds requirement is too high. A shade-tree mechanic[191] would recognize the lack of ever having called a convention of states as equivalent to a stuck valve in an engine. A software engineer would call this a process suffering from starvation. If the two methods of proposal represented tension and compression forces to make a truss, a mechanical engineer would see that the roof of the house would cave in. Before the Constitution was accepted, the states convened frequently.[192] It is doubtful that the framers intended to stifle that process. Some form of damping is only prudent because stability is very important. A document that is too heavily amended becomes useless. If two-thirds is too high, what should the threshold be? We have empirical data that helps.

Consider the rate of amendment that exists. It has happened twenty-seven times.[193] The first ten are the Bill of Rights and were passed together. The Twenty-Seventh Amendment was actually one of the first twelve proposed by Madison for the Bill of Rights.[194] That means that in reality, there have been sixteen amendments passed in approximately 225 years, or a rate of one amendment every fourteen years. They have all been proposed by the national legislature. Not one reduces national power. The requirement on state proposal should allow for a comparable rate so that the tug-of-war would be at equilibrium. There is a clear imbalance. The national government's self-interest will always concentrate power to itself. The states must have an equal tension to distribute power from the national government rather than to allow it to centralize. As a point of emphasis, lowering the threshold for calling a convention does not reduce the requirement for ratification. As such, it only strengthens the vertical check without opening a new potential for abuse.

---

191 Referring to a car hobbyist as opposed to a professional mechanic. The term refers to parking a car under a shade tree while working rather than a professional shop.

192 Ibid.

"State Initiation of Constitutional Amendments: A Guide for Lawyers and Legislative Drafters," Robert G. Natelson, Independence Institute, accessed June 30, 2016, https://www.i2i.org/wp-content/uploads/2015/01/Compendium-4.0-plain.pdf. See page 14.

193 US Const.

194 "US Constitution Online," Steve Mount, last modified March 6, 2011, http://www.usconstitution.net/xconst_Am27.html.

Inspection of the distribution of state applications gives insight into the potential for balancing the rate of amendment. To avoid the controversy of how to count requests, high-water marks of same-subject requests, one per state, are subtotaled.[195] We have the advantage of 225 years of empirical evidence that the founders did not have. A total of thirty-nine unique issues achieved the following distribution of states petitioning for a convention for that issue:

Table 2 Article V Convention of States Applications

Count of state petitions	Occurrences	Notes
5 or fewer	27	Below initial threshold of 8
8	1	
9	1	
10	1	
13	1	
14	1	
15	1	
16	1	
20	1	
28	2	
29	1	Led to 17th Amendment
33	1	13 rescinded; 3 reapplied.

We can now use a process similar to a Fermi estimate to derive a more effective threshold for balancing the tension between the national government and the states.[196] No petition with fewer than nine states could have ever succeeded. By 1860, there were thirty-three states in the union. Prior to that, there had only been a couple of petitions for an Article V convention of states. The year 1861 was significant in terms of

195 "Homepage," Bill Walker.

196 "Fermi Estimate," Brilliant.org, accessed July 06, 2016, https://brilliant.org/wiki/fermi-estimate/.

petitions in attempts to avoid the Civil War. Twelve states petitioned to address slavery. At the time, that was around 38 percent of the states. If the ratio from two-thirds to a simple majority of states had been lowered, the threshold would have been met four times in 225 years. This does not achieve parity with the national method that produced thirty-three proposals for ratification. Lowering to one-third only increases the rate to six times in 225 years. This is still not achieving parity.

Today, two-thirds of the states is thirty-four. If there were one hundred states, it would be sixty-seven. If thirty-four is not achievable, how could a higher number like this ever be achieved? What is missing here is the distinction between starting a discussion and approval. Requiring three-quarters for ratification reinforces a democratic principle for consensus; however, the same requirement for a percentage to *start* discussion actually inhibits the democratic process and enables implicit dictate because the citizenry is never engaged in the determination process. What if we abandon the idea of using a ratio and use a fixed number instead?

When the Constitution was ratified, there were only thirteen states. That means it took nine states to achieve the two-thirds ratio. A key insight here is that it is no easier today to get nine states to agree to something than it was in the founders' day. One concept for expansion during the founding generation was that the original states would grow westward to the West Coast. Jefferson's proposal for the checkerboard we see today had not yet been adopted.[197] If the threshold for calling a convention were a simple nine, it would have been achieved eleven times in 225 years. That is approaching parity with the national method, but we shouldn't lose sight of the fact that we're talking about just getting a convention called. Once the convention is called, there is no guarantee of success in producing an amendment. If it were fifty-fifty, that would produce five or six proposals (as opposed to thirty-three from the national legislature). The probability of ratification at this point is high, but it is not 100 percent. So, the net effect would be more like four or five amendments produced in 225 years.

197 Mark Stein, *How the States Got Their Shapes* (New York: Harper Paperbacks, 2009). 28.

This is still not pure parity, but it gives states a fighting chance to keep the division between state and national power in balance.

This exercise should demonstrate that lowering the requirement for simply *calling* a convention of states would not be as destabilizing as one might intuitively suspect. Furthermore, an argument that is totally ignored is that a bar that is too low is easily raised by using the process itself to make the correction. A bar that is too high cannot be easily lowered. We should err on the side of too low a bar, not too high. To ensure that the national government cannot oppress the states, it should be prohibited from adjusting the bar higher.

Going one step further, the second method could be switched from its current aperiodic scheme to a periodic scheme where states regularly meet with the full authority to propose amendments, just as the national legislature does for method one.

Consider the side effects of making this stuck valve work properly. On the positive side, history shows that the national legislature will react to just the threat of a convention being called. It would also increase citizen awareness because the issues would be closer to them. It is pure speculation, but a renewed sense of being able to affect one's destiny might cure a lot of apathy and encourage a more informed electorate. This would be analogous to putting better fuel in the engine of a car. Elections might actually produce better results.

So, what is the potential downside to frequent conventions of states? With the three-quarters requirement intact for ratification, a poor amendment is no more likely to be ratified than it was before. Fiscal waste is obviously a bad side effect. Technology can easily mitigate the expense of a convention. Telepresence renders the need to meet physically outdated.[198]

---

198 "Telepresence," *Wikipedia*, last modified June 10, 2016, http://en.wikipedia.org/wiki/Telepresence.

Tenth Amendment

The Tenth Amendment was meant to limit the national government in favor of the states—and consequently the people.[199] It has always been at odds with the supremacy clause (and the interpretation of the commerce clause). The Amendment *should* be considered an integral part of the Constitution and interpreted *before* the supremacy clause, but that has not always been the case. The founding generation's state-citizen-first attitude has diminished to the point where citizens today hardly acknowledge the existence of the states in governance, which is in line with Hamilton's view. The lack of balance in this dichotomy is the reason. An amendment to settle disputes on interpretation may well be justified to restore this balance and strengthen the intraconstitutional tension. At stake is the very existence of federalism.

Postconstitutional Ratification Modification

The Tenth Amendment is verbally intact as written; however, over time, the Supreme Court has largely negated this check on national power.[200] In so doing, it has assumed more power for itself and convinced the public that only horizontal checks and balances are meant to exist.

Analysis

The power of the Tenth Amendment was seriously tarnished by the Civil War. Today many seem to view restoring power to the states as sanctioning slavery. Their view is that the national government is morally superior to the states because the national government took slavery from the southern states. That is to ignore that it was actually half the states that vanquished the other half. Consider that most Civil War units were fielded by the states.[201] Ohio alone sent 197. There were only 19 national infantry regiments.

---

199 US Bill of Rights, amen. X.

200 "Supremacy Clause a Menace to State and Individual Rights," Sharon Kasica, Greensboro Guardian, November 16, 2012,

http://greensboroguardian.com/2012/11/16/supremacy-clause-a-menace-to-state-individual-rights/.

201 "Regimental Index," Civil War Archive, accessed July 06, 2016, http://www.civilwararchive.com/regim.htm.

Does it seem reasonable that the members of the national government themselves are universally more honorable than those in state government? If so, that implies that there is inherently increased morality in becoming a member of the national-level government than one in state-level government. How can that be? This thinking is counter to Lord Acton's assertion that "Power tends to corrupt, and absolute power corrupts absolutely."

Natelson makes an even more powerful argument against the moral superiority of the national government. He points to the Peace Conference of 1861. After the failure of the Crittenden Compromise in Congress, Virginia called for a convention of states.[202] The states did author amendments, but since it was not an Article V convention of states, they could only send them to Congress for consideration. According to Natelson, the wording of the amendments would have led to the end of slavery without the bloodshed.[203] The national government's inactivity cost over six hundred thousand Americans their lives and set the wheels in motion for diminishing the Tenth Amendment and elevating the perception of the power of the supremacy clause.

The truth is that all levels of government are composed of people of no better moral fiber than any other level. In fact, it could be argued that today the most ambitious people seek national office. Are we to ignore Madison's reference to ambition in his analysis of factions?[204] Likewise, are we to ignore Lord Acton's warnings?

In fact, the Tenth Amendment is the strongest statement of self-governance in the entire Constitution and Bill of Rights. The feeling of the American public that they have no say is largely due to the fact that

---

202 "Amendments Proposed by the Peace Conference, February 8–27, 1861," Avalon Project, accessed July 06, 2016, http://avalon.law.yale.edu/19th_century/peace.asp.

203 "Avalon Project - Amendments Proposed by the Peace Conference, February 8-27, 1861." Avalon Project - Amendments Proposed by the Peace Conference, February 8-27, 1861. N.p., n.d. Web. 13 Aug. 2016.

204 Madison, "Federalists Nos. 9 and 10."

this Amendment has been virtually abandoned.[205] That feeling of futility has led to apathy. Apathy has led to a less informed public that is not well suited to self-governance. The prophecy is self-fulfilling and enables the ancient Greek *kyklos* to turn to tyranny.[206] It's less a question of *if* the republic will descend into oligarchy than *how deeply* it will descend. When Mark Levin argues that we are living in a post-constitutional time,[207] is he not arguing that we may have already descended into oligarchy?

As noted in the section on horizontal checks and balances, the Supreme Court's power of judicial review is the single biggest impediment to establishing a better system of checks and balances that will encourage the national government to obey the Constitution and, consequently, the Tenth Amendment.

Summary

In *The Federalist Papers*, James Madison's discussions on factions present some of the best political theory of all time. Unfortunately, his arguments alone could not save us from ourselves. The fact is that the Constitution is the rule book that defines the rules of the game of American politics. As with any participant in any game, politicians will always try to bend or change the rules to their own advantage. Madison and the other founders recognized this concern and tried to create mechanisms strong enough to keep the game fair for the public's welfare.

Over the years, the intraconstitutional tensions established by the framers have given way to the extraconstitutional forces in the country today. This highlights a reality of human nature—someone will always try to cheat the system. Our challenge today is to strengthen the intraconstitutional tensions and reduce the extraconstitutional forces. The first part of this dichotomy requires that we ensure that the

---

205 The states are the agents of the people. When they are silenced, the people are silenced.

206 "Kyklos," digplanet

207 Mark R. Levin, *The Liberty Amendments: Restoring the American Republic* (New York: Threshold Editions, 2013), 2.

internal checks and balances are strengthened where they are weak. There is no way to strengthen the Constitution without amendment. Additionally, the power of political parties and other governmental and nongovernmental institutions promoting extraconstitutional forces must be reduced.

Anyone who understands human nature can see that a system of checks and balances that exists only at the national level of government is broken. The combination of judicial review and the supremacy clause conspire to keep the national jackboot on the throat of the states (our *agents*)—and, worse, "We the People." The Constitution was originally designed to retard or prevent the republic from descending into tyranny. As much as we all revere the founders, they were not perfect men. They knew it, and they knew that succeeding generations would likewise be imperfect. They gave us Article V to fix and adjust their miscalculations—and to fix those of generations between them and us.

We need to heed Jefferson's warning about judicial review. He was truly prescient. It has not only exposed a weak point for extraconstitutional forces to exploit, but it has all but destroyed the necessary vertical check of the Tenth Amendment. Frequent conventions among the colonies and states led to the creation of the United States. We should reignite this bottom-up, vertical methodology of governance. There are two ways to schedule any process—periodic and aperiodic. The convention of states process in Article V is aperiodic. That is, it takes two-thirds of the states to petition for a convention of states. History clearly shows that this requirement is too high to allow the states to check the amendment process of the national legislature. The author submits that this is an unrecognized flaw in the proper functioning of the Constitution. Without it, the national government will continue to assume more power. An Article V convention of states is the only constitutional means by which the states (and consequently the people) can check national abuses of any nature.

Periodic scheduling of processes is very familiar to software engineers. There is no accommodation in the Constitution for a periodic convention of states. A periodic convention of states for the express purpose of reviewing the constitutionality of all laws passed by the national government is but one possible way to replace judicial review. Such conventions could likewise be effective for considering proposing amendments. This would resolve the imbalance between the two methods of amendment proposal because the states would periodically meet, just as the national legislature does for the first method for proposal. On one hand, determining constitutionality is a power to negate, whereas the power to amend is a positive power. There is a synergy in this model. The author has left the rules undefined, as it is anticipated that the mere suggestion of this will probably cause enough controversy on its own merit.

To recap, the following are recommendations from this chapter to strengthen the system of checks and balances:

- **Remove judicial supremacy from the Supreme Court and limit the Court to its rightful place as the highest appeals court in the land.** Undoubtedly there will be times where rulings will by necessity confront constitutionality, but those should be the exception and finally settled by the states.
- **Give the power to determine constitutionality to the states (agents for the people).** It is recommended that a periodic convention of states be incorporated into a constitutional amendment to facilitate this. A yearly convention is just one possibility. This will restore the power of the Tenth Amendment and decentralize the tension between (extraconstitutional) political parties by diffusing the battle over Supreme Court justices.
- **Article V should be amended to reduce the number of states required to call a convention from the existing ratio of** two-thirds **to a small fixed number—perhaps nine, as the original two-thirds of thirteen.** Too low a number can be much more easily corrected than one that is too high. A viable alternative is to change the entire mechanism to a periodic convention rather than an aperiodic one. State conventions

would encourage more participation in the overall government by the states and restore the balance with the national government. "We the People" may wake up from our apathetic funk and become a more responsible electorate.

- **Restore the state appointment of national senators or substitute a new mechanism by which senators are directly responsible to the states.** The Seventeenth Amendment is recognized by many to have removed a crucial vertical check on the national government by the states. Data show a significant increase in the size and debt of the national government since 1913. Given the difficulties of the original appointment process, simply repealing the amendment may not be the best answer. There is no doubt a myriad of creative solutions to make senators directly accountable to their states. The national government will never address this situation. Just as the states promoted the removal of the check, they will have to initiate a substitute. Had the original Article V convention of states, which came very close to happening, proposed what turned out to be the Seventeenth Amendment, perhaps it may have substituted another check rather than merely removing it.

7

Maintaining Equilibrium

> We have no government armed with power capable of contending with human passions unbridled by morality and religion. Avarice, ambition, revenge and licentiousness would break the strongest cords of our Constitution as a whale goes through a net. Our Constitution was made only for a religious and moral people. It is wholly inadequate for the government of any other.
>
> *John Adams*

The section on constitutional checks and balances introduced the view of a constitutional tug-of-war between intraconstitutional tensions and extraconstitutional forces. For checks and balances to be effective, the former must be as strong as or stronger than the latter. The quote above by John Adams clearly shows that this view is consistent with the thinking of the founders. The goal is to achieve a stalemated tug-of-war at equilibrium. When recent polls show that a majority of US citizens sees the national government as a threat to individual liberty,[208] the tug-of-war is clearly not at equilibrium. The previous chapter explored and introduced how to strengthen the intraconstitutional tensions by reassessing the existing checks and balances. This chapter will explore reducing the strength of current extraconstitutional forces.

Today political issues are almost always assessed horizontally, based on the notions of left and right. Mindsets on both sides are so entrenched that this leads to Pavlovian reactions that spew talking points. In other words, the political landscape is populated with personality traps.[209] This is not how problem solvers approach a problem.

---

208 Several polls are summarized in the *New American*, Sunday, May 4, 2014.

209 See the section on recognizing personality traps in chapter 3, "Modern Tools."

A problem solver first takes notice of the effects of the problem. Once the effect is characterized, he or she then figures out the cause. Finally, the problem solver determines the remedy to the cause of the problem. This creates a chain of what-to-do and how-to-do-it questions that lead to the solution. In the previous paragraph, the top-level effect (what) is that US citizens see the national government as a threat to individual liberty. The cause (how) is that the constitutional tug-of-war is out of equilibrium. How is it out of equilibrium? The extraconstitutional forces are too strong for the intraconstitutional ones. The remedy is to determine what the extraconstitutional forces are that are disrupting the equilibrium and mitigate them.

Luckily, the founders were problem solvers and approached issues vertically. As it turns out, in *Federalist No. 10*, James Madison provides us with the clear definition of extraconstitutional forces that we seek. He recognizes the relevance of Newton's third law of physics keeping human nature in check. As we recognize that Madison had a solution for his time, it makes sense for us to investigate how we might modernize his solution to maintain equilibrium today. Unfortunately, now we need to go one step further to see how to restore equilibrium.

Understanding the Nature of Government

Understanding the nature of government requires reviewing some of the principles introduced in part 1. It is human nature to start by accepting the status quo rather than trying to understand the real nature of government. We have an emotional investment in our perspective. James L. Payne's *Six Political Illusions* is a powerful book for opening our eyes to understanding the true nature of government as the founders viewed it.

A difficulty in understanding documents from the founding period is that key words have changed meanings over time. Although we share a common language with the founding generation, the vernacular has changed—at times, radically—and the true meaning has been misinterpreted in our time. Academia is not immune to this mistake and, as a result, perpetuates many misunderstandings. This is extremely important when a singular word or phrase embodies an important principle or concept. A prime example of this is the true meaning in the Declaration of Independence of "pursuit of happiness." Thanks to the Irish philosopher Francis Hutcheson,[210] this phrase distinctively included a civic responsibility, not just self-gratification.[211] "Liberty" is another key word in that phrase of the Declaration. Today we talk more of freedom than liberty and conflate the terms.[212] "Liberty" specifically meant Locke's definition of liberty as a natural right—but it is constrained by law in Locke's view:

> Freedom is constrained by laws in both the state of nature and political society. Freedom of nature is to be under no other restraint but the law of nature. Freedom of people under government is to be under no restraint apart from standing rules to live by that are common to everyone in the society and made by the lawmaking power established in it. Persons have a right or liberty to (1) follow their own will in all things that the law has not prohibited and (2) not be subject to the inconstant, uncertain, unknown, and arbitrary wills of others.[213]

In Locke's usage, freedom is a *concept*, but liberty is a *right* constrained by the legitimate contextual laws—whether in a state of nature or civil society. The founders talked more of liberty than freedom. Our current vernacular has completely lost the key concept of restraint and civic responsibility embodied in "Life, Liberty, and the Pursuit of

210 Arthur Herman, *The Scottish Enlightenment: The Scots' Invention of the Modern World* (London: Fourth Estate, 2002), 77–86.

211 "Lexical Investigations: Happiness," Dictionary.com.

212 Geoffrey Nunberg, "The Nation: Freedom vs. Liberty; More Than Just Another Word for Nothing Left to Lose," *The New York Times*, March 23, 2003, accessed July 06, 2016, http://www.nytimes.com/2003/03/23/weekinreview/nation-freedom-vs-liberty-more-than-just-another-word-for-nothing-left-lose.html.

213 John Locke, and Lewis F. Abbott. Two Treatises of Government a Translation into Modern English. Schwechat Austria: Industrial Systems Research, 2013. pg. 117.

Happiness." Perhaps we need to add a Bill of Responsibilities to our foundational documents to clarify the point.

Another problem related to the shift in the English language is translation. A lot of the political theory has been based on ancient Greek and Latin sources.[214] The problem is compounded by the fact that modern Greek has moved from ancient Greek even more than English has moved since our nation's founding. Thankfully Latin hasn't moved, because it's dead. Although more than two millennia old, these manuscripts were important during the founding—and they are still foundational today.

Finally, we need to understand two key implications of complexity theory. First, complex systems surround us. They can be stable or unstable (in a critical state). The economist James Rickards uses the example of an avalanche on the side of a mountain to explain the theory.[215] Second, reactions to actions are not linear. We grow up gaining a notion of the ripple effect, but then we seem to lose sight of its prevalence in nature.

Linear reactions to actions occur with simple mechanisms. It is indeed Newton's third law of physics that to every action there is an equal and opposite reaction. Madison applies this law to politics in *Federalist No. 51*, where he says that "Ambition must be made to counteract ambition."

But linearity only applies to a simple mechanism. Any political-economic system is a complex system, where a myriad of these simple mechanisms are interdependently connected, not independent mechanisms. As such, these mechanisms exert varying degrees of influence on the effects within the aggregated system. The results are profoundly nonlinear. A small change to any component within the system can have a huge impact—for the better or for the worse. As such, we should not underestimate the impact that a small, overlooked change may have. It

---

214 See Plato's *Republic*; Aristotle's *Politics*; and Cicero's letters, essays, and orations. Digital editions can be found through the Perseus Project at http://www.perseus.tufts.edu.

215 Rickards, *Currency Wars*, 203–205.

is in human nature to overlook a simple solution to a complex problem. Rather than trying to untie the Gordian knot, Alexander the Great cut it.

On the other hand, problems within complex systems frequently defy a single, simple solution. Complex solutions need to be decomposed strategically to consider the short-, intermediate-, and long-term results. Previous American generations were inherently comfortable with this view. That gave rise to the American philosophy that each generation hopes for a better world for its offspring, in turn giving rise to an optimistic national mindset. It is not just a moral question. It is a problem-solving question, because some problems will persist beyond a lifetime. For the problem to be ultimately solved, a given generation must set up a subsequent generation for success and not failure. That is what the founders did to the best of their abilities. Of course, since they were imperfect, not everything was ultimately a success. The American public today is too impatient and expects immediate gratification. This impatience and selfishness abandons solutions that require multiple generations. Patience and unselfishness must be reintroduced into the public psyche.

Imperfect Society

Every nation gets the government it deserves.

Joseph de Maistre

The United States is a perfect ideal created by imperfect men.[216] Human nature being what it is, natural discontent arises from the fact that imperfect human beings can never achieve the goal of the perfect ideal. Society always has warts. The members of the first generation (the founders) knew that they were imperfect and that, as such, the founding documents were imperfect—but they were as good as they could produce. Each generation inherits the benefits and problems from prior generations. The founders were no different. In addition to the opportunity of the New World, they inherited slavery from their European predecessors. The issue was so divisive that they punted on the problem for twenty years (roughly

216 "Perfect" in the Constitution refers to "complete." Here, "perfect" is used in current vernacular.

a generation), but they did attempt to seed the Constitution such that it would not encourage propagation of what they .[217] (The three-fifths clause was a compromise.[218]) Ultimately their hopeful vision of slavery naturally dying failed because of the mistakes of subsequent generations.[219] Civil society degenerated into the Civil War.

Most Americans today recognize there is a lack of cohesion in civil society. We inherently know that the system is unstable. Many problems are inherited from our predecessors, but many are also of our own doing. Disputes arise because the population is divided between proliferating the mistakes and correcting them. The difficulty is recognizing the mistakes, because emotional (and financial) investments make us blind to the errors. No one wants to take a financial hit. Liberty allows everyone to disagree on topics; however, these disagreements should be based on civic responsibility rather than selfishness if we are to avoid another breakdown of civil society. The founders referred to following the golden rule as public virtue. As John Adams wrote, public virtue cannot exist without private virtue.[220]

Once we understand the original meanings and solutions of the founders, we can intelligently analyze how time has either reinforced or eroded their assumptions and weakened their solutions. Among the mechanisms that can weaken the framers' solutions are

- changes in the fabric of society,
- technological advances, and
- improper laws and regulations.

Of these three threats, no cure can be possible unless social attitudes cohesively align with the Constitution. Improper laws and regulations

---

217 "What the Founders Said About Slavery," Walter E. Williams, http://walterewilliams.com/quotations/slavery/.

218 "3/5 Clause: Annotations," ConText, http://context.montpelier.org/tags/35-clause. This page discusses the personal notes of John Dickinson from July 9, 1787.

219 "Trigger Events of the Civil War," Civil War Trust, http://www.civilwar.org/education/history/civil-war-overview/triggerevents.html.

220 John Adams to Mercy Otis Warren, letter, April 16, 1776, https://www.masshist.org/publications/apde2/view?id=ADMS-06-04-02-0044. Warren was an anti-Federalist.

can only be adopted and persist if society tolerates them. They reflect Aristotle's incongruent government. Technological advances only pose a problem if society uses them to attack rather than defend the Constitution.

The first section of this chapter develops the definition of extraconstitutional forces based on James Madison's writings. The second half of the chapter takes on weakening extraconstitutional forces today. This requires modernizing Madison's solution as well as restoring cohesion in civil society. Restoring equilibrium is the topic of the next chapter.

Every nation gets the government it deserves.

Opposition to the Constitution

The members of the founding generation themselves were divided on the Constitution from its inception, but the nature of the opposition to it was 180 degrees from the opposition today. The founding generation's members were cohesive in their desire for liberty and decentralization. There were those who sided with the British during the war, but even they viewed themselves as free men. Those who determined to build a new nation were united in that they wanted the individual to determine his or her own destiny without government interference. Today that cohesive view has been replaced by a schism where a large segment of the population appears to want government (specifically the national government) involved in every aspect not only of their lives but also of their fellow citizens' lives—whether the latter group desires it or not. This lack of cohesion threatens the civil society (and the union) at its core.

What Are Extraconstitutional Forces?

James Madison's "mortal diseases" in *Federalist No. 10* are extraconstitutional forces:

> The *instability, injustice, and confusion* introduced into the public councils, have, in truth, been the *mortal diseases* under which popular Governments have everywhere perished; as they continue to be the

> favorite and fruitful topics from which the adversaries to liberty derive their most specious declamations. (italics added)

These "mortal diseases" are the causes of governmental failure and a potential breakdown of civil society. Madison identifies three specific causes. It is no doubt an incomplete list,[221] but it informs us as to what the Constitution was designed to prevent. This chapter will only focus on the use of this enumeration of extraconstitutional forces. Weakening them is not so much about identifying Supreme Court decisions, legislative acts, and executive orders that are unconstitutional as it is determining those that have led to instability, injustice, and confusion. As a practical note, these diseases are not fully independent. In particular, it is quite likely that the source of instability or confusion is injustice—either real or perceived.

As important as it is to identify and correct those acts and decisions that have a negative impact, we need to find the sources that lead to these ills and address them.

Source of Mortal Diseases

How was the Constitution to prevent "instability, injustice, and confusion"? Later in *Federalist No. 10,* Madison identifies the source of "our heaviest misfortunes" as factions. Today we use the term "special interest group." Madison writes:

> But it will be found, at the same time, that other causes will not alone account for many of our *heaviest misfortunes*; and, particularly, for that prevailing and increasing distrust of public engagements, and alarm for private rights, which are echoed from one end of the continent to the other. These must be chiefly, if not wholly, effects of the unsteadiness and injustice, with which a *factious spirit* has tainted our public administrations. (italics added)

221 In fact, Aristotle defines his own set in *Politics*, Book 5. Perceived injustice is in both lists.

Although Madison does not use the visualization of a tug-of-war between the internal tension of the Constitution and extraconstitutional forces, he clearly recognizes that the existing state constitutions and the Articles of Confederation are not strong enough to prevent mortal diseases from destroying the existing union:

> The valuable improvements made by the American Constitutions on the popular models, both ancient and modern, cannot certainly be too much admired; but it would be an unwarrantable partiality, to contend that they have as effectually obviated the danger on this side, as was wished and expected.[222]

Of course, he argues that the new Constitution would be strong enough; however, he might see that today we are contending with stronger, consolidated factions. Madison was a champion of justice and liberty. He states this clearly in *Federalist No. 51* when he says, "Justice is the end[223] of government. It is the end of civil society. It ever has been and ever will be pursued until it be obtained, or until liberty be lost in the pursuit."

He does not specifically define either liberty or justice because the common understanding of these terms was an essential part of the cohesion of civil society at the time. Liberty was understood to mean Locke's definition. We can turn to Frederic Bastiat's *The Law* for a suitable definition of justice. Bastiat recognizes that force is the agent of law. In the chapter titled "Law is a Negative Concept," he argues that

> this negative concept of law is so true that the statement, "the purpose of the law is to cause justice to reign," is not a rigorously accurate statement. It ought to be stated that "the purpose of the law is to prevent injustice from reigning." In fact, it is injustice, instead of justice, that has an existence of its own. *Justice is achieved only when injustice is absent.*[224] (italics added)

---

222 *Federalist 10.*

223 "End of" means "reason for."

224 Frédéric Bastiat. The Law. Minneapolis, MN: Filiquarian Publishing, LLC, 2005. pg. 26.

Note that Bastiat's definition of justice actually reinforces Madison's enumeration of injustice as a mortal disease. Further note that *justice* is absolute, not relative. That is, an adjective cannot be put in front of the word "justice" without creating another form of *injustice.* Aristotle actually makes the distinction between the principle of justice and its practical implementation.[225] He notes that man's implementation is always imperfect. That fact is made worse if the blindfolded lady with the scale peeks and puts her thumb on one side. We can do no better than we can do. Makeup calls don't work in football games; they do even worse in real life. "We was robbed!" in a game translates to perceived injustice, leading to instability and confusion. The cohesion of society can be destroyed.

Definition of Faction

Madison defines "faction" in *Federalist No. 10*:

> By a *faction*, I understand a number of citizens, whether amounting to a majority or a minority of the whole, who are united and actuated by some common impulse of passion, or of interest, adverse to the rights of other citizens, or to the permanent and aggregate interests of the community. (italics added)

By this definition, any organized group of people can be a faction. What distinguishes a faction is that it influences the body politic in a self-serving way that is not in the best interest of the citizenry as a whole. Madison is cutting right to the chase of Aristotle's distinction between congruent and incongruent governments. He is addressing how to prevent the United States from degenerating into an incongruent one and ultimately failing. One reason incongruent governments fail is that the ruling body itself foments the mortal diseases in order to retain power by pitting factions within the citizenry to deflect dissatisfaction from themselves.[226]The specific concern the founders (anti-Federalists as well as Federalists) had was that democracies have always degenerated to catering to the indigent or the aristocracy at the expense of the middle

225 Aristotle, *Politics*, Book 3, section 1280a.

226 Ibid., Book 5.

class.[227] Aristotle documented this phenomenon over two millennia ago.[228] As Madison puts it in *Federalist No. 10*,

> Hence it is, that such Democracies have ever been spectacles of turbulence and contention; have ever been found incompatible with personal security, or the rights of property; and have in general been as short in their lives, as they have been violent in their deaths.

This, then, is why the founding generation universally championed a republic over democracy. Republics are more stable than democracies because they are designed to dampen emotional overreaction and enable reason to have a chance. The French Revolution was so bloody because they failed to see the significance of this distinction. It wasn't until the progressive educational reforms of John Dewey during the Wilson administration that the term "democracy" lost its negative connotation in the American psyche.[229]

Madison's Conclusions

After Madison identifies factions as the source of the mortal diseases that have killed popular government throughout the history of humankind,[230] he turns his attention to finding a cure for the mortal diseases.

The Argument for a Big Republic

In perhaps one of the more famous passages in *The Federalist Papers*, Madison first considers eliminating the source of the diseases: faction. He writes,

> There are again two methods of removing the causes of faction: the one, by destroying the liberty which is essential to its existence; the other, by giving to every citizen the same opinions, the same passions, and the same interests.

---

227 Ibid., Book 3, section 1279b.

228 Ibid.

229 John Dewey, preface, *Democracy and Education* (London: MacMillan, 1916).

230 Aristotle, *Politics*, Book 5.

> It could never be more truly said than of the first remedy, that it was worse than the disease. Liberty is to faction what air is to fire, an aliment without which it instantly expires. But it could not be less folly to abolish liberty, which is essential to political life, because it nourishes faction, than it would be to wish the annihilation of air, which is essential to animal life, because it imparts to fire its destructive agency.

The conclusion is that factions cannot be prevented without destroying liberty. That was not an option to the founders. Liberty was the absolute top priority. Since factions could not be eliminated, they needed to be controlled. Again, from *Federalist No. 10*, Madison concludes that "The inference to which we are brought is, that the *causes* of faction cannot be removed; and that relief is only to be sought in the means of controlling its *effects*" (italics added).

So it was the design of the republic to innately control factions from fostering the mortal diseases of instability, injustice, and confusion. Madison discusses human nature's propensity to quarrel over potentially frivolous issues, but he identifies the most enduringly divisive issue of all:

> But the *most common and durable source of factions has been the various and unequal distribution of property*. Those who hold, and those who are without property, have ever formed distinct interests in society. Those who are creditors, and those who are debtors, fall under a like discrimination. (italics added)

Turning his focus to structuring the government to control factions, Madison argues first that a republic is superior to a democracy because the smaller ruling body of representatives will be wiser than will be the general electorate. This argument is straight from Aristotle.[231] Madison's second point is that a republic can rule over a larger land mass and number of people than can a democracy. This is a matter of pragmatics. It was impossible for all the people from the thirteen states to assemble and vote on every issue that might require addressing. But representatives from all thirteen states

231 Ibid., Book 4, section 1295b.

clearly could. Both arguments resonated with the founding generation, as they universally believed in republicanism. This was an easy sell.

After arguing the superiority of republic over democracy, Madison argues that a larger republic has a significant advantage over a smaller one with respect to controlling factions. A smaller republic must have a higher ratio of representation to avoid dominance by a local cabal. On the other hand, a larger republic doesn't have this problem.[232] The larger republic can have a lower ratio of representatives to citizens because there is no concern about a local cabal. Having fewer representatives from a larger pool implies better quality of representatives.[233] The implication of this point is that the reason that earlier republics fell is because they weren't big enough. This refutes the prevailing wisdom of the time. Madison further argues that a larger republic, in fact, must reduce the ratio of representation in order to avoid confusion (another mortal disease) of overrepresentation. The result is that a larger republic would naturally get a better group of representatives because fewer representatives are chosen from a larger population. This is the "best and brightest" argument.

This appears to be a valid argument that a larger republic would control the effects of factions better because the larger pool with fewer representatives would ensure better leaders. Madison concludes that factions might indeed be able to dominate a locale or a state, but they could not dominate the union as a whole.[234]

Observations

Madison's coverage of factions is outstanding, but two key factors have changed since his day that compel us to revisit his arguments:

1. The social fabric has changed.
2. Technology has removed barriers beyond his consideration.

232 Madison, "Federalist No.10."

233 Of course, this argument assumes that the electorate is intelligent and well informed.

234 It is interesting that Aristotle makes this same argument in *Politics*, Book 4, section 1296a.

Over two centuries, a lot has changed with generational turns. Perhaps the biggest difference between today's generation and that of the founders is that very few in the founding generation even wanted a national government and instead looked to community first. There are many in today's generation who look first to the national government with little if any thought of local community. Economic issues may have served as the catalysts in the incremental changes, but technology has facilitated them.

The Middle Class

The first argument about the superiority of a republic is directly from Aristotle. To Aristotle, a democracy is an incongruent form of what we call a republic. Not normally attributed to Aristotle, one of his key observations is that a large middle class serves as a buffer against the natural enmity between the rich and the poor.[235] Note that this enmity is due to the same "unequal distribution of property" that Madison notes as the most durable source of faction.[236] Aristotle further notes that democracies favor the aristocracy or the indigent over a beleaguered middle class. Depletion of the middle class has always been a key factor in the failure of democracies.

Empirical evidence shows that the middle class has shrunk since 1967—into the upper class, not the lower class.[237] A study by Peter Lindert and Jeffrey Williamson suggests that the middle class was stronger in 1774 than today.[238] This demonstrates the arbitrary nature of where lines are drawn and the faulty conclusions that follow. The source of rich and poor factions is not so much about the real wealth as it is about perceived wealth. Those numerically in the middle class who perceive

---

235 Aristotle, *Politics*, Book 4, sections 1295b and 1297a.

236 Madison, "Federalist No. 10."

237 "Charts of the Day: Another Look at How America's Middle Class Is Disappearing into Higher Income Households," Mark J. Perry, AEI, https://www.aei.org/publication/charts-of-the-day-another-look-at-how-americas-middle-class-is-disappearing-into-higher-income-households/.

238 Jordan Weissman, "US Income Inequality: It's Worse Today Than It Was in 1774," *The Atlantic*, September 19, 2012.

they are poor will align with the poor faction. Oppressive taxation can make anyone feel less wealthy. Restoring both the middle class's actual and perceived wealth is important to weakening extraconstitutional forces. In *Politics*, both Books 4 and 5, Aristotle makes the point, clearly, that the middle class provides stability. He argues that the middle class aligns with the poor when attacked by the rich and vice versa. If it is the largest of the three classes, it keeps the other two in check. I explore the parameters about what makes one middle class in part 3 of this book.

Implicit Assumptions in Madison's Theory

There are weaknesses in Madison's argument for a larger republic over a smaller one. First, he implicitly assumes a uniform distribution of talent throughout the population. This is a surprising oversight on his part, because prior to pointing out that unequal distribution of property is the most durable source of faction, he notes that the inequality of talent among men is why it happens. What saves the argument (to a degree) is the effect of a composite function wherein talent tends to be fairly uniformly distributed across geographic areas. This doesn't change. According to Madison,

> The diversity in the faculties of men, from which the rights of property originate, is not less an insuperable obstacle to a uniformity of interests. The protection of these faculties is the first object of Government. From the protection of different and unequal faculties of acquiring property, the possession of different degrees and kinds of property immediately results; and from the influence of these on the sentiments and views of the respective proprietors, ensues a division of the society into different interests and parties.[239]

He also assumes what can be called *locality of faction*. That is, he only sees factions forming locally, from the bottom up. Implicit in factions forming from the bottom up is that they form independently. This was a perfectly understandable assumption in an era where one might travel thirty miles on horseback in a day. Letters were the common mode of

239 Madison, "Federalist No. 10."

communication before the invention of wired communications like the telegraph and telephone.

The technology and mobility two hundred years later challenge this assertion. With the Internet (social media in particular), factions can easily form without regard to geography and from the top down. Top-down formation of faction can invalidate the assumption that they form independently. Likewise, there is a much higher potential for the infusion of more money. Money is power, and the temptation is to use government for social solutions. It enables the activation of factions. Crowdfunding makes it easier than ever to fund factions, but the bigger injustice is from the wealthy. In fact, the United States is suffering mightily by the wealthy using their wealth as a force multiplier to distort the will of the people.[240]

Consider also that during Madison's day, people considered themselves citizens of a state first and of the union second. This continued until after the War Between the States. There was a strong sense of community that all but ensured that faction formation would be from the bottom up. Clearly, today's citizens have an inverted view of their loyalty and communicate at the speed of light between the coasts. This adds to the probability that, in fact, factions will form from the top down. Any sense of community formed by social media is virtual, not geographic.

Factions Today

In reality, the formation and activation of factions has always been a complex relationship between motivation and ease of communication. The more committed to a common goal people are, the more likely a faction will form—and activate. *Federalist No. 10* uses the term "rage." Easing communication has removed a resistance to factions forming in the presence of discontent. This same ease of communication enables

---

240 Eli Stokols, "Bloomberg Dismisses Colo. Springs, Pueblo as Roadless, Rural Backwaters," Fox 31 Denver, July 10, 2014, http://kdvr.com/2014/07/10/bloomberg-dismisses-colo-springs-pueblo-as-road-less-rural-backwaters/.

"Michael Bloomberg," Ballotpedia, https://ballotpedia.org/Michael_Bloomberg.

fostering rage on a massive scale. A local event may provide the catalyst, but fostering rage on a massive scale is a top-down process.[241] In the day of the Internet, there is little to allow cooler heads to prevail. This has rendered Madison's argument that factions are less likely to dominate in a large republic suspect today.

What about his argument that it is less likely that one faction will dominate a large society in which many factions opposing one another are present? This argument assumes the randomness of independent events in the same manner that computer simulations and queuing theory do. With our current two-party system, we do not have independence among factions. Not only has technology defeated the barriers of locality for faction formation and activation, but also factions no longer compete. They form alliances—and mostly under the supervision of a political party. This is consolidation.

The one encouraging sign of fracture among these factions is the growth of Independents within the political landscape. What is driving this growth? Rage, of course. As a party caters more and more to specific factions (the squeaky wheels) within the consolidated faction, more members become disillusioned and leave the party. Political scientists debate whether the current party system is the fifth-party system or the sixth-party system.[242] This is not as important as recognizing that the current party system is in a critical state.[243] Each twenty-first-century election appears to inch us closer and closer to the collapse of the current system. We can expect a major shift in party politics within the lifetime of the youngest generation of Americans today. It may even have already happened.

---

241 Howard, Koplowitz, "Of Michael Brown, Eric Garner Demonstrations Sites by State, Plus Justice for All March Details," *International Business Times*, December 12, 2014, http://www.ibtimes.com/week-outrage-protests-full-list-michael-brown-eric-garner-demonstration-sites-state-1751517.

242 Brewer and Maisel, *Parties and Elections in America*, 42.

243 That is, unstable.

Weakening Extraconstitutional Forces

The actual weakening of extraconstitutional forces involves a two-step process. First, the cohesion of civil society must be restored to a state of equilibrium. Disagreement is good; too strong a disagreement is unhealthy. In fact, no equilibrium can be achieved unless stability, a common sense of justice, and lack of confusion are brought to society.

The second step is to maintain long-term equilibrium once it's achieved. We can do this by modernizing Madison's solution. We must address the social and technological changes that have occurred since the Constitution was adopted.

Modernizing Madison's Solution

To quickly recap the previous observations, Madison's solution to restraining factions makes the following foundational assumptions that are suspect today:

- Locality of faction
  - Bottom-up, independent formation of factions
  - Sense of community meaning "state citizen" before "national citizen"
- A middle class to buffer the enmity between rich and poor
- Communication limitations of his day inhibiting rage

What is the first step in addressing these issues? We certainly can't—and don't want to—put the genie back in the bottle and return to eighteenth-century technology. All need to be addressed, but restoring locality of faction is the most important step to be made.

Locality of Faction

Is there any way to restore locality of faction without inhibiting freedom of speech and association? Current technology has removed the physical barriers on which Madison's original theory relied. Any replacement barriers must work in the virtual world of today. Activation of a faction requires money. It is as necessary in the virtual world as it is in the physical world. One possible path to a solution is through money.

Most Americans today recognize that money's influence is distorting our politics. In military terms, it is a *force multiplier* where one essentially gets more than one vote. When a wealthy donor (individual or collective special interest) uses the force multiplier of money to exert undue influence, injustice against the rest of the electorate exists. It is essentially theft. Preventing this injustice by restricting the disposition of the wealthy donor's money is in direct conflict with the donor's inalienable right to dispose of his property freely. On the other hand, the donor's action is an injustice that conflicts with the electorate's pursuit of happiness (buying office is not consistent with civic duty).

This is how professional protestors are activated today. It is also a driving force for campaign-finance laws. As with many laws, campaign-finance laws always make the mistake of affixing artificial numbers (limits) on donations. In a complex system, this approach is hopeless and leads to convoluted rules and exceptions. The wealthy will always adapt and defeat such rules. However, the desire to control campaign finance is aligned with and can be used to reestablish Madison's locality of faction. Solutions that are simple and enforceable are often the best within a complex adaptive system.

A simple, national law that *no money* can cross state boundaries for any political purposes would restore locality of faction. States could choose to impose any or no limits within their individual borders. As Madison writes, it is quite possible (even probable) that faction could dominate a locality or even a state, but the key to his argument is that the whole union would not be corrupted.[244] This principle could be echoed within a state by not allowing money to cross county boundaries, but that would be beyond the jurisdiction established by the US Constitution.

244 Madison, "Federalist No. 10."

Of course, the devil is in the details, but there is no adapting around an ironclad law. Of course, there would be a constitutional challenge, but current campaign-finance laws have already set precedence. Ultimately, the states could always override any judicial objection with an amendment to the Constitution. Capturing violations could be annoying, but we have the technology to enforce such a law. The key is to make it a criminal offense with stiff penalties.

One obvious objection to eliminating political money from crossing state lines is that we might never get another president from a poor state. This point misses the fact that the state of origin is not the issue. The issue is that a president represents the interests of the states as a whole adequately. Keeping track of the president's state of residence is a bragging-rights issue, little more. From the beginning of the nation, the balance to be struck is between the interests of the small states and that of the big states (poor versus wealthy). This is more of a legislative issue than an executive one. The founders came up with the Great Compromise of 1787. The Electoral College is a similar mathematically sound principle for diffusing the issue for the presidency.

An immediate benefit of the proposed law to prohibit interstate political funding is that members of Congress would be motivated to spend more time in the state they represent because that would be the sole source of funding for their election campaigns. Another side effect would be that national parties would be all but defunct because they would have no source of funding. George Washington cautioned against political parties in his farewell address.[245] Other founders echoed his sentiments. This would be making their vision come true. Another by-product of the proposed law is that it would diminish the use of money in politics overall. Without the motivation to spread a political view nationwide, an interested party would have no need to exceed the expenditures needed for his or her result. Aristotle enumerates "profit from office" as one of the major reasons for the failure of governments.[246]

---

245 "Washington's Farewell Address (1796)," Wikisource, https://en.wikisource.org/wiki/Washington's_Farewell_Address#22.

246 Aristotle, *Politics*, Book 5, section 1308b.

Profit from office is not confined to elected officials. There are many political apparatchiks who profit from not being in office. Their numbers would dwindle. Reducing the money in politics is a stabilizing goal.

Preventing money from crossing state lines would prevent wealthier states from overpowering the political process *within* the poorer states. Currently wealthier states do in fact create incongruent representation within poorer states by flooding money across state lines. A key part of this strategy would be to put more meaning behind *residency*. For the purpose of political contributions, there would have to be a single, primary residency to prevent owners with properties in multiple states from donating in multiple states. The same rule would have to apply to institutions.

Restoration of community- and state-aligned citizenship is perhaps not as difficult as it seems. If you live in Colorado, there's a good chance you're a Denver Broncos fan. If you live in North Carolina, you probably cheer for the Carolina Panthers. All that needs to transpire to shift this citizenship paradigm is to shift rightful power back from the national government to the states. A key element of this is to strengthen the meaning of residency as mentioned above. A huge part of the shift should include a reduction in tax money moving out of the states to the national government. Currently, some tax money flows to the national government and is returned to the states, minus overhead and with many strings attached. Federalism is based on dual sovereignty—state and national, not just national. State sovereignty has been weakening since the Civil War. That trend needs to stop, and we must obey the principle of the ancient Greek golden mean where parity exists.

Restoring the Middle Class

The middle class is not defined by its earnings. It is defined by its temperament. The modern middle class definitely feels squeezed and is not as stable as the classic middle class.[247] On one hand, restoring

247 Michele Dickerson, "Angry US Middle Classes Feel the Squeeze," BBC News, February 9, 2015, http://www.bbc.com/news/world-us-canada-31121518.

the middle class's stability is an economic problem. On the other hand, it is a legislative problem. Bad laws inhibit commerce. Production and consumption are symbiotic, and there are too many laws that discourage the producer side of the economic producer-consumer model. These laws can be divided into three categories:

1. Tax laws
2. Regulatory laws
3. Civil suits

In addition to bad laws, mishandling of the value of the dollar has a direct negative impact on the net worth of any citizen. Debasing the currency can decimate the middle class because it robs everyone of existing wealth.

Tax Law

Tax laws that tax production need to be reduced, if not eliminated, and balanced by consumption-side taxation. Early progressives pushed hard for the progressive tax system we have today.[248] The goal was to increase revenue to grow government and to make the rich pay their "fair share." Of course, there was no objective measurement as to what constituted a fair share, and this lack of metric continues today. The fair-share chant is the enmity between rich and poor of which Aristotle and Madison write. Inflation and the pressure for more revenue by a growing government quickly imposed the tax system on the middle class. The progressive tax system hurts the middle class more than either of the other two classes because the aggregate income is the largest of the three classes. The "regressive" taxation system that progressive taxation replaced taxed the consumption side of the economic model, and it indeed inhibited growth of government—consistent with the founders' goal of limited government.

248 Ajay K. Mehrota, "The Lost Promise of Progressive Taxes," Reuters, April 15, 2014, http://blogs.reuters.com/great-debate/2014/04/15/the-lost-promise-of-progressive-taxes/.

Objectivity can build a tax system that is neither regressive nor progressive. It is not intellectually challenging at all. It is emotionally ἀρετῆ[249] (arete) or the founders' public virtue. Tax law cannot encourage commerce. It can be neutral and opaque if it achieves two goals:

1. It balances its impact on both production and consumption (not necessarily at the same rate but with the same effect). This means rates must change according to market sensitivities (the business cycle).
2. It is insignificant in expense to the average citizen. A tax of 50 percent of one's income is *not* insignificant. An honest and open discussion would probably peg this at more like 10 percent, including all forms of taxation. Tainter's research into collapse of civil societies clearly shows that the cost-benefit shift over time (diminishing returns) is a major contributor to collapse.[250] Tax revenue should not increase to support a bigger government. Government size should balance with tax revenue that is not oppressive.

Regulatory Law

The administrative state imposes excessive regulatory costs on business. The phenomenal growth in government agencies is the result of Congress delegating its responsibility to legislate to unelected officials in these agencies. Since a majority of agencies are under the executive branch, this amounts to a complete subversion of the expressed power in the Constitution for all legislation to be held by the legislative branch.[251] This arrangement suits elected officials because they aren't held responsible for excessive regulation. Unelected officials are protected by agreements between public-sector unions and the government.[252] The

249 Normally translated as "virtue," Aristotle's meaning emphasizes the golden mean and avoids excess. The founder's public virtue stressed the golden rule of "Do unto others . . ."

250 Tainter, *Collapse of Complex Societies*, 92.

251 US Const., art. I, sec. 1.

252 "John F. Kennedy: Executive Order 10988—Employee-Management Cooperation in the Federal Service," American Presidency Project, accessed July 06, 2016, http://www.presidency.ucsb.edu/ws/?pid=58926.

cost of meeting regulations discourages many among "We the People" from starting our own businesses. This is because regulations are written based on recommendations of "experts." These experts almost always represent the interest of big companies, which are motivated to use regulation to prohibit new competition from smaller ventures.[253]

The issue is not just that regulation destroys competition. The issue is that it destroys *opportunity* by making the entry fee to production too high. Economists have demonstrated that even an imperfect system with fewer, larger companies drives prices down as well as a market with many, smaller companies.[254] That measures the benefit to the consumer. On the other hand, it does not account for the loss to the production side of the relationship. Monopolistic tendencies stifle production opportunities—in other words, jobs. This hurts the middle class and destroys opportunity.

Three forces limit the natural lifetime of a monopoly. The problem appears to be that none of these forces seems to work at a rate acceptable to impatient humans. The result has been regulations that actually reinforce monopolies more often than they help limit them. The three forces are the following:

1. **Slower reaction to market changes**. This is the economic equivalent of inertia. Smaller companies can respond to market conditions much faster than larger ones. The more technological markets of today change much more quickly than those in the Progressive Era.
2. **Pournelle's iron law**. Monopolies may be more focused on the market, but they still grow a control group that is more focused on the organization than on its goals. Eventually, this will alienate a customer base.
3. **Generational inconsistency**. As another byproduct of Pournelle's law, it is unusual for succeeding generations to be as driven or competent as one that creates a monopoly.

---

253 Burton Folsom, Jr, *New Deal or Raw Deal: How FDR's Economic Legacy Has Damaged America* (New York: Threshold Editions, 2008), 33–66.

254 Skousen, *Big Three in Economics*, 228.

Civil Suits

Finally, civil suits impose excessive fines on questionable cases, especially with respect to negligence. The same lack of public virtue that inhibits a better tax code drives an indulgent society to excessively reward "victims" in favor of hard-working folks. Larger companies proliferate the lottery-winning mentality of these rewards because settling is cheaper than the legal fees to fight the suits. This means that our entire civil law system is corrupted when that tradeoff is consistently made for village idiots who spill hot coffee on their laps in drive-throughs.[255]

Debasing the Currency

Returning to purely economic concerns, the value of a dollar is of preeminent importance for our sovereignty and also our older years. If we live long enough, we all live on a fixed income. Erosion of the dollar during fixed-income years threatens the lives of the elderly. It also places additional financial burdens on their families. The founders were very aware of the evil of paper money. In the period from 1777 to 1781, the Continental Congress printed "continentals" to the point where the purchasing power dropped from one-third of hard specie to 1/165. This is why the states were, per Article I, Section 10 of the Constitution, prohibited from using anything but silver or gold for tendering debts.

Tainter details the valuation of the denarius through the Roman Empire.[256] The negative impact of debasement is clear to see in the demise of the empire. John Maynard Keynes himself quotes Lenin: "There is no subtler, no surer means of overturning the existing basis of society than to debauch the currency."[257] Debasing the currency always works in favor of a debtor government. It repays in cheaper currency. In the first part of the twentieth century, the United States was the world's largest creditor. Today it is its largest debtor.

---

255 *Liebeck v. McDonald's Restaurants*. (New Mexico District Court 1994).

256 Tainter, *Collapse of Complex Societies*, 128–152.

257 "Keynes Quote On Currency Debasement." EconomicGreenfield. 2011. Accessed July 30, 2016. http://www.economicgreenfield.com/2011/01/26/keynes-quote-on-currency-debasement/.

Our incomes rise linearly, but our costs rise geometrically as everyone else's increases and the higher dollars for resources are aggregated into them. That means that our purchasing power declines over time due to devaluation. The declining value of the dollar discourages saving. The opposite is true for deflation. A transition from inflation to deflation is tough because of the loss of income in quantity of currency. Debtors get hurt because the value of their debt increases. Savers benefit immediately with real increased wealth from a more valuable dollar. The debt spiral is a death spiral, financially for citizens and economically for the nation.

There is an insane fear of deflation at the Fed and on Capitol Hill. This is an artifact of the theory that the cause of the Great Depression was underconsumption. Most economists (though not all) acknowledge that this theory is flat-out wrong.[258] In reality, the yearly number for our income that we report to the IRS is of no consequence with respect to our individual wealth (or lack thereof). It is the purchasing power of our dollars that matters.

Peter Schiff points out that the value of currency tends to increase as we get more efficient in production processes.[259] He uses the period between 1813 and 1913, when no major economic legislation was enacted, to demonstrate that the dollar actually bought more in 1913 than it did in 1813. The website *measuringworth.com* has a fascinating calculator for determining meaningful metrics on the value of the dollar. The GDP deflator is a measure of the average price of all goods and services. It shows that indeed what did cost one dollar in 1813 cost eighty-three cents in 1913. This is natural deflation. Baselining one dollar in 1913 with the same GDP deflator shows an equivalent value at $17.50 in 2013—a 1750% increase. It's fascinating to check the numbers between 1913 and 1929. In fact, this was an inflationary period, not a deflationary one. Deflation did not occur until after the Depression started. The same dollar in 1913 required $1.62 in 1813 for equivalent purchasing power.

---

258 See Rickards, *Currency Wars*, page range; Skousen, *Big Three in Economics*, 50; and Peter Schiff, *The Real Crash: America's Coming Bankruptcy—How to Save Yourself and Your Country* (New York: St. Martin's Press, 2014), 37.

259 Schiff, *Real Crash*, 110.

The question becomes, who really gets hurt with natural deflation? It only hurts the average citizen if the money supply is too small and creates a liquidity problem—which is exactly what the Fed did in 1929. Without a liquidity problem, the average citizen has more purchasing power.

Rage Versus Communication

In our high-technology world, rage can travel at the speed of light. This means factions can form from the top-down, consolidate, and become active quickly. The only hope to control rage is education and maturity. That is, we must develop a society that includes what the founders called public virtue.

Myers-Briggs testing informs us that 60 percent of the population instinctively wants to make decisions based on feeling rather than reason.[260] Learned behavior can slow this tendency so that rage can be overridden. Learned behavior should be the implementation of public virtue. Competition and participation in sports with a sense of fair play have always been the best education for this.

Reduction of rage is a goal in the next chapter.

Summary

Madison identifies faction as the source for the mortal diseases of injustice, instability, and confusion. These mortal diseases are the extraconstitutional forces that the intraconstitutional tensions within the Constitution are designed to control. This is why the military swears to protect and defend the Constitution, not government officials, who might promote mortal diseases. Factions today have found all the weaknesses in the Constitution and our legal system, thereby enabling injustice, instability, and confusion to overpower the intraconstitutional tensions. Many of these mortal diseases are promoted by government officials.

---

260 "How Frequent Is My Type?" The Myers and Briggs Foundation, http://www.myersbriggs.org/my-mbti-personality-type/my-mbti-results/how-frequent-is-my-type.htm.

The reasoning behind Madison's model for the control of faction is sound and appears to have worked well for the first one hundred years of the republic. The advent of technology has exposed some of his assumptions that no longer apply. This dictates that his model must be modernized to stabilize the control of faction. High-level goals include the following:

- **Constructing virtual locality of faction to update Madison's physical locality of faction.** Geographic locality is still key, but technology has overcome the limitations of travel and communications. The states are still the key geographic entities, and federalism is even more important than in Madison's time.
- **Stabilizing the middle class so that it can buffer the enmity between rich and poor, as Aristotle advises.** This natural enmity empowers the enemies of the Constitution. This requires a combination of economic and legislative measures.
- **Reinvigorating the sense of community.** In particular, federalism needs a rebirth where state citizenship is revived. A natural affinity exists among human beings who communicate frequently. Local communication needs to be strengthened.

Restoring a virtual locality of faction is both a legal issue and a societal one. But it is first a legal one. A law that makes it a felony to move money across state lines for political purposes has a number of benefits:

- Congressional representatives would return to spending time in and representing their state.
- It would prevent wealthier states from dominating poorer states politically.
- National parties would become unfunded—and probably extinct.
- It would diminish the overall money in politics.
    - This would remove one of Aristotle's threats to social stability.
- It would have the side benefit of reducing the number of annoying campaign ads.

As Aristotle identified over two millennia ago, a strong middle class is the key to national stability. The government is what is destroying the middle class by falling into the classic failure of democracies throughout history. It is catering to the poor to satisfy the avarice of the wealthy and powerful (elites). Restoration of the middle class is a foundational issue, and it would benefit from the government observing the Constitution. It also requires restoration of public virtue through the following:

- Establishing a producer-consumer neutral tax system
- Reducing the size of the national government so that taxation becomes tolerable
- Reducing regulations that are severely inhibiting producers and opportunity
- Stopping the lottery syndrome in civil-suit awards
- Halting nonstop inflation so that natural deflation can occur to offset the endless debasing of the currency

Many economists point to eliminating the Fed as a solution to nonstop inflation. No doubt the Fed is an inflation machine, but some entity needs to regulate the money supply. It is the constitutional responsibility of Congress to do this. Obviously, there aren't many rocket scientists (or economists) in Congress. This is a problem that has never been satisfactorily addressed throughout the history of the republic. Economic theory could be useful, but the key may be that today's big-data capabilities allow for a lot tighter curve follow. That means that objective metrics can be more responsive than at any time in history—if we quit trying to cook the books.

"We the People" get the government we deserve. We appear to have a lot of rage. Our political discourse today is shallow and is biased with the belief in using government to fix all problems. Our impatience focuses us only on the short term, which reinforces the belief in using government because it can exert the largest force possible to exert change quickly. We need to tackle the nature of our society head-on. The next chapter will do so to show a path toward reestablishing equilibrium.

8

Reestablishing Equilibrium

Before constitutional equilibrium can be maintained, it must be restored. This is analogous to an American going on a diet. Society has been on a long binge of growing government faster than a middle-aged man's waistline. Just as diets don't work in the long run, any temporary measures to cut government spending are doomed to failure. Society needs a change in lifestyle.

There is irony today in the way Americans view themselves. Many Americans believe that they want small government, yet they want all the benefits that only a big government can provide. Many believe they are staunch advocates of liberty, yet they insist on big, centralized government. They suffer from James Payne's six political illusions.[261] A simple adjustment to the left-right model is to rotate the axis clockwise ninety degrees. One side wants top-down governance: the other wants bottom-up governance.

The Greatest Generation grew up during the Depression. Then they fought and won World War II. The whole nation went to war. Public virtue was alive and well then. The nation was still a creditor nation after the war. Things changed when the baby boomer generation took the helm. The same irresponsibility and lack of public virtue that fueled the hippie movement took over society's institutions. The boomers (a prophet archetype) made a mess of it, but the seeds of the pending debacle had been sown years before by the prior "prophets,"[262] the Missionary Generation.[263]

---

261 Payne, *Six Political Illusions*.

262 Strauss and Howe, *Fourth Turning*, 20.

263 *Ibid.*, 60.

Society: Perception Versus Reality

Bastiat proclaimed that "law is force."[264] The role of government includes passing and enforcing laws. James Payne's voluntary illusion echoes Bastiat's claim that (physical) force is central to government's function but that people lose sight of the force. By Locke's definition of liberty, law restrains liberty—more law, less liberty. The logical conclusion is that every law robs us of a little liberty. Members of civil societies willingly give up a little liberty for the benefits they gain. But the pride with which lawmakers take in increasing the sheer number of laws as an indicator of success should alarm us. The implication is that diminishing liberty without bound is the measure of successful governance. This is exactly the opposite of the intention behind the Constitution.

As stated before, we have inherited the benefits and problems from previous generations. What we have inherited are the institutions of civil society as established by the founders and subsequently molded by intervening generations. We should be grateful for the benefits and honest about the problems. What we recognize as problems in our complex social system are really the effects of the root cause(s). We can only see the original cause if we know history and realize that effects are not linear.

One way to identify a root cause is to look to history for instability, confusion, and perceived injustice—in other words, look for outcry and objection at the time of legislation. If metrics trend in the wrong direction shortly thereafter, it may indicate when the root cause was introduced. Use of key economic metrics is one sound device. For example, economic graphs are very enlightening with respect to the effects of legislation passed that year. Figure 2 below clearly shows the effect of ending the gold standard in 1970.[265]

---

264 Frederic Bastiat, *The Law*, pg. 25.

265 Carmen M. Reinhart and Kenneth S. Rogoff, "Shifting Mandates: The Federal Reserve's First Centennial," Scholars at Harvard, accessed July 6, 2016, http://scholar.harvard.edu/files/rogoff/files/shifting_mandates_aer.pdf.

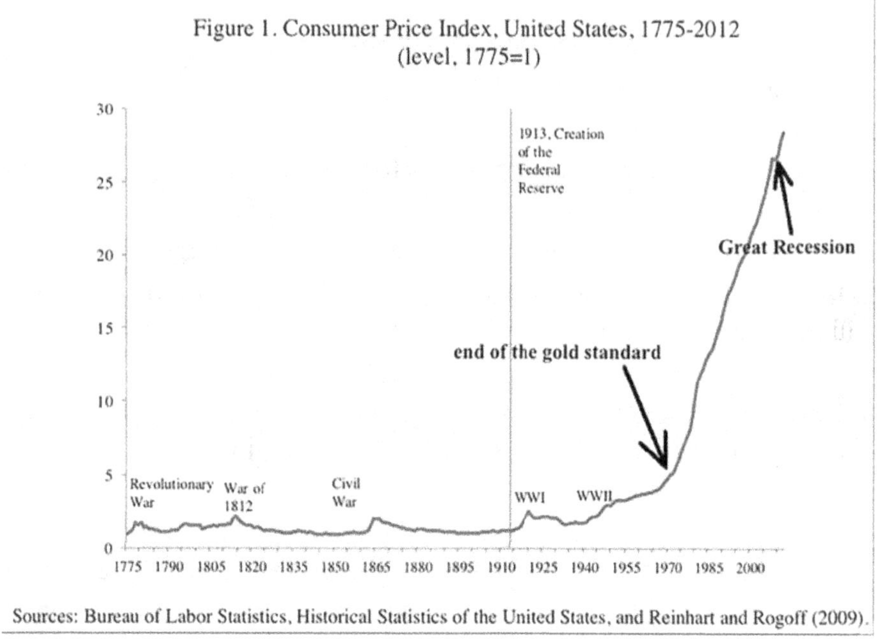

Figure 1. Consumer Price Index, United States, 1775-2012
(level, 1775=1)

1913, Creation of the Federal Reserve

Great Recession

end of the gold standard

Revolutionary War

War of 1812

Civil War

WWI

WWII

Sources: Bureau of Labor Statistics, Historical Statistics of the United States, and Reinhart and Rogoff (2009).

Figure 2 CPI

The fabric of civil society has static and dynamic components. The static nature of institutions provides stability. No generation can be held hostage by its predecessors, so priorities will shift within the population. These shifts give rise to social movements, a dynamic component. The usual motivation behind a movement is correction of a perceived injustice, and such movements usually target at least one of the existing institutions. The perceived injustice may not be an injustice at all, in which case the movement may actually *create* an injustice. Even if the perceived injustice is real, the movement risks creating instability and confusion. By their very nature, then, social movements are risky. Society adapts to the resulting institutional changes and loses awareness of the effect with generational turns.

Institutions themselves can promote their own mortal disease(s).[266] Let us consider the history of just one: the *original sin* of the United States,

266 They are instability, injustice, and confusion. See Madison, "Federalist No. 10."

slavery.[267] No one should dispute that its very existence as a national institution was an injustice. It was a legislative mistake promoted by the original special interest group, the slave industry. The conclusion of the founding generation was that attempting to remove this injustice would have had more dire consequences in fomenting other mortal diseases that would have made the new republic stillborn.

Their concern was validated by the subsequent growth of the abolition movement, which led to a breakdown in civil society. Instead of these two factions checking each other, as Madison (and other founders) had hoped, the mortal disease of injustice (slavery) spawned instability and the Civil War. The end of the war eventually restored a modicum of stability. The Emancipation Proclamation and the Thirteenth Amendment corrected the legislative mistakes in the Constitution and removed the injustice of slavery. That was not the end of injustice and instability. The Fourteenth and Fifteenth Amendments had to address residual injustice. That was still not the end of related injustice against a specific segment of the population (black Americans).

The slave industry is the first example of a special interest group that succeeded in promoting improper law—into the original Constitution. Slavery itself was both a social movement and an institution that supported and was supported by improper law. The Civil War demonstrated how deadly the confluence of an institution (slavery) and the fomenting a movement can be. It just took another movement of equivalent force to ignite hostilities—abolition.

Although the term "War Between the States" is used today, the true meaning of this term is not internalized by current generations. It truly was a war between states. It was not a war of the national government against the antebellum South. There were only nineteen national infantry regiments in the war. But Ohio alone had 197.[268] Little Rhode Island fielded twelve. This misconception fuels a number of today's factions. Moreover, in addition to being a war to correct injustice, it was the start

267 Slavery was inherited from the United States' origin as a British colony.
268 "Regimental Index," Civil War Archive.

of a social conflict over *federalism*. Americans stopped shooting one another, but the conflict morphed into the mortal disease of *confusion* about federalism.

It has degenerated to the point where many of today's Americans view states' rights as an evil concept. This tears at the very fabric of the Constitution. The dual sovereignty was devised to have the states serve as agents of the people in order to check the power of the national government. The fact that a powerful faction geographically located in a portion of the country stubbornly promoted an injustice does not invalidate the concept of bottom-up federalism. The fact that the other half of the nation corrected the injustice actually validates it.

It makes sense to consider the following:

- What **improper laws** exist that are supported by and fuel special interest groups?
- What **social movements** spawn improper laws or foment mortal disease(s)?
- What **institutions** perpetuate improper laws?
- What **institutions** foment one or more of the mortal diseases?

These are the first questions to ask to determine how to remove the existing mortal diseases that are fermenting. Improper laws can be rescinded or replaced on their own merit. Social movements and institutions are more difficult to defuse because they both promote and are fueled by improper laws. All social movements and institutions have a life cycle. They usually (but not always) start out with a positive intent, but good intent does not always translate into good effect. Both movements and institutions are prone to degeneration or misguidance as less competent or malevolent leadership takes over. Whereas social movements could wither and die, such a happenstance usually requires a generational turn.[269] People tend to wed themselves to a movement

269 Strauss, William, and Neil Howe. The Fourth Turning: an American Prophecy: What the Cycles of History Tell Us about America's next Rendezvous with Destiny. New York, NY: Three Rivers Press, 1997. Pg.15.

for life—even if the movement morphs into something completely different. On the other hand, a subsequent generation *may* lose interest in the movement.[270]

The very stability that institutions provide makes them very difficult to correct or destroy once they have gone awry. One view of institutions is that they are "the rules of the game." As such, there may well be improper laws that need to be addressed. The biggest danger is the confluence of a movement and one or more institutions. An institutionalized movement (like slavery) is the deadliest of circumstances.

Improper Laws and Regulations

How can a law or regulation be improper? National law is (in theory) confined by the Constitution, but it is also improper if it infringes on liberty or promotes one of the mortal diseases. The enumeration is if the law

- exceeds the bounds of the Constitution,
- infringes on liberty unnecessarily,
- creates instability,
- promotes injustice, or
- creates confusion.

As an example, segregation laws existed until the Civil Rights Act of 1964 abolished them. The Civil Rights Act clearly removed an injustice; however, it also infused confusion by adding racial quotas. It is arguable whether racial quotas were necessary, but if we assume some force of law was necessary to make a social reform, we need to realize that it infringes on liberty. Any such force that infringes on liberty should not persist once the reform is complete.

What is the metric for completeness? Bluntly put, it cannot be the elimination of bigotry without destroying liberty. Liberty implies that a citizen has a right to be a bigot, but that citizen doesn't have the right to

270 The hippie movement is an example.

negatively affect the well-being and liberty of another by such bigotry. The metric for completed social reform should be that the disadvantaged segment of the population is no longer institutionally disadvantaged. In other words, individuals can be bigots, but institutions cannot be.

If we consider the Strauss-Howe generations theory, such a reform is subject to the turning of a generation. This is the ideal situation for a sunset provision. In the final analysis, the Civil Rights Act of 1964 was mostly proper, but it was somewhat improper because it infringed on liberty while risking a mix of Madison's mortal diseases. The infringement could have been curtailed with a provision for the sunset of the law in twenty-five years' time, thereby restoring liberty. Did bigotry disappear by 1989? No, but the social inertia necessary for stopping the (new) injustice was established. Continuing quotas risks resentment (which is perceived injustice) that could lead to a new rage and swing the pendulum in the opposite direction. There is no statute of limitations on mood eras.[271]

We need to keep the correction of improper laws in perspective. They are short-term corrections, but they will have nonlinear effects. Nonlinear effects are normally not instantaneous. The effect we can expect from removing an improper law is that it will stimulate social change, just as the enactment of the improper law did in the first place. We need to analyze whether the momentum established by this stimulation should be sustained or checked at some point, just as it should have been done when the improper law was enacted. The goal should always be to avoid both long-term injustice and infringement of liberty.

Social Movements

The strength of a social movement can overpower any boundaries between independent factions to create consolidated factions. It would be dishonest to deny that we suffer from this circumstance today. If we have any hope of correcting our current path away from the Constitution, we need to recognize these movements and loosen their hold on our

271 Strauss and Howe, *Fourth Turning*, 2–5.

society. Some movements are obvious; others are not. One of each is discussed below. A full enumeration of movements is beyond the scope of this book. Again, the goal is to stimulate a removal of injustice with as little infringement on liberty as possible—without introducing undue instability and confusion.

Progressivism in the United States

> The whole modern world has divided itself into Conservatives and Progressives. The business of Progressives is to go on making mistakes. The business of the Conservatives is to prevent the mistakes from being corrected.
>
> *G. K. Chesterton*

The progressive movement in the United States started in response to grievances mainly caused by the industrial revolution. Historian William Leuchtenburg, a leading scholar on FDR,[272] defines progressivism in the United States as follows:

> The Progressives believed in the Hamiltonian concept of positive government, of a national government directing the destinies of the nation at home and abroad. They had little but contempt for the strict construction of the Constitution by conservative judges, who would restrict the power of the national government to act against social evils and to extend the blessings of democracy to less favored lands. The real enemy was particularism, state rights, limited government.[273]

By this definition, can there be a clearer enemy of the Constitution than the progressive movement? The principal intention of the Constitution was to limit the national government to protect individual rights from it. By Leuchtenburg's definition, progressives fundamentally declared war on the Constitution. Progressives clearly suffered from Payne's illusion of government preeminence—the belief that only

272 FDR is a hero of progressivism. This is a progressive historian's definition.

273 William Leuchtenburg, "Progressivism and Imperialism: The Progressive Movement and American Foreign Policy, 1898–1916," *The Mississippi Valley Historical Review* 39, no. 3 (1952): 483–5.

government can solve social problems. If one accepts that society itself can be a problem solver, there is no reason to have government cure social evils. Likewise, one has to be suffering from Payne's voluntary illusion to believe that the use of government force can "extend the blessings of democracy." The blessings of democracy include liberty; however, democracy, as the founders well understood, could become the tyranny of the majority. That is a curse, not a blessing. The progressives' goal of "bringing the government closer to the people" was a movement away from a republic to a democracy. In fact, the progressive movement is the root cause of all six of Payne's political illusions—and it persists to this day. Progressives also suffered from the additional cognitive trap that kept them from seeing the consequences of Pournelle's iron law. That is, they didn't see that the second group of bureaucrats will dominate. As such, the government will serve itself rather than the people. The only way to avoid this is to limit the government, as the Constitution was designed.

Are progressives and liberals the same? Modern liberals draw a distinction between progressivism and modern liberalism. Indeed, Walter Lippmann writes about the distinction in 1914, during the original Progressive Era (1890-1920). As he defines it, progressivism's goal is to overthrow authority, and liberalism is the "gap" between this destruction and the creation of a substitute—"a period of drift and doubt."[274] "Drift and doubt" is synonymous with "instability and confusion." Therefore, according to Lippmann, progressives purposely created the mortal diseases of instability and confusion—and liberalism was the resulting period with two of Madison's mortal diseases.

Liberals draw the distinction that progressives were only concerned about "movement away from something."[275] Some of them want to distance themselves from the progressive label because they recognize the

---

274 Walter Lippmann and William E. Leuchtenburg. *Drift and Mastery: An Attempt to Diagnose the Current Unrest* (Englewood Cliffs, N.J: Prentice-Hall, 1961), 221.

275 Eric Rauchway, "What's the Difference Between Progressives and Liberals?" *The New Republic*, September 25, 2006, accessed July 02, 2016, https://newrepublic.com/article/37705/whats-the-difference-between-progressives-and-liberals.

damage done by early progressives.[276] Progressives take the view that the movement has evolved.[277] These arguments may or may not be valid, but they obscure the fact that today's progressives and liberals share the desire to unbind the national government from the Constitution as written. The "living Constitution" is one device invented to realize this goal. Like the original progressives, both perpetuate all six of Payne's political illusions.

It is important to note that Lippmann's definition of modern liberalism has absolutely nothing to do with personal liberty. The theory promotes freedom of experimentation—*by government*. If we remove the veil of the voluntary illusion, we see clearly that this is a threat to personal liberty, not a reinforcement of it. Labels in American politics are frequently misleading. (From the beginning, Alexander Hamilton took the label "Federalist" for his nationalist movement. He then labeled the true Federalists as "anti-Federalists" when they objected that they were the true champions of federalism. This move alone went a long way to winning the argument for the Constitution—despite the fact that it was really championed by nationalists who wanted tighter coupling than the national mood era.)[278] Lippmann's use of the term "liberal" is likewise misleading.

Some contemporary liberals argue that those who are using the "progressive" label are damaging the term "liberalism" and that they are not related to the original progressives.[279] In truth, those who call themselves progressives today are different people from those of the Progressive Era. Likewise, the list of grievances has changed—but there is a thread of continuity. Like their forebears, progressives suffer from all six of the cognitive traps enumerated by Payne. In addition, they

---

276 Matthew Yglesias, "The Trouble with 'Progressive,'" *The Atlantic*, February 6, 2008, accessed July 03, 2016, http://www.theatlantic.com/politics/archive/2008/02/the-trouble-with-progressive/48351/.

277 "Progressive Traditions: The Progressive Intellectual Tradition in America," Center for American Progress, accessed July 03, 2016, https://www.americanprogress.org/issues/progressive-movement/report/2010/04/14/7677/the-progressive-intellectual-tradition-in-america/.

278 Smith and McIlroy, *The Federalist Papers*.

279 Yglesias, "Trouble with 'Progressive.'"

suffer the cognitive trap that progressivism is about technical progress and that it can only be achieved via political progressivism. They confuse *change* with *progress*. Change can be regression or deterioration, as well as true progress. As Rauchway states, progressivism is about "moving away from something. Essentially the view is that progressivism is about the 'destruction' part of 'creative destruction.' " True to the American tradition of mislabeling, the label "progressive" really has nothing to do with progress.[280]

What about the creative side of creative destruction? Lippmann did not really define liberalism as the resolution but as the period of drift and doubt. In theory, there is a lot of experimentation during this period. Unfortunately, there does not seem to be a method of closure. One problem-solving technique that would be reasonable to employ would be the scientific method. Regrettably, the destructive part of this creative-destruction model removes the first essential part of the scientific method—a baseline from which to measure results. The second problem is that there is no advocacy for using metrics for success or failure anywhere in the process.

So, can progressivism and liberalism be separated? The truth is that being creative with social norms requires destruction of the old norms by definition. In reality, both self-proclaimed progressives and liberals are a continuation of the original progressive movement. The details of the issues may have evolved, but they still advocate "moving away from today" without measuring the consequences to social cohesion. Many of the ideals are fundamentally the same as of the original Progressive Era.[281] The fact that the ideals persist despite a century of progressive solutions demonstrates the inadequacy of the goals and the ineffectiveness of the solutions.[282]

In addition to outlining grievances resulting from the industrial revolution, progressivism in the 1890s emphasized making society more

280 Rauchway, "What's the Difference."
281 "Progressive Traditions," Center for American Progress.
282 Ibid.

efficient.[283] Top-down government gives the illusion of being the way to do so. Socialism swept through Europe in the 1870s. Historians have noted that social movements in the United States have tended to lag behind Europe by ten to twenty years. This is consistent with a generational turning. On the other hand, the culture of the United States inevitably morphs movements. Outright socialism has historically been repulsive to Americans; however, it influenced the progressive movement at its inception.[284] Each successive generation has become more accepting of socialist ideals, and progressivism has embraced more of these ideals over time as generations turn.

Early progressive action items included the following:

- Labor issues
    - Worker compensation
    - Improved child labor laws
    - Minimum wage legislation
    - Maximum worker hours
- Graduated income tax
- Women's suffrage
- Prohibition[285]

We have already seen that the progressive movement promoted Payne's illusion of government preeminence and the voluntary illusion by Leuchtenburg's definition. If we scrutinize the list above, we see that the labor issues also promoted the philanthropic illusion and the materialistic illusion. The graduated income tax was based upon the voluntary, frictionless state, materialistic, and philanthropic illusions. Prohibition was based upon the watchful-eye illusion and the illusion of government preeminence.

---

283 Samuel Haber, *Efficiency and Uplift: Scientific Management in the Progressive Era*, 1890-1920 (Chicago: University of Chicago Press, 1964).

284 "Progressive Traditions," Center for American Progress.

285 "Overview of the Progressive Era," Digital History, accessed July 01, 2016, http://www.digitalhistory.uh.edu/era.cfm?eraID=11.

The United States has both prospered and suffered in the wake of progressivism. No doubt improved child labor laws and women's suffrage corrected injustices. The rest of the labor laws are a mixed bag. One of the original progressive targets encouraging offshoring—and more—is unilaterally overlooked because of linear thinking. The minimum wage has become untouchable. It encourages offshoring and illegal immigration, and it is an ever-present inflationary pressure.

A large part of a modern company's overhead is labor. To reduce this overhead, companies move overseas in order to pay lower wages (and taxes). Businesses that don't have the option of offshoring (like farming) seek cheaper sources of labor via illegal immigrants. The more-regulated small businesses have no option but to eliminate jobs. Finally, minimum wage does not exist in a vacuum within the labor market. It logically follows that wages above the minimum increase to keep the pecking order intact. The cost of labor is embedded in the prices of all products—more than once. Its inflationary effects are nonlinear because the economy is a complex system. Not every job needs to pay a living wage. Dependents need a starting point into the job market. Frequently, couples both have to work more than one job each just to make ends meet because of hidden inflation. So, how are we better off? Throughout the generations after the Progressive Era, we have lost sight of the fact that labor is a market that obeys supply and demand. This is amplified by the global market.

If we look at some of our heaviest misfortunes today (borrowing from Madison), we see that the roots of these miseries trace directly to progressivism's earliest targets. In particular, the current tax code has become a leviathan in its own right. Taxation is a complex problem beyond the scope of this book, but the current tax code encourages business to go offshore to escape excessive taxation. Obviously, progressives consider progressive taxation just; however, a large segment of the population considers it unjust. In particular, a large part of the middle class (Aristotle's "best") considers it unjust.[286]

---

286 Bonnie Kavoussi, "Most Americans Say Tax Code Unfair to Poor, Middle Class: Survey," *The Huffington Post*, accessed July 05, 2016, http://www.huffingtonpost.com/2012/04/18/tax-code-unfair_n_1432178.html.

At a minimum, the complexity of filing taxes is in fact the mortal disease of confusion. The simple fact that businesses and individuals alike react energetically to changes in the tax code speaks to the instability it injects. Long-term business and individual decisions are impacted by it. A good tax code would affect neither personal nor business decisions significantly. The progressive movement achieved its goal of graduated income tax so that it could redistribute wealth and increase the size of government, but it never weighed the results of so doing. The increased size of government increases our exposure to complex system failure. Clinging to progressive ideals prevents us from extricating ourselves from its influences.

Another example from the original progressive movement was the temperance movement, resulting in the Eighteenth Amendment. Prohibition was such a resounding failure that it was repealed by the Twenty-First Amendment. As a result, the term "progressive" became a pejorative. The more positive use of 'liberal' in the sense that Lippmann discussed became popular. Liberals continued promoting the welfare state without missing a beat. Regardless of what label is used, what we see today is the evolution of the progressive movement. We have already seen that the movement was based upon the illusion of government preeminence and the voluntary illusion by Leuchtenburg's definition. We can see all six of Payne's illusions by looking at the enumeration of political values (ideals) promoted by the Center for American Progress.[287] For example, the initial value on the list is freedom. The paradox of promoting freedom by enlarging government and the body of laws reveals the intensity of the voluntary illusion and the illusion of government preeminence in the movement.

A reoccurring theme of progressivism is social justice. Recall that Bastiat identifies that justice itself is merely the absence of injustice. The implication is that any qualifier (adjective) to the term "justice" means that only certain injustices are unacceptable. By implication, other injustices are sanctioned. Lady Justice is depicted with a blindfold for a

---

287 "Progressive Traditions," Center for American Progress.

reason. Once we consider to whom a law is applied, we enter the realm of the makeup call—an application of injustice to make up for an earlier injustice. This erodes the sense of and application of justice in society. Many solutions address an injustice by creating another injustice that may be as bad as or worse than the injustice it purports to resolve. On top of that, there is no consideration of the fact that any institutional change (new law) can also create the remaining mortal diseases of instability and confusion.

It should be emphasized that this critique of progressivism is not a critique of a single political party. Today, progressivism infects both major political parties and has done so since the Progressive Era. It is like a virus that attacks the principle of obeying the Constitution and has grown stronger with each generation. The only difference between the parties is the social change that the respective parties want to inflict.

If there is any doubt, consider the Republican response to the Democrats' (and media) accusation that they have no better idea than the Affordable Care Act. Some national laws that affect the health care industry are perhaps unavoidable, but the Republican response should have been that there should only be laws to remove national injustice, instability, or confusion. That is not what they did. All Americans alive today have been afflicted with the progressive virus because we have been conditioned to believe that it is more important to use government to solve a problem *first* rather than *last and least*. This is Payne's illusion of government preeminence. Both major political parties have abandoned the very cornerstone principle of limited government.

Progressivism has not stood still, but it still promotes solutions that penalize productivity. As G. K. Chesterton put it, they continue to make mistakes. Most social movements today are spin-offs from progressivism or a reaction to it. A side effect of progressivism's pervasiveness is the myth of the advanced society. This arrogant myth confuses our advances in technology with social evolution—or, even more brazenly, evolution as a species. Embedded in this view is the pretension that one does not believe in progress if he or she is not politically progressive. This is a naïve notion of how technological progress works. It is also blind to Lippmann's assessment of progressivism. The progressive methodology is actually the antithesis of the scientific method, where results are always measured and the information fed back into the improvement cycle. As a result, the progressive solution to everything has devolved to using the national government to throw money at any and every problem.[288] Of course, this is a combination of Payne's materialistic illusion and the illusion of government preeminence.

Nonetheless, the progressive movement has been extremely successful at undermining the Constitution. It has done so by recruiting through a number of institutions—not least of which the formal educational system. Instead of educating the next generation in the wisdom behind the Constitution, it has reinforced Payne's six political illusions for over a century. Today it goes further and inculcates the young in social justice, fair share, safe spaces, and other progressive mechanisms. Restoring the stature of the Constitution will require minimizing or destroying the influence of the progressive movement. For a half-dozen generational turns, the movement has been a constant source of instability, confusion, and promotion of injustice under the guise of social justice. The socialist basis of the movement has been on full display since the 2016 presidential election. The historic failures of socialism should diminish the movement's ability to inject confusion into society henceforth. It just requires enlightenment to the true nature of progressivism.

The American public at large suffers the largest cognitive trap of all. Americans do not see the dangers of progressivism—to their liberty and to their well-being.

Consolidation

Consolidation by its very nature reduces competition. There are fewer competitors. Monopoly is the ultimate consolidation. Economists have demonstrated that competition reduces prices even in an imperfect

288 This is Payne's materialistic illusion.

market with few competitors,[289] but that only considers the consumer's benefit, not the overall impact on society.

Perhaps no single syndrome has shifted the nature of factions from Madison's time more than consolidation. Consolidated factions create a complex system of factions as opposed to the simple factional mechanisms of Madison's time. Newton's third law of physics[290] applies with simple factions; however, consolidated factions introduce nonlinear effects.

Teddy Roosevelt was famous for being the "Trust Buster" during the Progressive Era (1890–1920).[291] The mood era of the country was fueled by a rage against monopoly, where one company controls a market. The rage of that generation over monopoly was twofold, in that a monopoly can

- charge whatever price it dictates with the market unable to do anything to correct it and
- abuse labor through unfair wages and working conditions.

Both of these effects are unjust. The president's solution was to use government to force the breakup of monopolies. It is ironic to consider the existence of "too big to fail" in the current business world. Whereas companies in Teddy Roosevelt's day purportedly captured a vertical market, consider the consolidated complex of just ten companies that dominate the food industry today (see figure 3).[292] It is truly a leviathan

---

289 Skousen, *Big Three in Economics*, 215.

290 Newton's third law of physics states that **"For every action, there is an equal and opposite reaction."**

291 Dominick T. Armentano refutes the notion that there really was a monopoly problem, but that is outside our scope here. For his argument, see Dominick T. Armentano, *Myths of Antitrust: Economic Theory and Legal Cases*. Alington House: New Rochelle, NY. 1972

292 Clarissa A. León, "These Top 10 Food Companies Control Nearly Everything We Eat," Alternet, July 21, 2014, accesssed July 2016, http://www.alternet.org/food/food-brands-climate-change.

that dominates multiple markets horizontally. There is little room for new producers to enter the market.

Figure 3 Top-Ten Companies

Consolidation can be a natural occurrence, or it can be forced. It is natural when there is a natural affinity or survival dictates the consolidation. This is how civil societies form in the first place. In a free-market system, producers consolidate when the market matures, saturates, or collapses. This is a bottom-up process of cohesion. On the other hand, it is unnatural when it is imposed by force (law or by faction—which could be an unscrupulous business person). This is a process of coupling. The typical way this happens is that businesses are unable to meet associated regulatory costs and close or sell to a larger company. This is a top-down process where the last man standing inherits the market. In a larger context, conquest is a top-down process of consolidation. Hostile takeovers are a form of conquest.

In the bottom-up process, all participants have equal potential, and the process stops at a point of equilibrium. In the top-down process, winners are arbitrary, and there is no determinant halt to the process.

Note that the latter case is contrary to Locke's description of liberty: "Not be subject to the inconstant, uncertain, unknown, and arbitrary wills of others."[293] In point of fact, the goal of the Sherman Antitrust Act (and subsequent legislation) was not to protect competitors but to protect competition.[294] Top-down consolidation (whether inflicted by government or private party) destroys competition but protects certain competitors.

There is something very striking about the adoption of the Constitution. Whereas the Articles of Confederation were adopted to forge an alliance among independent colonies (loose coupling), the Constitution consolidated those colonies into a tighter union of states. It is often argued that the main distinction between the Constitution and Articles of Confederation was the power of the purse. Moreover, it was the first time that the power of the states was consolidated by the purse. The nationalists (Federalists) pushed consolidation, while the Whigs (anti-Federalists) opposed consolidation and favored decentralization. The Constitution was ratified by speed and cunning despite the fact that the mood era of the country was opposed to consolidation in general.[295] It remained that way until the (mood) Progressive Era reignited a natural human tendency for consolidation.

During the ratification debate, the nationalists' argument was that the very survival of the union required consolidation. This excerpt from *Antifederalist No. 38* refutes that position:

> I deny that we are in immediate danger of anarchy and commotions. Nothing but the passions of wicked and ambitious men will put us in the least danger on this head. Those who are anxious to precipitate a measure will always tell us that the present is the critical moment; now is the time, the crisis is arrived, and the present minute must be seized. Tyrants have always made use of this plea; but nothing in our circumstances can justify it.

293 Locke, *Two Treatises of Government.*

294 *Spectrum Sports, Inc. v. McQuillan* 506 US 447 (1993).

295 Smithand McIlroy, *The Federalist Papers.*

Patrick Henry proclaimed the same position in the Virginia ratification debates. The Constitution itself was born from a disagreement as to whether or not the consolidation was necessary—that is, natural.

The anti-Federalists' objections to the Constitution illuminate a powerful tool used perpetually by enemies of liberty throughout human history. Today, we hear the phrase "scare tactics," but this epithet is used to blunt and negate potentially valid positions by triggering a Pavlovian rejection of the proposition. Throughout history, tyrants and the shills of tyrants have promoted true scare tactics wherein they persuade the citizens to give up liberty for security. During the ratification debates, the accusation of a threat to liberty was seriously considered by both sides. Today, our Pavlovian response is to ignore threats to liberty as unfounded because of the resilient stability of the United States. As David Hume put it in 1742, "Seldom is liberty of any kind lost all at once."[296] We should worry that we discount threats to our liberty so cavalierly. It is hubris to think that incremental loss of liberty cannot happen in the United States. In fact, it has already happened.

In general, consolidation is a companion to the human affinity for top-down solutions. A top-down organization will always appear to be more efficient than a bottom-up one because it directly addresses the most visible "what?" question. The irony of human nature is that we are lured to the desire for efficiency, but we are captivated by the few examples in history when the little guy (usually a bottom-up institution) defeats the big guy—David and Goliath, the ancient Greeks defeating the Persian Empire, and so forth. Moreover, the apparent efficiency of top-down solutions is specious. Efficiency is really achieved near or at the bottom level where the most repetitive tasks are routinely performed—where the "how?" question gets answered—where things get done. This was the basis for Adam Smith's argument for the "division of labor."[297] It is also where the true ingenuity of the classic American has always resided.

---

296 "David Hume, Of the Liberty of the Press," Founders' Constitution, http://press-pubs.uchicago.edu/founders/documents/amendI_speechs2.html.

297 Smith, *Wealth of Nations,* Book I, chapter 1, pg. 1.

Consolidation is insidious. *Star Trek: The Next Generation* emphasizes the term "assimilation." The evil Borg assimilate unwilling individuals, sapping them of their individuality. When one's group is consolidated into another, larger group, it is assimilated. Today we see this phenomenon everywhere in the United States with mergers and acquisitions—which leads to companies that are "too big to fail." "Too big to fail" is an acknowledgment that these corporations are complex systems that can become unstable and collapse. It further acknowledges that such a failure could destabilize the larger complex system that is the national economy—and potentially the even larger global economy. The computing world turns to distribution and not consolidation to provide robust solutions. A single point of failure is a catastrophe waiting to happen.

There has been no movement to reverse the effects of consolidation. There could and should be. The original Sherman Antitrust Act of 1890 was passed with the correct intent of protecting competition, not competitors, but it failed miserably. Unfortunately, it fueled mergers. The subsequent Clayton Antitrust Act of 1914 and Robison-Patman Act of 1936 both amended it. They, too, have failed to stem consolidation. Perhaps it is time to review history, remove laws from the books, and let nature take its course. The problem is—and always has been—that we want nature to work more quickly than it does. As cited in the section on regulatory law in the last chapter, monopolies will naturally lose their grip (in a truly free market) on competition because of slower reaction times than more nimble entrants in the market, generational turns, and Pournelle's iron law.

Institutions

Civil society establishes institutions to ensure stability. The ultimate institution is government. As Aristotle frames it, governments can be either congruent or incongruent with the interests of society.[298] We can

298 The usual translation of ὀρθάς and παρεκβεβηκυίας is "good" and "perverted," but this is not a very accurate translation. The Perseus project uses "right constitution" instead of "congruent" and "divergent" as opposed to "perverted" or "incongruent." The specific meaning is that the government diverges from the interests of the people. For the original Greek, see the Perseus Project, http://www.perseus.tufts.edu/hopper/text?doc=Perseus:text:1999.01.0058:book=3:section=1282b&highlight=perverted.

extrapolate that logic to all institutions.[299] That is, an institution can either act in the best interests of society or against them. Hippies might take heart because "it's the corporations, man." The problem with the hippie view is that it is a myopic focus on one set of institutions. There are many societal institutions, and they all have a life cycle. Their life cycles are subject to periods of both congruence and incongruence.

The catalyst for an institution's nature is society's nature and any consequential social movements. When an institution is formed because of a social movement, there is a crossover between the dynamic movement to the static institution that is like concrete hardening. Social movements are a response to a perceived injustice. Once the injustice is addressed, stability can return, by either the dissolution of the movement or the adaptation of the institution. The former case is preferable and sustainable only within a virtuous society. The latter case is indicative of a society in need of public virtue. The more those institutions created by social movements persist, the less likely that society is capable of self-governance.

No institutional repair is possible unless the existing Strauss-Howe mood era is repaired. In the United States, the most consequential social movement since 1890 has been the progressive movement. This movement has benefited society in some areas; however, it is also the root cause of our heaviest misfortunes. The movement is rooted in grievance. Some grievances are justified. Some are not. The insatiable feeling of being aggrieved is a cancer that spreads through society destroying any public virtue. The persistence of any institution that divides the population along *any* line draws political battle lines based solely on grievance, real or contrived. Society descends into Hobbes's "war of all against all." It is a mood era within the current generation that has been created by a half-dozen generational turns of progressive thought that have promoted Payne's six political illusions.

---

299 Aristotle actually uses "household management" (οἰκονομία) in Book 1 of *Politics* to develop his entire theory on political systems. This actually reverses his argument and expands it to all institutions.

Institutions are a reflection of the society that builds them. They are normally congruent when they are established. However, the very stability that motivates creating an institution can become a detriment. Pournelle's iron law applies. Whether an institution is beneficial or detrimental to society is the first question to ask. If it's detrimental, the next step is asking which of the following phenomena is most applicable:

- The need for the institution disappears, but the institution perseveres. The institution should be destroyed.
- Society's needs change, but the institution does not adapt accordingly. The institution should be replaced.
- Bad leadership misdirects the institution to work against society's interests. The leadership (Pournelle's second group) needs to be replaced.

The appropriate action should then be apparent.

The Family

The family is the cornerstone institution of any society. It is a phenomenon of our natural existence. It is where public and private virtue are commonly either created or destroyed. The most important element of public virtue a family can instill is the ability to respect another human being. That is the single most lacking element in the character of many Americans. Since the late twentieth century, the family has not adapted well to either the changes in generational mood eras or to technological advances. These forces have overcome the internal strength of the family.

Book 1 of Aristotle's *Politics* uses the family to define a system of roles and responsibilities. He expands on this baseline to develop his general theory of government. If we look at Maslow's hierarchy of needs, the family unit first provides the basic needs of food, water, shelter, and protection. The family then provides the initial educational needs of the young, teaching society's norms. The family is a unique institution in that it also assists individual development up through the higher levels of Maslow's hierarchy—or not.

The family is the first and best line of defense against the mortal diseases of instability, injustice, and confusion. Once again, we can gain a better understanding of the true state of the family as an institution by looking at it as a dynamic dichotomy—a tug-of-war. On one side, the family has a natural cohesion. The strength of that cohesion varies by the individuals comprising the family. On the other side of the rope is a world of external forces. For prior generations, these forces included the immediate community—in particular, schools, houses of worship, fairs, businesses, and so forth. In a congruent society, these forces are positive, reinforcing the family. (The prevalence of gangs is a very negative communal influence that spotlights the incongruence of society itself.) The positive influences of community and houses of worship are much weaker while the influence of technology has grown stronger.[300] The largest external influences in the United States today are schools and the Internet.

Most analysts go straight to marriage and single-parent statistics to highlight the failure of the family as an institution.[301] The failure is more about weak parenting than out-of-wedlock births. A single, strong parent can be an amazing role model. Consider Dr. Ben Carson's mother. A parent's role is first to provide stability. The educational role of a parent is to provide consistency and instill a sense of virtue—both personal and public. That begins with earning the child's respect, not being a friend. Widespread failure to perform these parental duties sets up society for failure with the next generational turn. There are five ways this widespread failure has occurred in the United States:

1. Weak parenting at home leaving a void to be filled
2. Poor parenting overriding discipline within the school system
3. Parental absenteeism
4. Confusion of a broken home—even with two parents
5. Overpowering external influences

300 Robert D. Putnam, *Bowling Alone: The Collapse and Revival of American Community* (New York: Simon & Schuster, 2000), 34, 142–537.

301 George Will, "The Sobering Evidence of Social Science," Freedom's Back, July 7, 2016, accessed July 10, 2016, http://freedomsback.com/george-will/the-sobering-evidence-of-social-science/.

No doubt, poor parenting has been with mankind since the beginning, but discipline between parents and children has collapsed since the post–World War II era. The Greatest Generation spoiled their kids—the baby boomers. Many boomers then turned their backs on classic parent-child relationships by eschewing discipline. Boomers lacked this key aspect of public virtue. This shows up in spades financially with personal debt, but it has been most damaging in parenting. It is hard to be a good parent. It is easy to give into kids. The loss of discipline has had many bad side effects. The biggest problem is that many children are unguided. They do what they want instead of what is to the benefit of themselves and society. It is a pattern they continue through life. It is a total breakdown of personal and public virtue.

Bad parenting has extended from the home to the schools. There was a time when schools disciplined children. The boomers were still subjected to corporal punishment—on rare occasions. More and more families became indignant about schools laying a finger on their precious darlings. The removal of discipline didn't stop with corporal punishment. The long-term result has been a complete breakdown of discipline in the schools. What was once a minority of families with bad parenting has led to chaos in the school system. Good parents must now compensate for the bad influences prevalent in public schools and are also fleeing the public system.[302] There is a complete breakdown of public virtue in the public education system.

There is a problem with parental absenteeism. Demographers have collected a plethora of statistics that support the weakening of the family as an institution since World War II.[303] In October 2000, the CDC published a report about births out of wedlock.[304] The report shows that out-of-wedlock births went from about 5 percent in 1940 to 32 percent

302 "Students Names on Charter Schools Waiting Lists Top One Million for the First Time," National Alliance for Public Charter Schools, accessed July 10, 2016, http://www.publiccharters.org/press/waiting-list-2014/.

303 "Four in Ten Children Are Born to Unwed Mothers," FamilyFacts, http://www.familyfacts.org/charts/205/four-in-10-children-are-born-to-unwed-mothers.

304 Stephanie J. Ventura and Christine A. Bachrach, "Nonmarital Childbearing in the United States, 1940–99," *National Vital Statistics Reports* 48, no. 16 (2000).

in 1999, over a six-fold increase. Other statistics show that marriage itself is on the decline, but it is possible that parents stay together and raise a family without the marriage contract. The statistics show that 60 percent of cohabiting parents end up marrying.[305] All these statistics reflect that the legal device of the marriage contract no longer binds the family. That is not the problem. The problem is a shift in society brought on by technology and the welfare state promoted by the progressive movement:

- The progressive movement has forgotten about public virtue:
    - It weakens the bond between parents, independent of the legal contract.
    - Fathers do not take responsibility for fathering.
    - Parents are focused on careers rather than on parenting.
    - Some parents let society raise children rather than take responsibility themselves.
    - The Internet is easily accessible and is full of sites unfit for children.
- The government welfare state has distorted finances and directly damaged the family. This is reflected in Moynihan's Scissors:[306]
    - It encourages fathers not to take responsibility for fathering.
    - It encourages poor mothers to have more children.
    - The War on Poverty has been a catastrophe for the middle class.[307]

305 Patricia H. Shiono and Linda Sandham Quinn, "Epidemiology of Divorce," *The Future of Children* 4, no. 1 (1994): 15–28, http://futureofchildren.org/publications/journals/article/index.xml?journalid=63&articleid=408§ionid=2781.

306 "Social Disruptions," PBS, http://www.pbs.org/fmc/timeline/ddisruption.htm.
George F. Will, "What Patrick Moynihan Knew About the Importance of Two Parents," The Washington Post, March 13, 2015, https://www.washingtonpost.com/opinions/what-patrick-moynihan-knew-about-the-importance-of-two-parents/2015/03/13/2cdf9bae-c9a4-11e4-aa1a-86135599fb0f_story.html.

307 Louis Woodhill, "The War on Poverty Wasn't a Failure—It was a Catastrophe," *Forbes*, March 19, 2014, http://www.forbes.com/sites/louiswoodhill/2014/03/19/the-war-on-poverty-wasnt-a-failure-it-was-a-catastrophe/#209e1a5f7b6c.

Another form of parental absenteeism happens with the family intact. Often, both parents work to make ends meet. (The national tendency to live above our means started with the baby boomers). Many adults now focus on career first, not the family. But decades of bad economic policies have made life expensive. Many working-class couples are trapped in a state where they could afford their station in life had economic factors not eroded their financial capabilities—by increased taxation, hidden inflation, and/or loss of income. Either scenario leaves the middle class under pressure and reduces the priority on parenting. The focus on financial stability shortchanges the educational duties of parents.

Busy and stressed-out parents place too much trust in other institutions. Many parents aren't aware of the undue influence the media and schools have on their children. Often, these institutions are imparting values that are counter to the parents' own and destructive to public virtue.

The increase in divorce rates can add confusion, even in two-parent households. Stepparents may be a source of stability, but they can also be a source of confusion. Additional adult influences compromise consistency. Children know how to play parents against each other. With more parents in the family comes more opportunity for children to do so. All parents involved need to provide consistent guidance—and discipline.

Finally, there is no escaping the fact that technology has created stronger opposing forces to family cohesion. Children escape to technological devices because they are entertaining. The Internet is open—regardless of age. Both problems are addressable by strong parenting; however, the Internet is so accessible that it is virtually impossible to shut it off. Society can assist families by limiting unfettered access to the Internet by youths. Rather than immediately going to government, the Internet community (World Wide Web Consortium, W3C) could address the problem via software standards. Movies have had an age-appropriate rating system for decades. Parallel Internet standards could be adopted that would be enforceable via software.

Social media is a blessing and a curse. Bad behavior is unchecked. Cowards bully, embarrass, and spread rumors. It leaves children and women open to exploitation. This spreads Madison's mortal diseases. The lack of decorum in social media is more an indicator of society's state than it is a driver of it. On the other hand, many families use sites like Facebook and Photobucket to stay in touch. Sites like Nextdoor have the potential of restoring a sense of community. The problem with social media is that it is dependent on the public virtue of society. A virtuous society will eventually use these tools to enhance itself. The first hurdle is the same as the one when dealing with any addiction. It's OK for an adult to drink as long as the drinker controls the alcohol. Once the alcohol takes control, problems ensue. Social media is addictive, just like alcohol. Alcohol truly can enhance leisure time as long as Aristotle's golden mean is observed. Social media can enhance a sense of community—as long it isn't in excess and doesn't take control of us.

The family and public virtue are inseparable. Failure of the family negatively influences society's ability to rule itself. Classically the family and the community had an important synergy. Without these interactions, the family loses a valuable support system and is more susceptible to negative external forces. We need to figure out how to better support families in our current high technology, low-kinship environment. This is imperative for restoring society's equilibrium.

Academia

> A primary object of such a national institution should be the education of our youth in the science of government. In a republic what species of knowledge can be equally important and what duty more pressing on its legislature than to patronize a plan for communicating it to those who are to be the future guardians of the liberties of the country?
>
> *George Washington*

Aristotle declares that the role of education is to instill the values of society into the young.[308] The founders agreed.[309] Therefore, academic institutions in the United States are congruent if they instill the values of life, liberty, the pursuit of happiness, and loyalty to the Constitution. As we have seen, this goal is diametrically opposed to those of the progressive movement.

The importance of education in perpetuating the republic is what has made it the major target of the enemies of the Constitution. Our educational institutions are a prime example of the third detrimental phenomenon of institutions: bad leadership. The leadership is progressive, and it exists at all grade levels. It is intentional, and it is insidious. The results are quantified in test results and the ballot box. Emphasis on progressive principles has replaced sound basics—even in mathematics. The educational system teaches the horizontal left-right axis of political science. This model should be replaced by a vertical axis that reveals the true top-down nature of progressivism and the bottom-up intention of the founders.

The fact that academic institutions have become bastions of progressivism makes them incongruent with the principles of the United States. John Dewey implanted progressive ideals into the educational system during the Wilson administration.[310] The effectiveness of educational progressivism can be seen by considering how historians and political scientists rate presidents. A survey of these polls reveals the extreme bias these people have for progressivism.[311]

Polls of historians and political scientists always place FDR and Woodrow Wilson near or at the top of lists of best presidents. These men had no respect for their constitutional limits. Wilson redefined

---

308 Aristotle, *Politics*, Book 1, section 1260b.

309 "Educational Quotes from Our Founding Fathers," Rasmussen College, http://www.rasmussen.edu/student-life/blogs/main/educational-quotes-from-our-founding-fathers/.

310 Dewey, *Democracy and Education*, 153–159.

311 "Overall Rank," Siena College, https://www.siena.edu/assets/files/news/Presidents_2010_Rank_by_Category.pdf.

liberty from the people's liberty to the government's liberty.[312] He put the administrative state on steroids. The enumeration of FDR's contempt for the Constitution also warranted a book.[313] His noteworthy accomplishments include Executive Order 9066, which violated the rights of 117,000 Japanese-Americans by imprisoning them during WWII—for being who they were, not for what they had done.[314]

Once boomer radicals took over the reins of the schools, the youths were inculcated into a more aggressive progressivism.[315] Even if the schools were now purged of this extreme progressivism, damage has been done. They have already inculcated more than a full generation. Free speech is assaulted instead of respected,[316] yet the assailants perpetually raise the First Amendment to justify their assaults. The assailants are frequently the teachers.

Tenure is unheard of anywhere in the United States except for the Mafia "made man" and academic institutions. Given a choice, eliminating academic tenure would be more effective. Academic tenure has caused much more harm than the Mafia, and it is much easier to eliminate. A bad tenured instructor is a bad instructor who can indefinitely corrupt students. Professors like Ward Churchill flaunt their hatred of this country. There is a difference between acknowledging the wrongs in our history, like slavery and the Trail of Tears, and calling our current youths "Little Eichmanns."[317] The former is required to improve our public virtue. The latter is damnation of the nation from a hypocrite. The

---

312 Pestritto, *Woodrow Wilson*, 110–123.

313 Folsom, *New Deal or Raw Deal?*

314 "Teaching with Documents: Documents and Photographs Related to Japanese Relocation During World War II," National Archives, https://www.archives.gov/education/lessons/japanese-relocation/.

315 Saul D. Alinsky, *Rules for Radicals: A Practical Primer for Realistic Radicals* (New York: Vintage Books, 1989), 5, 160–195.

316 Richard Pérez-Peña and Christine Hauser, "University of Missouri Professor Who Confronted Photographer Quits Journalism Post," *The New York Times*, November 15, 2015.

317 Dan Elliott, "Colorado Prof Fired After 9-11 Remarks," *The Washington Post*, July 24, 2007, http://www.washingtonpost.com/wp-dyn/content/article/2007/07/24/AR2007072402000.html.

president who violated the rights of the Native Americans on the Trail of Tears, Andrew Jackson, is usually rated in the top quarter of presidents by academics.[318] This ranking reveals the preference of academics for strong, top-down governance.

The materialistic illusion is pervasive throughout academia. Bringing in money is a very high priority. Sporting events and facilities are just one noneducational means by which these institutions profit.

Americans are very generous, especially when it comes to education. There is a legitimate need to spend on the tools of research. Today's advanced research requires highly controlled environments; however, advanced research should be separated from mainline learning institutions. Luxurious accommodations are a wasteful expense that exposes bad priorities on the part of school administrations. Nicola Tesla built a crude wood tower in Colorado Springs to do some of his most intense experiments. Aristotle taught students while they went for a walk. His main schoolhouse was a cave. Thomas Edison learned at home. Earlier generations of Americans learned in one-room schoolhouses. Learning only requires minimal facilities and the desire to learn. The misalignment of priorities is a by-product of the materialistic illusion. We don't want students learning in a dingy decrepit room, but they don't need the Taj Mahal.

Just how necessary is a four-year degree? According to CareerBuilder, between 32 percent and 47 percent of graduates never work in the field they studied in college.[319] With monumental student-loan obligations, graduates are starting adult life as debtors. Currency deflation, which is natural to a free-market economy where production naturally becomes

318 Arthur Schlesinger, Jr, "Rating the Presidents: Washington to Clinton," *Frontline*, accessed July 06, 2016, http://www.pbs.org/wgbh/pages/frontline/shows/choice2004/leadership/schlesinger.html.

319 O'Shaughnessy, Lynn. "New Study Shows Careers and College Majors Often Don't Match." CBS News. CBS Interactive, November 15, 2013. https://www.cbsnews.com/news/new-study-shows-careers-and-college-majors-often-dont-match/.

more efficient, harms debtors. Fortunately for new graduates, Keynesian economists won't let a much-needed deflation happen.

So, how does obtaining a sheepskin help young adults financially? How does it help one be a better worker or a better entrepreneur? Thomas Edison was homeschooled. He held 1,093 patents and founded General Electric.[320] George Washington was always self-conscious about his lack of formal education, but he more than made up for it by reading, thinking, and doing. He founded the United States. They had *enough* education, and they had the drive to self-educate further. This was directed education with a purpose. Too many youths attend college with no goals for their education. No one should be prevented from getting any degree, and certainly, we want to encourage breadth and depth of knowledge. But no degree should be required to be a productive member of society. Four years of drinking in a dormitory is not an indicator of character and capability.

Artificial requirements for formal education are pushed by a process of occupational licensing. Licensing an individual's occupation makes sense when the errant practice of the occupation can harm the public. An obvious example of this would be a doctor. On the other hand, someone doing a poor job of braiding hair threatens no one's wellbeing.[321] A version of John Stuart Mill's "harm principle" should be applied to such licensing. Dr. Dick M. Carpenter of the Institute for Justice exposes the questionable activities of academics as expert witnesses in occupational licensing cases in his book, *Bottleneckers*.[322] Occupational licensing has become a corrupt practice whereby competition is stifled. Of course,

---

320 "Edison's Patents," Thomas Edison Papers, accessed July 06, 2016, http://edison.rutgers.edu/patents.htm.

321 Sanchez, Moses. "Occupational License or Business License? 7 Expert Answers." Phoenix Narrative, September 1, 2020. https://phoenixnarrative.com/2020/06/what-is-an-occupational-license/.

322 Mellor, William H., and Dick Michael Carpenter. *Bottleneckers Gaming the Government for Power and Private Profit*. New York: Encounter Books, 2016. Dick M. Carpenter II, "Bottleneckers" (lecture, Bastiat Society, Colorado Springs, June 16, 2016). Mellor, William H., and Dick Michael Carpenter. *Bottleneckers Gaming the Government for Power and Private Profit*. New York: Encounter Books, 2016.

educational institutes profit, and politicians get reelected in the process. Profit incentives for universities have led to degree inflation and barriers to entering occupations. The errant assumption is that someone becomes an expert by procuring a higher degree. This is just one way that the rise of experts has become problematic.

Before the baby boomer generation took over the reins, vocational education produced a productive workforce of blue-collar workers who could actually make things (welders, plumbers, and so on). Mike Rowe's mikeroweWORKS Foundation is championing a return of vocational education. In addition to laying a solid foundation in character, vocational education prepares youths for the production side of the economic producer-consumer model.

Too many youths with degrees find themselves in service jobs today. Adam Smith labeled these jobs as "unproductive labor."[323] Service jobs provide no long-term benefit to society. There is an exchange of money, but it doesn't contribute to what Smith called "opulence." A welder or plumber will create functional pieces that endure. We all know where a meal eventually ends up within twenty-four hours after a server brings it to a customer's table.

Public schools were designed to be run by the states, not the national government. The founders intended that they would first teach the principles of the Constitution and other founding documents.[324] The schools were intended to be congruent with society's needs. The schools were indeed congruent while we were an agrarian society. They have not adapted well to the urban society of today. Instead of redirecting the focus from the requirements of an agrarian society, they gutted the foundational societal requirements of government, history, and economics. Even worse, they have actually become degenerate models for behavior that tear at the first principles of self-governance—character and public virtue.

---

323 Smith, *Wealth of Nations,* Book II, chapter 3.

324 "Eighth Annual Message of George Washington," Avalon Project, accessed July 06, 2016, http://avalon.law.yale.edu/18th_century/washs08.asp.

Reforming contemporary academic institutions is a daunting task. First, school administrators are completely inculcated in the progressive mindset—which means they are opposed to the Constitution and founding principles. They meet and reinforce one another. The only way to redirect the incongruence of these organizations is reformation at the state level. Like other government-imposed standards, educational standards perpetuate the progressive culture of the administrators. One possibility for reformation is to turn to military personnel, who understand and pledged allegiance to the Constitution. Many of these folks are well educated and can meet the standards currently imposed. It would likewise be good to revisit the educational standards in order to eliminate pieces of the progressive agenda totally from the educational system—all at the state level. Let the states compete. Like dominos, the first state can set the trend with results.

The Press

On one hand, the contemporary media is really a composite of corporations. As such, each media source is prone to all the same pitfalls as any other corporation. On the other hand, the (intended) product of these corporations is so essential to the proper function of the republic that the founders gave it special protection in the Bill of Rights. In the founders' vision, a right is counterbalanced with a responsibility. This was baked in the cake of the pursuit of happiness.[325]

The role of the news media is to keep the public informed of current events. This is really an extension of the educational system's civics training. Honest disclosure of events is a tricky business. The first problem is that the media is composed of businesses that compete for an audience and funding from advertisers. Advertisers have biases of their own, and these biases can influence coverage.

In addition, they compete to get the story out first, instead of accurately and thoroughly. The pressure to break a story encourages disinformation that causes confusion. Unfortunately, people usually cling to the first story instead of the best researched.

325 "Lexical Investigations: Happiness," Dictionary.com.

The media as an institution suffers from the second detrimental phenomenon of institutions. It has not adapted properly to changes in technology and demography. Catering to the darker side of human nature is destructive and not supportive of public virtue.

It would be naïve to think that human beings are capable of being unbiased. The fundamental problem is that the predominant news media are centralized in the small enclaves within large population centers like New York City and Washington, DC. When newspapers were the main distribution channel, the system was more evenly distributed. The advent of radio and television shifted the paradigm to central sources, now broadcast 24x7. The nature of these enclaves makes the system inherently prone to a single, progressive view. Because of the role of news dissemination, this progressive view eventually becomes that of society. There is a fine line between information and propaganda. It is a precarious informational model.

The founders' view of the country was one that was both bottom-up and distributed. If we rotate the traditional left-right axis clockwise, the founders would be on the bottom side of the vertical axis. The distributed media during the founders' time emulated the checks and balances in the Constitution. Society was accustomed to divergent views in publications that were analyzed on a personal basis. Analytic discussion has never been free of emotion, and certainly disagreements could become disagreeable, possibly escalating to becoming physical. The main difference today is that the minority view is the one supportive of constitutional principles. This is a direct result of the incongruence of both the educational system and the media to founding principles. As generations have turned, more of the population has become more inculcated in the progressive, anti-constitutional view.

The prime example of the start of the transformation from watchdog journalism to propaganda outlets happened during FDR's administration. Moses Annenberg ran the *Philadelphia Daily News* and other printed media. While many papers were very favorable to FDR, Annenberg's papers were consistently a thorn in his side, always pointing out FDR's overreach of power. FDR retaliated by jailing Annenberg in 1940 for tax evasion, silencing him forever. Saying that FDR's respect for the First Amendment was suspect is an understatement. The IRS was FDR's favorite weapon against political adversaries. He also tried to jail former secretary of the treasury Andrew Carnegie, but Carnegie had his books in order.[326] The media got the message. Add in the National Recovery Administration (NRA) and his court-packing scheme, and FDR's top-tier ranking as a president by the media and academia does not seem to be based on his respect for the Constitution.

A writer is supposedly trained to remove individual bias during the writing process. A casual comment on radio or television, however, can have a subtle but major impact. The media has been inculcated into the progressive movement's philosophy of top-down force by academic institutions. They inherently distrust their fellow citizens to create solutions without the force of the national government behind it (Payne's illusion of government preeminence). Nothing screams the danger more than Thomas Friedman's promotion of "one-party democracy."[327] He promotes the misguided notion that there is a difference between one-party democracy and one-party autocracy. Apparently, he was absent the day Lord Acton's tautology on absolute power was covered. Being a Pulitzer Prize winner at the *New York Times,* he is very influential, and his belief is now prevalent in the halls of government in Washington, DC.[328] Repeated promotion of this attitude programs rather than informs the public.

Online outlets have the potential to restore the checks and balances in the media system that were lost by centralization. Unfortunately, getting these counterviews requires more effort than just pressing

326 Folsom, New Deal or Raw Deal?,. 231–262.

327 Balan, Matthew. "Friedman Again Hails Communist China's 'One-Party Autocracy' as Superior to American Democracy." Media Research Center, August 12, 2014. https://www.mrc.org/articles/friedman-again-hails-communist-chinas-one-party-autocracy-superior-american-democracy.

328 A former roommate of mine who has worked in the State Department for years is infected with this belief. His wife is currently Kamala Harris' national security advisor.

a button on a remote. So, the bulk of the population is still fed the progressive view. What used to be mainstream American views are now countercultural, and "big tech" companies like Facebook, Twitter, and Amazon are not just censoring but blacking out those views. This is what totalitarian regimes do.

Corporations

Companies are the engines of the economy. At birth, they are congruent with society's needs. In a free market, an incongruent company will cease to exist. Of all institutions, corporations are unique in this. The only way an incongruent company can survive is in a market with government intervention—which is the market in the United States today.

Corporations are the institutions that Marxists everywhere love to target the most. Yet, they actually promote a form of neo-Marxism. They are both a proliferator and a by-product of consolidation. Large corporations conspire with regulators to destroy competition from smaller, newer challengers. They provide stability, but they affect the opportunity and liberty of those who would compete if it weren't for regulations designed to prevent them from doing just that. Large corporations can pass the high cost of regulations onto the consumer. They can also use the most incongruent means of all to avoid their own regulations—offshoring.

Starting with the "Trust Buster" Teddy Roosevelt, regulations have been used in an attempt to inhibit the damage from monopoly. "Too big to fail" makes it obvious that this technique has failed to improve on the free market after a century of effort. We might consider that the regulators themselves are incongruent with society's needs. The nature of the problem defies the use of Madison's reasoning in the *Federalist No. 51* argument for a big republic. It really predicts the course of a free market unguided by public virtue. We are left with an oligopoly where there are few competitors that dictate the market instead of reacting to it. Ironically, this is what "too big to fail" means. We are in the same place as before Teddy Roosevelt's reforms. Today's market is antithetical to public virtue. Public virtue may be the sole means to inhibit oligopoly, but we may never know.

The baby boomer generational turn has introduced a new form of injustice into corporations. According to the Census Bureau, (prior to Covid-19), there are about twenty-seven million companies in the United States. Of those, about six million have employees. Approximately eighty million out of the 120 million employees in the United States are employed by less than four thousand of the largest companies.[329] That means that two out of three workers are dependent on a publicly traded firm for a paycheck. Between 1977 and 2005, approximately one million jobs per year have been destroyed by these firms.[330] The natural enmity between rich and poor exposes itself today with the realization that the ratio of CEO pay to employee pay is unjustifiable.[331] Even worse, the lack of accountability among these C-level officers is astounding. They secure golden parachutes before taking control, so subsequent company failure is of little or no consequence to their personal financial states, whereas average workers face abrupt termination of their paychecks.

Just as individual investors in the stock market know to diversify to protect wealth, corporations know to diversify in order to weather ever-changing market conditions. This leads either to a natural, broadened growth or to mergers and acquisitions. Broadening a company's market makes a stronger company that is both more stable and more capable of adapting to market conditions. Mergers and acquisitions in order to broaden lead to layoffs and reduced competition. Consumer prices may benefit from offshoring, but consumption is only one-half of the

---

329 "Statistics of US Business (SUSB)," US Census Bureau, https://www.census.gov/econ/susb/introduction.html.

330 Steve Denning, "The Surprising Truth About Where New Jobs Come From," *Forbes*, October 29, 2014, http://www.forbes.com/sites/stevedenning/2014/10/29/the-surprising-truth-about-where-new-jobs-come-from/#255170047d99.

331 The public narrative on this distorts the picture, but there are valid points on both sides. See Mark J. Perry, "The Great CEO-Worker 'Pay Gap' Is Nothing but a Union-Built Myth," *Investor's Business Daily*, June 10, 2016, accessed July 10, 2016, http://www.investors.com/politics/commentary/the-great-ceo-pay-gap-is-nothing-but-a-union-built-myth/.

economic engine. Production and employment in the United States are reduced by twenty-first-century robber barons—CEOs. Focus on the bottom line has led to real job loss for real people.

Family-held companies' managements turn at about the same speed as society's generations. Publicly held companies turn much faster. The effect of this is analogous to the difference between a republic and a democracy. Democracies respond too quickly to the will (rage) of the people. Republics are designed to slow the process to enable more thought so that the response is more concerned about the good of the people rather than their will. The shift from family ownership to public ownership exposes corporations to a similar phenomenon. Instead of focusing on the long-term health of the company and its employees, executives focus on the short-term bottom line and return on investment for stakeholders (including themselves). The interests of the stakeholders may be congruent with the interests of the company, or they may not. In the past, holding stock in a company was rare.[332] Those who did hold stock predominantly bought and then held the stock. This was the source of stability and congruence. That is not the condition in today's stock market. There is no loyalty between employer and employee. Stakeholders are fair-weather friends to a company, and that introduces instability.

Wall Street is really like a huge casino. The house (consisting of brokers) is the only guaranteed moneymaker. Money is raised for infusing companies with needed funds to grow and prosper. This is a good thing, but it has inherent risk to the investor. Privately held company pension plans provided for stability, because these funds were not Wall Street bets. The workers' and company's interests were aligned (congruent), and the investment was internal. Workers might agree to pay cuts and other drastic measures in a time of crisis to keep the company afloat. The natural deflation of a nonmanipulated currency might actually reward workers by increasing the value of their wages despite the fewer dollars of income. The result of the push for everyone to be in the stock market

---

332 "Historical Timeline: The 1920s," FDIC, https://www.fdic.gov/about/history/timeline/1920s.html, 10 percent in 1920s vs. >50 percent today.

is that people are financially unstable because they do not control their destinies. The cancellation of most pension plans on 1 Jan 2006 was Wall Street's ultimate dream. Virtually all pension money now goes through Wall Street.

Unions

No one should object to employees uniting to provide a check on the interests of the company for which they work. It is the fundamental principle of equal and opposite force. The idea is to promote justice. Like all institutions, unions have a life cycle that is subject to Pournelle's iron law.[333] The problem with unions is that they outlive their usefulness and can become detrimental. Just as corporations can become monopolies, labor can become a monopoly. There are two issues associated with this: industrial unionization and forced unionization.

The Wagner Act of 1935 legalized industrial unionization. Under this act, unions can represent all labor in an entire industry. For example, the Union of Automobile Workers (UAW) represents workers against all US automobile companies, not just a single employer. Like any other monopoly, labor can dictate price and benefits to the companies. Coupled with forced unionization, labor competition is eliminated. Labor strikes can completely cripple an entire industry. Labor unions all but destroyed the American automobile industry. As for the rank and file union members, most have been replaced by automation or offshoring, but the union bosses are very wealthy.[334]

Marx and Engels saw labor unions as the cornerstone of promoting socialism and communism. The progressive movement in the United States has done likewise. It has not been in the best interest of the individual worker, in the long run, to financially feed a persistent union where those at the top profit. Many union bosses have functioned like

---

333 See the chapter 3 on modern tools or "The Iron Law of Bureaucracy," Jerry Pournelle.

334 Luke Rosiak, "Union Bosses' Salaries Put 'Big' in Big Labor," *The Washington Times*, January 10, 2013, http://www.washingtontimes.com/news/2013/jan/10/labor-union-bosses-salaries-put-big-in-big-labor/.

demagogues to get more. Any collective that loses its moral compass (public virtue) creates injustice and instability in the system. Unions have had the power to overvalue labor. The labor market is a part of an adaptive complex system. That system has reacted with offshoring and automation to reduce labor costs. In the end, workers and their families ultimately do not prosper. Likewise, their communities suffer. One need only look at the story of Detroit.

Public Unions

Government is overhead, not a producer. As such, government employees should *serve* the citizens of the country. Unionizing government employees has changed the relationship between government and the citizenry. The average wage for "federal" employees is higher than in the private sector for all equivalent education levels except PhDs.[335] The taxpayers pay the wages, but they are not represented at the table when public unions bargain with the government. Essentially, the government is on both sides of the table.

Unelected government officials create regulations and inflict them on the citizenry with impunity. Couple this with higher wages, and it can be seen that the question of who serves whom has been turned upside down.

Many first-time elected officials go to Washington, DC, to make a difference. They have a desire to "fix" DC. Then, freshmen representatives get hit between the eyes by the reality that the unelected government employees will be there long after they're gone. Enlightenment usually occurs after being confronted directly by one of the unelected officials. So much for DC fixing itself.

Longevity for unelected government employees provides some stability in government, but that's the problem. The government is too stable. Length of employment and benefits for unelected government

335 "Comparing the Compensation of Federal and Private-Sector Employees," CBO, http://www.cbo.gov/sites/default/files/cbofiles/attachments/01-30-FedPay.pdf.

employees need to be restricted to restore the relationship to serving the people instead of the people serving the government. That will not happen as long as public unions exist. Executive Order 10988 established public unions.[336] Rescinding it would be a good start.

Political Parties

The national government of the United States has become the leviathan that the founders feared,[337] but the salient question at hand is if it is incongruent with the American public at large. Recent polls show that the American people believe that it is incongruent, going so far as to consider the government an immediate threat.[338] Given that politicians measure success by the number of laws they pass, it is a reasonable conclusion. As mentioned earlier, more laws lead to less liberty. It is encouraging that almost half the citizens in the United States recognize the threat that the national government poses to their rights. The next question is whether they have the will to do anything about it.

The political system in the United States is, theoretically, a two-party system. Indeed, there are two separate institutions in each of the several states that send money to Washington, DC. Within the DC corridor, there are two progressive teams that compete viciously to win. They do so by fomenting factions all over the country with contrivances (scare tactics) familiar to tyrants throughout history. Once in power, both parties do one thing—move power and money to DC from the states.

The Democrats are at least honest in stating that is what they intend to do. At one time, the Republican Party did honestly try to prevent said dynamic, but that changed after the 1936 election when FDR

---

336 Exec. Order No. 10988. (17 January 1962)

337 Hobbes, *Leviathan*.

338 Frank Newport, "Half in US Continue to Say Gov't Is an Immediate Threat," Gallup, September 21, 2015, http://www.gallup.com/poll/185720/half-continue-say-gov-immediate-threat.aspx.

"Trust in Government," Gallup, http://www.gallup.com/poll/5392/trust-government.aspx.

won a landslide victory.[339] At that point, the national sentiment moved from preserving liberty to promoting progressive agendas. Since then, the Republican Party has degenerated into no more than a different brand of progressivism that speaks of core values but acts differently. Americans have become complacent with the assumption that liberty is assured because, of course, this is the United States.

The only way the national government is going to shrink is to starve it. Until the populace is willing to shut the government down, the leviathan will continue to feed.

Regulatory Agencies

One cannot talk about liberty in the United States without addressing the issue of regulatory law. Likewise, when talking about the enormous size of the national government, one needs to address regulatory agencies since that is where the growth has been. Philip Hamburger advocates small, incremental steps where Congress eliminates a small, insignificant agency first and proceeds incrementally.[340] His hope is that Congress might find out they like shrinking the executive branch. Many of us would prefer the subtlety of an atomic bomb. But we should champion any possible approach to shrink the size of government, and Hamburger's approach is in keeping with the patient optimism of prior generations of Americans. In addition to affecting liberty, the size of government directly correlates to its cost—and taxation.

Regulators are unelected officials, and the agencies are prone to Pournelle's iron law of bureaucracy. Their interests are not congruent with society. A free society wants to regulate itself and put regulators out of a job. Most agencies are under the executive branch. Therefore, the president can reform (reduce) the regulatory agencies that threaten liberty and severely impact commerce and industry. It is questionable

339 Folsom, *New Deal or Raw Deal?*,. 7–10, 42.

340 Philip Hamburger, *Is Administrative Law Unlawful?* (Chicago: University of Chicago Press, 2014), 491.

that such a reformer could get elected with the current mood era within the nation.[341]

Conclusion

Civil society is composed of static and dynamic elements. Institutions are static elements that provide stability. They result from the acceptance of social norms and a need. Social movements are dynamic elements that target social norms. Generational turns are the dynamics that these social movements use to change social norms. Liberty dictates that a new generation should not be held hostage by a prior one. On the other hand, the main goal of the Constitution is protecting liberty. Abandoning the Constitution risks the loss of liberty. Once lost, it is nearly impossible to regain.[342]

Before control of factions can be stabilized, equilibrium must be reestablished. In a general sense, the two political parties today are a facade for a collection of underlying factions that spread injustice, instability, and confusion. All these factions within both parties are the result of one social movement that has spread the six political illusions identified by James Payne—progressivism.

Leuchtenburg reveals that the goals of the progressive movement are diametrically opposed to the Constitution. The Progressive Era occurred while the Missionary Generation was coming of age. Strauss and Howe identify the missionaries as the prophet archetype, just like the baby boomers. It should be no surprise that the mood era of the 1880s would be similar to that of the 1960s. The decimation of the Lost Generation during World War I left the progressive leaders of the Missionary Generation (FDR and Upton Sinclair) in charge for double the usual length of time to solidify progressivism in the American psyche.

341 Charles J. Cooper, "Confronting the Administrative State," *National Affairs*, no. 25 (Fall 2015), accessed July 10, 2016, http://www.nationalaffairs.com/publications/detail/confronting-the-administrative-state.

342 John Adams writes, "But a Constitution of Government once changed from Freedom, can never be restored. Liberty, once lost, is lost forever." John Adams to Abigail Adams, letter, July 7, 1775.

Breaking the cognitive traps of Payne's six political illusions requires awareness. Myers-Briggs testing shows that more of the American public naturally makes decisions based on feeling rather than thinking. This means that the appeal against progressivism must not be made merely based on reason, but it must also have an emotional component. Restoring constitutional equilibrium would require a social movement equal in appeal and force to the progressive movement.

Standing in the way of a counter-movement to progressivism is academia and the press. There is nearly a complete blackout of traditional opinions and supporting facts online and on television. As a result, necessary facts and opinions are not being received by a lot of Americans. Restoring classic Americanism must use techniques like the radical progressive takeover of academia did.[343] But it is essential that honest facts are disseminated instead of squelched.

The wild divergence seen in the 2016 presidential election indicates that there is a pending emotional realignment in the party system. The growing discontent on both sides may signal an opportunity to infuse new thinking into the public discourse.

"We the People" get the government we deserve. Our political discourse today is shallow and biased with the belief of using government to fix all problems (Payne's government preeminence). Our impatience focuses us only on the short term, which reinforces the belief in using government because it can exert the largest force possible. The left-right axis needs to be rotated clockwise ninety degrees to show the true nature of progressivism. The progressives want a big top-down government. Believing a large top-down government will enhance liberty requires all six of Payne's political illusions and a belief that Pournelle's iron law is incorrect.

343 Alinsky has some interesting ideas in *Rules for Radicals*, 1–10.

Part 3

Beyond the Constitution

9

Political Vertigo

Part 2 of this book assumed a strict constructionist approach to the Constitution. Part 3 does not. This part assumes that we continue on our current path of political divergence. That path is based upon the concept of a living Constitution to promote the Hamiltonian active government embraced by the progressive movement. Spin doctors are able to create the political vertigo we experience today because we let them use this device to propagate Payne's political illusions. The Constitution defines a structure of national government *and* behavioral limitations on that government. The concept of a living Constitution ignores the behavioral limitations to augment both the size and power of the national government.

Nations throughout history have not had a written constitution and have survived. The people of these nations endured potentially centuries of unstable governance before their societies finally collapsed. The theory behind a written constitution is to provide stability, avoid confusion, and promote a consistent sense of justice. It attempts to reduce the number and magnitude of phase transitions the complex system of society must endure to survive and to strengthen society against those that do occur. There is no way to prevent phase transitions because of generational turnings. Crises will happen. Education can blunt the mood swings, but it cannot prevent them.

Today's political vertigo is a combination of Madison's mortal diseases of injustice, instability, and confusion and the manifestation of Payne's political illusions. The original sin of slavery injected both injustice and instability into the republic, but society saw the merit of the written Constitution after the Civil War. It appears that today's society is now poised to reject the safeguards provided by the Constitution against

Madison's mortal diseases. The best we can do is assess our social and economic stability. There is no solution to the problems so long as the mood era prevents it. Only a mood era focused on true problem solving can address these problems effectively. Such a mood era requires public virtue as opposed to personal avarice or greed. My hope here is to lay the foundation for an intellectual discussion of the problems facing the nation.

10

Transition or Collapse?

This chapter will explore what scholars have discovered about the collapse of complex societies. Traditional thinking is covered, but preference is given to the modern tools introduced in part 1—in particular, complex systems. We all really have an innate understanding of complex systems. Lincoln's prediction that "a house divided against itself cannot stand"[344] is a reflection of such an understanding. Clearly, the following are true:

- The US is a complex system poised for a phase transition.
- The current turning is analogous to the 1930s.
  - There are big economic problems.
  - The US has internal social crises testing social cohesion.

Empire?

Most Americans go into denial when Europeans accuse the United States of being a modern-day Roman Empire, but there are parallels to consider. Turning our backs on the Constitution is very much like the Roman Republic being superseded by the Roman Empire. Both events are examples of complex-system phase transitions. They are reflections of society's generational turning where the entire value system changes.

The United States has been the dominant economic and military power in the world since the end of World War II. Rome dominated Europe from the Punic Wars until its downfall circa 500 AD. The Roman Republic began around 250 BC. Once Julius Caesar was assassinated in 44 BC, the republic was soon replaced by the Roman Empire. The

344 Abraham Lincoln, "Speech at the Republican State Convention" (speech, Springfield, Illinois, June 16, 1858).

Roman Republic lasted about two hundred years. The Constitution was ratified in 1788, over 225 years ago.

Another similarity to Rome that is often overlooked is immigration. Despite the fact that the Roman Empire grew through a conquest ethic, many people on the border of the empire wanted to *be* citizens of the empire. Throughout most of US history, the immigrants coming to this country wanted to be citizens. Immigration has not slowed, but the intention of those coming to this country now must be questioned. Their intentions will affect phase transitions.

Rome did not collapse after the republic gave way to the empire. As stated in the chapter on foundations, the civil society can change the government at any time. The Romans chose to abandon the republic and submit to an emperor. The empire then dominated the Mediterranean and Europe for approximately five hundred years. The same potential exists for the United States—or does it? There are some disturbing differences.

Collapse?

In looking forward to the future of the United States, we have no choice but to consider the past. Aristotle devotes Book 5 of *Politics* to a study of the subject of why governments collapse and how to prevent it. He considers each of the permutations of society-government pairings in his analysis. In short, his conclusion is that the cornerstone to stability is the sense of justice within society. The implementation of it by the government must be consistent. Any perception of injustice threatens to destabilize the government, which can have a domino effect on society itself. In particular, he highlights corruption and profit from office as root-cause concerns. We enumerated some of his recommendations for stability in the chapter on foundations. If we look at Aristotle's overall position of advocating the golden mean, we see that he really gives advice to keep society away from a critical state. The goal is similar to that of a written constitution. In fact, Aristotle references the benefits of a written constitution a number of times in Books 2 and 3 of *Politics*.

At the time the United States was created, Edward Gibbon was writing *The Decline and Fall of the Roman Empire.* His thesis is that that Roman society gradually lost public virtue. In particular, they outsourced their military defense. Put another way, they had no citizens who cared enough about the empire that they would risk their lives to defend it. The United States does not appear to have this problem; however, immigrants can achieve citizenship through service. This is an excellent program, but we should worry if that program becomes the rule instead of the exception because it would signal that existing citizens have lost their patriotic zeal.

Aristotle largely documents active destruction of government by societies that retained their cohesion and replaced the government. Gibbon observes that Rome basically died out with a whimper. No one cared. The resulting dark ages left European society fractured because nothing filled the vacuum left by the Roman collapse.

There are many more recent writers who have addressed collapse as well. In 2009, Donald Przebowski released *The Rise and Fall of the United States.*[345] He covers the subject at hand more thoroughly than I do here. He and the others all build on Aristotle's observations. Two other modern writers are worthy of special note here.

Igor Panarin

In 1998, Russian political science PhD (and former KGB analyst) Igor Panarin predicted that the United States would break up into six separate countries due to economic degradation, mass immigration, and moral decay.[346] We all sense that the United States is unstable because society itself is so divided on foundational issues. We should always take

345 Przebowski, Donald. The Rise and Fall of the United States: An Interpretation of History. www.xlibris.com: Xlibris, 2009.

346 Andrew Osborn, "As If Things Weren't Bad Enough, Russian Professor Predicts End of US," *The Wall Street Journal*, December 29, 2008, http://www.wsj.com/articles/SB123051100709638419.

an educated foreigner's perceptions seriously. It provides a perspective that is not biased by being an American. Panarin is a Russian, and a degree of his analysis may be wishful thinking. His prediction hasn't come true, but the possibility is still out there.

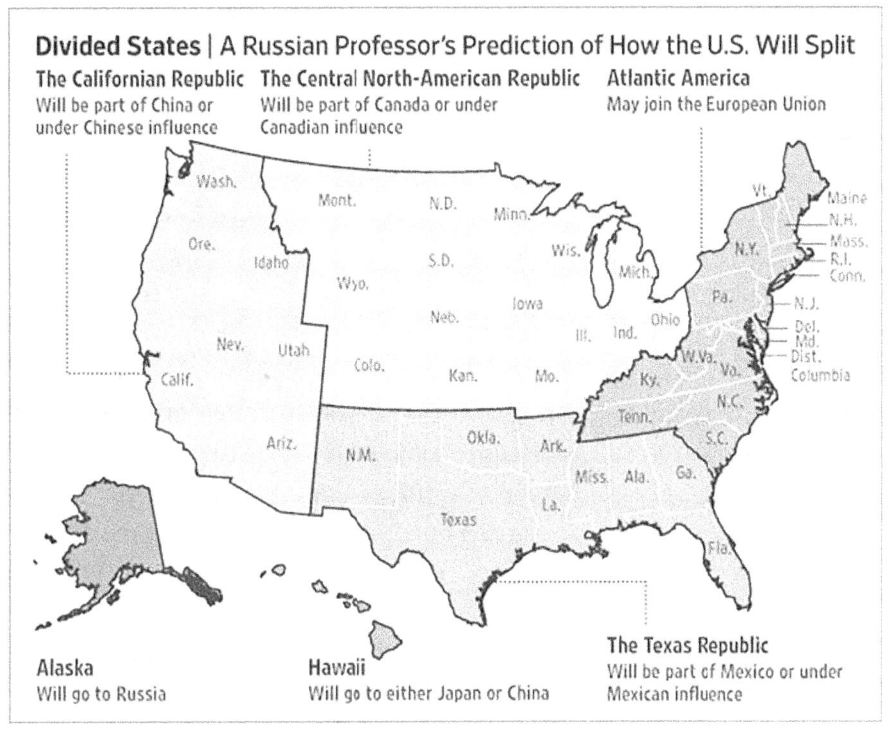

Figure 4 Igor Panarin's Map

Panarin's predictions are speculative and no doubt biased (he predicts Russia will take over Alaska). On the other hand, he correctly sees that the United States is in a critical state and could collapse. His identification of the sources of instability is astute. The economic degradation is obvious the world over. He is not speaking with a religious inclination when he speaks of moral decay. He is referring to an absence of public virtue. What is very interesting is that he sees mass immigration as causing instability. I return to this subject later when I discuss the melting pot.

Joseph Tainter

Joseph Tainter is an anthropologist and historian who applies complexity theory to his disciplines. He published *The Collapse of Complex Societies* in 1988. The book contains an analysis of the collapse of twenty-seven separate cultures over four thousand five hundred years using complexity theory. James Rickards points out how Tainter's use of complexity theory is reinforced by Eric Chaisson's use of it in astrophysics.[347]

Traditional thinking has been that natural disasters (like earthquakes or drought) or invasion cause the collapse of societies. Tainter shows that these very same societies had repelled invasions many times before the collapse. Likewise, societies that were destroyed by natural disasters had rebuilt repeatedly prior to their ultimate collapse. What matters is society's *response*. His conclusion is that societies that are not beaten down rebound from any disaster—man-made or natural.[348] The key is society's resilience. In complexity terms, a state that is subcritical will rebound. One that is supercritical will collapse. What beats society down? Government—via abuse of power and taxation.

Whether society is in a critical state or not reflects the founding principle behind why societies form in the first place. That is, the strength of society depends on the belief that its members hold that they are better off in society. The main contributor to one's perception of that has always been financial. The equivalent of government finance is the economy. A government that oppresses the economy will eventually be purged. Social collapse depends on the resulting vacuum. If society is cohesive, it might merely change the government. In the case of ancient Rome, it eventually lost its cohesion.

Avoiding collapse is really surviving the next phase transition.

---

347 Rickards, *Currency Wars*, 141.
348 Tainter, *Collapse of Complex Societies*, 93–213.

Currency Comparison

A big indicator of a society's stability is the strength of its currency. Debasing the currency is beyond ignoring maintenance of a car. It's like purposely running a car without oil. Yet debtor governments do it for their benefit, not for that of society. It destroys the wealth of the citizens, but it enables repayment with cheaper currency. It's the equivalent of international theft from a lending nation and leads to currency war.

One of the astounding things about the Roman Republic is that the currency retained virtually 100 percent of its initial value for the two hundred years for which we have data. Why Romans chose to abandon the republic after two hundred years and accept the empire is not apparent from looking at its currency value over time. On the other hand, the collapse of society at the end of the empire is very apparent from looking at the value of its currency around 500 AD (year 700 on the x-axis). The denarius started failing in about 350 AD (year 600), but it really started collapsing around the time the Goths sacked Rome in 404 AD (year 654). The empire lasted almost another one hundred years, but it was definitely over by the time the denarius reached less than 10 percent of its original value.[349]

The US dollar shows very different behavior from the denarius. Figure 5 plots the fractional value of each currency from its inception over time. The zero year is 250 BC for Rome and 1800 for the United States. These are the start dates for existing data. A value of 1.0 means the currency is at the same value as it started. A value of 2.0 means it is worth double its original value, and a value of 0.5 means it's worth half. There is cause for Americans to be concerned about the value of the dollar. From 1800 to 1950, the dollar was in great shape. Through most of that time, the value of the dollar was actually better than in 1800. As the chart shows, the dollar has been in trouble since 1975 (year 175). The

349 Data in this chart are taken from two sources. See Tainter, *Collapse of Complex Societies*, 135 and "Consumer Price Index (Estimate) 1800," Federal Reserve Bank of Minneapolis, https://www.minneapolisfed.org/community/teaching-aids/cpi-calculator-information/consumer-price-index-1800.

slope of its decline matches the end of the Roman Empire too closely for comfort. It is worth noting that 1975 correlates with the coming of age of the baby boomer generation. The really scary part of this information is that in 1970 James Lawler predicted the fall of the United States by 2040[350] (year 240). Unfortunately, the graph supports that conclusion.

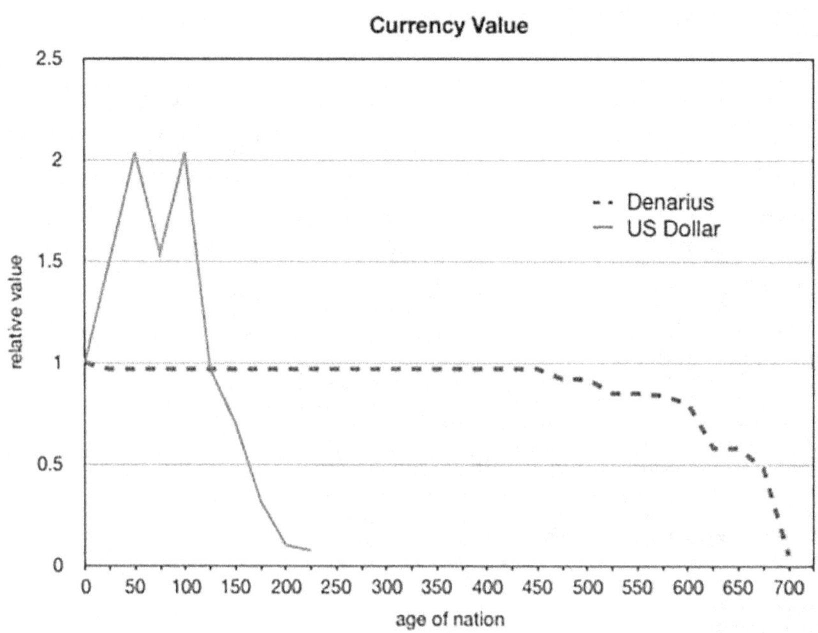

Figure 5 Denarius versus Dollar Chronology

Social Disorder

We can pick any of a multitude of reference points in history to demonstrate our neglect of maintaining society. Remember JFK's famous inauguration speech? JFK said, "Ask not what your country can do for you. Ask what you can do for your country." He spoke those words almost sixty years ago. There have been two complete generational turnings since, and those words do not inspire today as they did then. It

350 Tainter, *Collapse of Complex Societies,* 75. Tainter refers to James H. L. Lawler, *Socio-Mathematics and Cyclic History* (Provo, Utah: J. Grant Stevenson, 1970).

was a clarion call for public virtue. JFK is still idolized, but these words are not internalized by most of those who do idolize him.

Putting oneself first is the opposite of public virtue. Being a burden on society is the opposite of virtue as well. Permissiveness removes the peer pressure during a youth's formative years that encourages one to follow either the golden rule or the golden mean. It also removes the awareness that one becomes happy through selfless rather than selfish deeds ("pursuit of happiness"[351] in the Declaration).

Despite the disdain for founding principles as arcane, most Americans today want a better tomorrow. Almost all still want liberty, but not all are able to see that they can't deprive liberty from others and retain their own. They also refuse to believe that some problems are unsolvable in practice. This leads to the threats to society that are independent of one's attitude towards founding principles.

The three biggest threats to our cohesion as a society today have been enabled by the loss of public virtue. They are relatively new and actually quite counter to what most Americans want in their society:

1. Winning justifies the means.
2. There are way too many people trying to tell all other people how they must live their lives—what they can say and more. There is a belief that government can legislate good behavior.
3. We believe that we can overcome nature. "If a lot didn't work, it must not have been enough money" is driving uncontrolled expenditures. (Payne's materialistic illusion)

Winning with excellence is a virtue, but winning without excellence totally lacks virtue. Competition with fair play is a wonderful thing. It makes us better both as individuals and as a society. Remove fair play, and the situation changes. Opponents become enemies who need to be conquered. Once it becomes common knowledge that cheating or

351 "Lexical Investigations: Happiness," Dictionary.com.

bullying is required to win, everyone cheats and bullies. Society loses its sense of justice. On the opposite side of the coin, once it is more profitable to be a burden to society, everyone becomes a burden. This is the fatal flaw in socialism, but the welfare state is prone to it as well.

The second problem is outright tyranny. This does not end with speech or action. It ends with demanding how someone thinks. These folks are so fixated on one issue going their way that they will give up everything to force their opponents into submitting—because they are enemies. Submission is ensured by putting the issue into law. Such individuals will use government to get their way—and they mean to do it at the national level. They never consider the ramifications of their excess. It is the exact opposite of the golden mean. In order to get their way, they have formed alliances with like-minded parties who have a different pet issue.

The nation was founded on the reality that man cannot control nature. The legal term used to be "act of God." It was an open acknowledgment of our limitations. The root of the fixation problem is a refusal to live with what can't be helped. The original progressive movement held a belief that our technological capabilities could overcome nature. Morgan Robertson took note of this phenomenon and published a book called *Futility, or The Wreck of the Titan* in 1898. Fourteen years before the Titanic disaster, this book predicted it in eerie detail. The name of the mythic ship is the Titan, and there aren't enough lifeboats because the ship is "unsinkable."[352] We now spend uncontrollably to do what is infeasible.

Once again, repeating the introduction, "We the People" are to blame for this mess because we have let demagogues be in charge. We haven't maintained our government—or our society. It has morphed into more of an oligarchy while we've been asleep. Fixation leads to tyranny of the majority, but it also makes us susceptible to the "Big Lie."

---

352 "'The Wreck of the Titan' or 'Futility,'" Morgan Robertson, Titanic-Titanic.com, http://www.titanic-titanic.com/wreck_of_the_titan_1.shtml.

Spin in politics is normal, but the Big Lie is spin on steroids. It is how totalitarians take over societies. Adolph Hitler coined the term (*große Lüge*) in *Mein Kampf* (1925). The idea is to distort the truth so grotesquely that no one dare make the accusation of lying. A process of repetition and rewriting history establishes the lie.[353]

The United States has not reached the point of totalitarianism (or has it?); however, distortions of inflated proportion have given rise to demagogues and destabilizing social movements.

353 Joe Nocera, "The Big Lie," *The New York Times*, December 23, 2011, accessed July 06, 2016, http://www.nytimes.com/2011/12/24/opinion/nocera-the-big-lie.html.

11

Society

Civil society and government have a symbiotic relationship. If society is stable, so is its government. On the other hand, government can destabilize society through poor laws and heavy-handed enforcement.

As mentioned in the chapter on reestablishing equilibrium, Aristotle enumerated five keys to sociopolitical stability in Book 5 of *Politics*:

- Common sense of justice
- Large middle class
- Education system that perpetuates social norms and traditions
- Rotation of office
- Prevention of the enrichment of political officials

The United States has serious problems in all five categories. A common sense of justice does not seem possible without common agreement on the form of government. That agreement cannot be sustained unless the education system supports it. This section of the book acknowledges the failure of the educational system to do that.

Cohesion

The first schism in US politics was, technically, whether to go to war with Britain or not, but it started in earnest when the Constitutional Convention adjourned. Of course, one side supported the new Constitution. The other attacked it. At that time, the attack came from opponents who wanted less centralization than the Constitution defined. They wanted the decentralization of the Articles of Confederation. Fortunately, both sides of the schism could agree that they wanted "life, liberty, and the pursuit of happiness."

Society in 1788

We can visualize the contention between supporters and opponents of the Constitution with the following graph. It is a representation that the founders would recognize. First, the horizontal axis represents support for the Constitution such that the left represents a population that has an affinity for centralized control. The ultimate in centralized control is monarchy. As we proceed to the right, the preference is for decentralization. This represents the continuum of government as Aristotle described.

The vertical line on the left depicts where society's sentiment aligns with the Constitution as it was written. We can assume this because the Constitution was in fact ratified. The vertical line on the right represents the same for the Articles of Confederation. The normal distributions are theoretical representations of the distributions of opponents and supporters of the Constitution, respectively. Opponents are represented by the distribution on the right; supporters are on the left. The dotted line is a theoretical aggregate of the whole society.

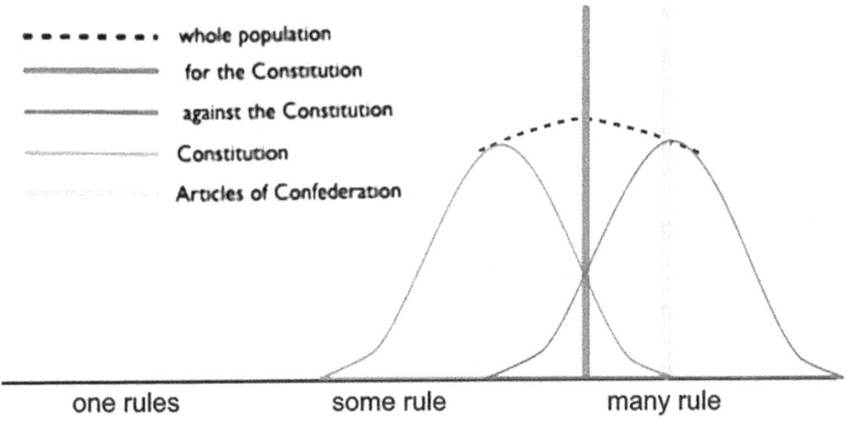

Figure 6 Constitutional Positions 1788

Figure 6 is a very abstract representation of society in 1788. It shows that society was cohesive enough to weather some significant phase transitions. Even more importantly, although there was clear disagreement between the two factions, they were close enough that they both wanted a republic.

A more accurate representation would probably show that the opposition distribution was larger than proponents of the Constitution. The mood era of the country was dominated by a desire for decentralization. 95 percent of the population was rural,[354] and they didn't want a centralized government bothering them. The urban areas were more accepting of a central government, and the Federalists (nationalists) exploited this by using speed to get the Constitution ratified. The distance to travel from rural areas worked against the opponents.[355]

With respect to moderates, the threat of European powers surrounded the nascent country. Spain was in Florida; France was west of the Mississippi; and Britain both was in Canada and had refused to vacate its forts in the western territories.[356] Historians have long puzzled over Madison's apparent switch from nationalist (during *The Federalist Papers*) to decentralist (upon Jefferson's return). If we observe that the threat was real, even a moderate would be concerned about national security. This probably best explains why George Washington gave preference to Hamilton over Jefferson within his cabinet. It also may explain why Madison championed a central government in the first place. In this day of ideology, we forget that an unbiased mind can be won by a solid argument.

Security

The family was extremely strong in the agrarian society of 1788. It provided food, shelter, clothing—not to mention defense. Society universally believed in self-defense. Due to public virtue, the community responded to assist one another, but distance and time dictated self-reliance first.

---

354 "Population: 1790 to 1990," US Census Bureau, accessed July 7, 2016, https://www.census.gov/population/censusdata/table-4.pdf.

355 Smith and McIlroy, *The Federalist Papers*.

356 Ibid.

Justice

Society's concept of justice was consistently based on Anglo-Saxon tradition. Quakers and other sects were pacifists, but they recognized the Anglo-Saxon tradition as well.

Economy

Adam Smith's *Wealth of Nations* dominated the world (and the United States) during the founding period. Envy was replaced with a belief in the *mutual benefit* of Adam Smith's invisible hand.

Civil Society Now

Attacks on the Constitution today are quite the opposite of those in 1788. Those who assail it today want more centralization—more consolidation. The same graph above takes on a very different look with today's society. The opposition distribution is now on the left.

The following graph is for representation only and not to any scale. It depicts a house divided. If the mean approximates the government's match with society, then an oligarchy may be more appropriate than a republic. More importantly, the gap between supporters and opponents visually demonstrates the width of the divide in society. Society itself is unstable. If the government were to collapse, it is unclear whether society would fracture. Panarin's prediction might be more prescient than we wish to believe.

Social cohesion is displaced by a social gap. The graph depicts a society in a critical state. Cohesion could be restored by moving the two distributions closer so that a dotted line could be drawn as in figure 6. Movement to the left represents abandoning the Constitution. Movement to the right would be a recommitment to it. A movement of each toward the other is still a movement away from the Constitution because the mean moves to the left. Where reality lies is speculative, but figure 7 seems about right for 2020.

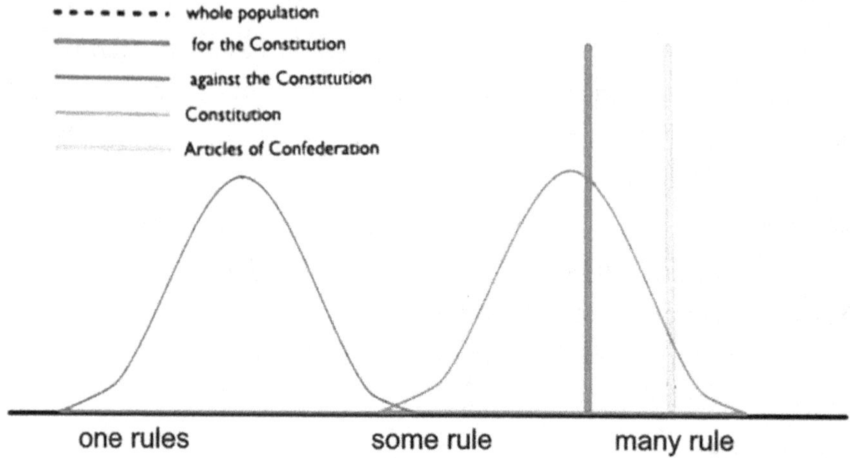

Figure 7 Constitutional Positions 2016

The recommendations in part 2 of this book were intended to move the opposition distribution on the left toward the right. This part of the book ignores that possibility and accepts either of the other two options mentioned above as viable for social stability.

With respect to Strauss-Howe mood eras, crises can reinvigorate public virtue in a heartbeat. No doubt both distributions above pulled to the right sharply after 9/11 in 2001. Unfortunately, this effect was not sustained. The generations old enough to be aware of the crises became disconnected from the threat. Only military families, not all of society as during World War II, shouldered the load of protecting the nation. This mistake allowed society to disengage emotionally from the threat. The academic institutions' disdain for the Constitution solidified the momentum away from it in the next generation. There was no renewed commitment to the Constitution as the anchor to society. The next generation had no clearly defined lessons to support the Constitution.

Security

The same split seen in figure 7 exists with respect to security. Many people today still believe, as the founding generation did, in self-defense first. On the other hand, a large share of the population believes in outsourcing defense. They have a belief that the police will always be able to protect them. In point of fact, response times vary wildly. Each city has its own distribution of response times. In 2008, the average response time by police to a violent crime was 9.1 minutes in New York City. In Denver, it was between 11.4 and 14.3 minutes. Dallas response times averaged eight minutes.[357] A lot can happen in eight minutes.

The term "first responder" is defined in US Homeland Security Presidential Directive, HSPD-8, 2d.[358] Response times of less than fifteen minutes are a testament to the dedication of the police. It would take a *Star Trek* transporter to reduce the response times significantly. In truth, the term in HSPD-8.330 should rightfully be "second responder." The real first responders are the people who are present at the instant a crisis occurs. Those who want to outsource their security are suffering from a cognitive trap that instantaneous response to a crisis is possible. This demonstrates Payne's illusion of government preeminence and the watchful-eye illusion. HSPD-8.330 reinforces the illusions. These are illusions with potentially dire consequences.

Justice

> Rule of Law: The authority and influence of law in society, esp. when viewed as a constraint on individual and institutional behaviour; (hence) the principle whereby all members of a society (including those in government) are considered equally subject to publicly disclosed legal codes and processes.
>
> —*Oxford English Dictionary*

Once again, figure 7 can be used to represent the divide in the country with respect to a sense of justice. This is the most dangerous divide in society. About half the nation still believes in the Anglo-Saxon sense of justice; however, progressivism promotes social justice. These

357 Kara Pendleton, "Here's How Long on Average It Takes for Police to Respond to a 911 Call," Independent Journal Review, http://www.ijreview.com/2016/03/554002-heres-how-long-on-average-it-takes-for-police-to-respond-to-a-911-call/.

358 See glossary for definition or "Homeland Security Presidential Directive / HSPD-8." Homeland Security Presidential Directive / HSPD-8. Accessed July 30, 2016. http://fas.org/irp/offdocs/nspd/hspd-8.html.

two senses of justice are not compatible. Anglo-Saxon tradition is *blind to who* the individual is. This is the key to the principle of the rule of law. On the other hand, social justice is *based on who* is involved. This is counter to the principle of the rule of law. This is a pivotal issue for phase transitioning. Aristotle identifies that loss of confidence in the government's administration of justice as the primary cause of collapse.[359]

Economy

Since the founding generation, two more major theories have been introduced: Marxism and Keynesianism. Smith's free markets and Keynes's general theory differ, but advocates of each have some common ground. Smith's banner has been picked up by the "sweet water school" (for University of Chicago). Keynes's has been labeled the "saltwater school" (for MIT/Harvard). At a minimum, the saltwater school has been responsible for much more government spending than the sweet water school would like.

Despite the fact that Marx has lost credibility in economics, socialism seems to be alive and well. In fact, Bernie Sanders's rise in the United States highlights how divided the nation is. Envy seems to have reappeared and replaced the belief in mutual benefit.

Institutions

The institutions in the chapter on reestablishing equilibrium can be referenced for this section but with a different perspective. It is still correct to weaken the mortal diseases of instability, injustice, and confusion, but the goals are different. The key is eliminating instability. Instead of trying to move society back to the right as depicted in figure 6, the goal here is one of the other two options. That is, either society needs to shift completely left or both sides need to move toward each other. Closing the gap between the distributions in any way pushes society through the pending phase transition. As with all complex systems, the question is whether this can be accomplished without catastrophic collapse.

---

359 Aristotle, *Politics*, Book 5, section 1301b.

Most of the institutions today are a direct reflection of society. There is no real reason to consider any change of direction unless there are compelling problems that threaten stability. Some definitely require maintenance and repair:

- **The family:** This is always the building block of society. The breakdown of the family must be addressed. Most of the chapter on reestablishing equilibrium is applicable, even without consideration for the Constitution. The family must reinforce social norms—whatever they are.
- **Academia:** The results are just too bad to ignore anymore. The problem starts with a lack of discipline.
- **The media:** The biggest concern is sufficient and accurate reporting of external threats. The world is burning, and there is a dearth of coverage of it. There might actually be benefit to less *internal* reporting, as it might stabilize society by refocusing it on the *external* threats.

Government

Government deserves special consideration because it is the ultimate institution of society.

If we look honestly at the US government today, it really is more of an oligarchy than most would admit. The predominance of incumbency is fundamentally the entrenchment of an oligarchy. The founding generation (and Aristotle) promoted the republican principle of rotation of office specifically to prevent incumbency. Political office becoming a family affair is also oligarchic. Aristotle specifically points out that tyranny and oligarchy distrust the multitude. As a result, they both disarm the people.[360] The constant attack on the Second Amendment is also evidence of oligarchy.

At least a part of the system of government proposed by Alexander Hamilton on 18 Jun 1787 has been adopted in recent years. The states have

360 Ibid., Book 5, section 1311a.

been reduced to, basically, administrative entities. The national government regularly bypasses them. Funding goes directly to local entities from the national government, not through the states. The national executive branch dictates policies on college campuses, which are state enterprises. These dictates influence all institutions, including corporate policies. It is all enabled by the collection of "federal" taxes *directly* from "We the People" and the abandonment of the Ninth and Tenth Amendments.

The Party System

The two separate distributions of figure 7 do not represent the two major parties. In fact, the distribution on the left may represent an aggregate from the two major parties. The distribution on the right probably is composed mostly of Independents.

The two major parties are both progressive. They just exhibit different goals for centralization. The Democratic Party is directly derived from the original progressive movement. On the other hand, the Republican Party never was the same after the 1936 election.[361] It has responded according to Newton's third law of physics. It speaks of decentralization but merely promotes different strains of centralization. Whereas the Democratic Party wants to spend without limit on entitlements, the Republicans want to spend without limit on a national military and different centralized solutions.

The distribution on the right of figure 7 may continue to grow as citizens leave both parties. The net result depends upon immigration. Immigration could swell the ranks of either distribution. It depends on the intentions of the immigrants.

It will be interesting to see what happens with the political party system going forward. It appears that realignment has started in 2016. Either or both parties could collapse. We could wind up with just one dominant party. In reality, the parties are dominating the national government. If there is a clear winner, that agenda may dominate. Without an effective check from another party, the whole system may become supercritical quickly.

---

361 Folsom, *New Deal or Raw Deal?*,. 7–10, 42.

12

The Melting Pot
(Versus the Salad Bowl)

The importance of the melting pot has been underemphasized for far too long. It was a part of civics curriculum for years, but it was viewed as more of a novelty than an essential part of social maintenance and preservation. This chapter emphasizes its importance.

The term "melting pot" goes back to 1782. In *Letters from an American Farmer*, John Hector Saint John de Crevecoeur, born in Normandy, France, asks the rhetorical question, "What then is the American, this new man?" He answers his own question. The American

> leaving behind him all his ancient prejudices and manners, receives new ones from the new mode of life he has embraced, the government he obeys, and the new rank he holds. He becomes an American by being received in the broad lap of our great Alma Mater. Here individuals of all nations are *melted into a new race of men*, whose labors and posterity will one day cause great changes in the world.[362] (italics added)

In "The Examination," Alexander Hamilton writes:

> The safety of a republic depends essentially on the energy of a *common national sentiment*; on a uniformity of principles and habits; on the exemption of the citizens from foreign bias, and prejudice; and on that love of country which will almost invariably be found to be closely connected with birth, education, and family.[363] (italics added)

---

362 John Hector St. John, *Letters from an American Farmer*, 1782. Accessed July 30, 2016. http://xroads.virginia.edu/~hyper/crev/home.html.

363 Alexander Hamilton, "The Examination." In *Papers of Alexander Hamilton*, ed. Harold C. Syrett (New York: Columbia University Press, 1961–87), 25: 491–501.

The melting pot model was no accident. The founders realized that civil society could not be sustained without a "common national sentiment." Hamilton, always defensive in nature, writes:

> The United States have already felt the evils of incorporating a large number of foreigners into their national mass; by promoting in different classes different predilections in favor of particular foreign nations, and antipathies against others, it has served very much to divide the community and to distract our councils. It has been often likely to compromise the interests of our own country in favor of another. The permanent effect of such a policy will be, that in times of great public danger there will be always a numerous body of men, of whom there may be just grounds of distrust; the suspicion alone will weaken the strength of the nation, but their force may be actually employed in assisting an invader.[364]

As time progressed, immigrants who left the Old World for the New World wrote home and used the phrase "the land of opportunity" to describe the United States. Through much of the life of the republic, this belief assisted in making the United States a true melting pot because people who immigrated here wanted to be Americans. The process was not pretty, to be sure. Some would cling to their old customs. It is human nature to surround oneself with folks of similar origin. Even in today's mobile society, we just naturally gravitate toward folks from our neck of the woods. It could get ugly in the cities where new immigrants might clash (like in the movie *Gangs of New York*). But the new generations would go to school together, and eventually they became "new men" (and women), Americans. The process was analogous to societal fusion.

True to a complex system, the melting pot was a bottom-up process of spontaneous order, guided by public virtue. Each iteration of immigration broadened the concept of public virtue, which strengthened society. This process created the complex system that became the society of the United States. The key was that immigrants willingly obeyed

364 Alexander Hamilton, *The Complete Works of Alexander Hamilton*, ed. Henry Cabot Lodge (New York: G. P. Putnam's Sons, 1904), 776.

the adage "when in Rome, do as the Romans do."[365] At the same time, the process the Greeks point to—"Rome conquered Greece, and then Greece conquered Rome"—occurred. That is, the best parts of what new immigrants brought were bonded into the new society. A two-way *melting* occurred. Thus, the United States is truly a nation of immigrants, but only because the immigrants wanted to be Americans.

The opposite appears to be true today.[366] When immigrants do not truly want to become Americans, they want to change it—usually to the land they left. This disrupts society's cohesion. New immigrants always clustered into ethnic parts of town, but as generations passed, they blended into society and it just became an opportunity for food diversity.

The use of law has disrupted the melting pot and shifted the process to a top-down salad bowl. Improper laws enable immigrants to stay in their enclaves rather than to melt.[367] The salad-bowl approach will pull society apart from within. It promotes a process of fission. Europe is existing proof in front of our eyes.

We should not care from where immigrants come. We should only care if they want to adopt their new country or if they want to change it—or, worse, conquer it. That means that they must adopt the principles that enable the melting pot. American society has always been changing. The melting pot ensured cohesion. The Europeans have learned the hard way that the salad bowl leads to disunity.

The melting pot is how the United States conquered the world with virtually no blood. The demise of the melting pot will allow the world to conquer the United States—and it won't be as bloodless. The choice is ours as a society.

---

[365] This axiom was first attributed to St. Ambrose. See "When in Rome, Do as the Romans Do," *Wikipedia*, https://en.wiktionary.org/wiki/when_in_Rome,_do_as_the_Romans_do.

366 Kevin OBrien, "Illegal Immigrants Don't Want to Be Americans; They Want Money," Cleveland.com, April 8, 2014, accessed July 07, 2016, http://www.cleveland.com/obrien/index.ssf/2014/04/illegal_immigrants_want_money.html.

367 Ashley Pettus, "End of the Melting Pot?" *Harvard Magazine,* May-June 2007, accessed July 12, 2016, http://harvardmagazine.com/2007/05/end-of-the-melting-pot-html.

13

Rights

This chapter compares and contrasts rights as the founders understood them with those understood by progressives today. Many in the United States today still believe in the founders' concept of rights. The disagreement in these building blocks is a source of the schism within society. An understanding of both sides for the other is a step toward unity.

The founding generation believed in "inalienable, natural rights," as defined by the Age of Enlightenment. Inalienable rights can neither be given nor taken away. They exist whether one is a member of a society or a hermit. A consistent attribute of these rights is that they do not adversely affect another inalienable right for someone else. That is, nothing is taken from anyone in bestowing said rights. There is no injustice. There are two tests that can be applied to determine if a right is inalienable:

1. Does it exist if one is not a member of society?
2. Does it prevent someone else's inalienable right?

FDR's Four Freedoms

FDR's State of the Union speech in 1941 has become known as the Four Freedoms Speech. It laid down the basis for the United Nations' Universal Declaration of Human Rights (UDHR). They are

- freedom of speech,
- freedom of worship,
- freedom from want, and
- freedom from fear.

These are indeed good freedoms to wish for everyone. Does wishing for something establish it as a right? To legitimately categorize something as a right, it should meet some standard. Inalienable rights have a clear standard. What is the standard applied for UDHR? Let's consider each one at a time.

Freedom of Speech

The First Amendment guarantees freedom of speech—without abridgment. John Stuart Mill established the "harm principle" in the nineteenth century. In 1985, Joel Feinberg introduced the "offense principle." Locke's theory of property was clear that the right was based on having no one else's permission. Feinberg requires that the right to speak freely requires the permission of everyone who can or may ever hear it. The logical contradiction is astounding.

This is a clear example of the creeping incrementalism of progressivism in the United States. Mill believed that freedom of expression even to the point of offense was important to push arguments to their logical limits. Feinberg's principle turns this view and that of Locke on their heads. Unfortunately, Mill opens Pandora's box when he states, "The only purpose for which power can be rightfully exercised over any member of a civilized community, against his will, is to prevent harm to others."[368] Predictably, lawyers have twisted and pulled on the definition of "harm" to the point of meaninglessness.

Laws have repeatedly been passed to abridge free speech, despite the First Amendment's ban on abridgment. Limiting free speech because of offense logically leads to total suppression of speech. This is perhaps why there was no right not to be offended in the Constitution.

---

368 "Freedom of Speech," *Stanford Encyclopedia of Philosophy*, April 17, 2008, http://plato.stanford.edu/entries/freedom-speech/.

Inalienable Rights Test

- Does it exist if one is not a member of society? Nature never censors one's speech.
- Does it prevent someone else's inalienable right? No. Speech cannot prevent anyone's rights.[369]

Words do not cause bodily harm. Mill's point really should strengthen the argument for public virtue, where one does not abuse the right. Harm can only result from a word when a complex system within society is at a flashpoint (critical state). Yelling "fire" in a crowded room is only dangerous because the people in the room might panic and react in a disorderly fashion. It is the threat to the right of life that justifies the limitation to liberty. The harm principle really focuses a tradeoff between inalienable rights. There is no inalienable right not to be offended. Feinberg's offense principle is without justifiable basis.

Freedom of Worship

With respect to freedom of worship, the First Amendment guarantees no law prohibiting the free exercise "thereof." Unfortunately, there are a number of people in the United States who can't understand the difference between "thereof" and "therefrom." If we restate it more simply and lose "there," it might be better understood: "Congress shall make no law prohibiting the free exercise of religion."

Inalienable Rights Test

- Does it exist if one is not a member of society? Yes.
- Does it prevent someone else's inalienable right? Not unless human sacrifice is involved.

369 "Sticks and stones will break my bones, but words will never harm me" is traceable at least as far back as 1862.

Freedom from Want

The word "from" is a departure from classic rights. Rather than denoting a positive like "of," "from" is a negative. Likewise, "want" is a subjective term that involves degrees. We can want ice cream more than broccoli. Where do we draw the line where we can say that want is abolished? It seems that any standard for a right should require that it be definable.

It is even more confounding to determine if eliminating want is a good thing. If we don't *want* anything, we have no reason to strive to procure anything. Does this not remove motivation from our being? If there is no motivation, how do we improve the human condition? If want were eliminated, invention would be as well.

According to FDR, this freedom as "translated into world terms, means economic understandings which will secure to every nation a healthy peacetime life for its inhabitants—everywhere in the world."[370] Article XXV of the Universal Declaration of Human Rights (UDHR) declares this freedom as a right. It states:

> (1) Everyone has the right to a standard of living adequate for the health and well-being of himself and his family, including food, clothing, housing and medical care and necessary social services, and the right to security in the event of unemployment, sickness, disability, widowhood, old age or other lack of livelihood in circumstances beyond his control.
> (2) Motherhood and childhood are entitled to special care and assistance. All Children, whether born in or out of wedlock, shall enjoy the same social protection.

---

370 "Franklin D. Roosevelt, The "Four Freedoms" Address to Congress." Franklin D. Roosevelt, The "Four Freedoms" Address to Congress. January 6, 1941. Accessed July 30, 2016. http://www.wwnorton.com/college/history/ralph/workbook/ralprs36b.htm.

Inalienable Rights Test

- Does it exist if one is not a member of society? No. Unless you're a doctor who is somehow out of society, medical care doesn't exist at all. None of the other issues is even applicable outside of society.
- Does it prevent someone else's inalienable right? Possibly. During redistribution, too much can be taken from one to give to another.

There are several problems with Article XXV. First, what exactly does "adequate" mean? Certainly, all people have a right *to pursue* all these things, but do they have a right to them—just for being human? During a time of plenty, we may be able to achieve them by redistribution. During hard times, as much as we might wish, these are not necessarily achievable. The fact that hard times will happen strikes these from the ranks of inalienable rights because they cannot be given during bad times. Likewise, at its most basic, redistribution takes property from some to give to others. If the redistribution is voluntary, as through charity, there is no injustice. The use of governmental force is another issue.

Freedom from Fear

Again, the use of "from" denotes a negative, not a positive. Fear is a basic emotion that triggers a fight or flight response. We have to call into doubt the wisdom of wishing to remove fear itself. It only makes sense to remove the stimuli for fear. The problem then is that the fear reaction to stimuli is dependent on the individual. It is also, like want, a matter of degrees. We can be *more* afraid of snakes than spiders—or vice versa. Some people fear clowns. Again, we have a problem determining how to define a standard for eliminating fear. Actually, eliminating clowns has an appeal.

Article III of UDHR reads as follows:

> Everyone has the right to life, liberty and security of person.

"Security of person" is an interesting right to enumerate. Security is a precipice. No one is absolutely secure in every second of his or her life. No one is ever completely secure. Any worker can be out of a job the next day. Anyone living where poisonous snakes dwell can be fatally bitten in an instant.

Inalienable Rights Test

- Does it exist if one is not a member of society? No.
- Does it prevent someone else's inalienable right? Only if money is taken from someone in this aimless pursuit.

What Is the Standard for a Right?

The Age of Enlightenment established some clear standards for rights as the people understood them. There is nothing wrong with establishing another standard, but whim is not an acceptable standard. At a minimum, a right must be definable and objectively understandable.

Many of the rights enumerated in UHDR are derived from the founding documents of the United States. Several of them are abstracted to an international meaning, where the national laws are simply required to be equally applied. However, many have entered into whimsical territory that can neither be rigorously understood nor enforced. There is no standard that can ensure against fear.

Professor Malham Wakin (USAF Brig Gen retired) was the head of the Philosophy Department at the US Air Force Academy for five decades. He defines a difference between a *human* right and a *civil* right. By his definition, one has a human right just for being born human.[371] They are *unqualified* rights and are synonymous with inalienable rights. On the other hand, one attains a civil right by being a member of a civil society. These rights are *qualified*. Civil society grants them, and civil society can take them away. The *qualified* rights that a civil society can grant are *quantitatively* limited by what society can afford. There is a *social contract* where the member agrees to *responsibilities* in receiving the

371 from personal correspondence with Brig Gen Wakin on 30 Jul 2016. It is also documented in his book. Malham M. Wakin, Integrity First: Reflections of a Military Philosopher. Lanham: Lexington Books, 2000. pg. 34.

right. In general, civil society grants these rights through its institution of government.

The US Citizenship and Immigration Services list both citizenship rights and responsibilities. The rights listed are:

- Freedom to express yourself.
- Freedom to worship as you wish.
- Right to a prompt, fair trial by jury.
- Right to vote in elections for public officials.
- Right to apply for federal employment requiring U.S. citizenship.
- Right to run for elected office.
- Freedom to pursue "life, liberty, and the pursuit of happiness."[372]

The Bill of Rights enumerates the first three rights. The next three are covered by a combination of laws and amendments to the Constitution. The last one is straight out of the Declaration of Independence. According to Dr. Wakin's definition, they are all civil rights, but the last one lists human rights. A distinction that can be drawn between a human right and a civil right is the cost to society. If we look at the list above, the first two rights have no cost. They are enumerated, but are they not both included by the right of liberty? The next four cost society. Trial by jury and the overhead of managing elections are necessary costs to a republic. Imposing justice requires trials that cost, and determining officeholders is not free.

One right that is popular among progressives today is the "right to health care," which is in Article XXV of UHDR. It is absent from US citizenship site. As with most of these new rights, the most confounding problem is to determine the precise meaning. There are degrees of health care. Even worse, for any particular medical issue, there are a number of possible diagnostic techniques and subsequent treatments. Where and how are the lines drawn?

---

372 "Citizenship Rights and Responsibilities." USCIS. Accessed July 31, 2016. https://www.uscis.gov/citizenship/learners/citizenship-rights-and-responsibilities.

If society is to be relied on to grant a right, cost is an unavoidable factor. Cost always includes a moral hazard. With healthcare, *mutual plunder* and the *tragedy of the commons* loom large.[373] From society's perspective, it becomes analogous to determining if it is cost-effective to keep an old car running. Not to be coldhearted, but there are always new models on the way. The problem is that the right to health care sets up a dichotomy between society's interests and those of the individual who claims the right. It is an untenable position. The individual will claim both the *human* right to life and the *civil* right to health. At some point, the *civil* right of health can become too costly and society is forced to withdraw the right. At that point, society may be also withdrawing the *human* right to life by default. The challenge is that society has a responsibility to its citizens that it never overcommits its resources to grant a *civil* right. Doing so can infringe upon *human* rights.

Civil rights are a tricky proposition. There is no question that some civil rights must be granted if civil society is to be civil at all. Overhead functions and promotion of justice are necessary. On the other hand, a civil society that grants rights that it cannot afford invites phase transitions that can lead to systemic collapse. Systemic collapse takes a very real toll on human life. This is a fact that any civil society should consider before granting rights with a moral hazard. There will always be good times, but there will always be bad times as well. The budget must always consider the latter.

---

373 Tom G. Palmer, David T. Beito, David G. Green, Aristides N. Hatzis, Johan Norberg, and Michael Tanner. After the Welfare State: Politicians Stole Your Future—You Can Get It Back. Ottawa, IL: Jameson Books, 2012. pg. 5.

14

The Economy

James Carville hung the phrase "The economy, stupid" in Bill Clinton's 1992 campaign headquarters. Guess who won the election? No political book would be complete without a discussion about the economy. There are three major economic systems:[374]

1. Capitalism (more correctly, free markets)
2. Socialism
3. Keynesianism

The Big Three

Free-market principles are a natural extension of the barter system. Adam Smith establishes the current principles of free markets in *Wealth of Nations*, published in 1776. The French economists, including J. B. Say and Frederic Bastiat, promoted and extended his thinking. After Marx, the Austrian School resurrected Smith's economics around 1870. They were further reinvigorated by marginal utility theory, which addressed the "diamond-water paradox."[375] We know this as something being worth what the market will bear.

The principles of socialism go back to antiquity. Ancient Egypt has been classified as "theocratic socialism."[376] Plato idolized the Spartan form of socialism, leading to his *Republic*. Today's concept of socialism is derived from Marxism. David Ricardo unfortunately paved the way for Marx with his labor theory of value. This theory is that an item's value is based solely on the labor to make it. Later disproven by the

374 Skousen, *Big Three in Economics*, ix.

375 Skousen, *Big Three in Economics*, 108.

376 "Ancient Socialism," Phora, http://www.thephora.net/forum/showthread.php?t=19226.

marginal utility theory,[377] Marx used the labor theory of value to accuse capitalists of stealing their workers' labor. Although Marx's appeal in political circles still has influence, his theories are no longer considered economically credible.[378]

The United States was founded on John Locke's principles of natural rights, which are harmonious with free markets. There doesn't appear to be total consensus on what socialism is precisely; however, state ownership of the means of production is widely accepted as a minimum. It is at odds with Locke's theory. In *The Road to Serfdom*, Hayek warns the world that socialism can only be implemented by totalitarians. History reinforces his thesis with numerous examples like Stalin, Hitler, Pol Pot, and Castro. Modern-day socialists make the argument that capitalism only works better than socialism because we're not good people.[379] They use Adam Smith's famous quote in *Wealth of Nations* that "it is not from the benevolence of the butcher, the brewer, or the baker, that we expect our dinner, but from their regard to their own interest"[380] as a basis for the theory. Jason Brennan takes this argument head-on and demonstrates that even if we were all angels, capitalism would still be superior to socialism.[381] His argument includes a taxonomy of economic systems that is analogous to Aristotle's governmental taxonomy. Public virtue is a pivotal factor.

Keynes's goal was overcoming the business cycle—the ups and downs of the market. His *General Theory* burst onto the scene in 1936 when the Austrian economists had no answers to the Depression. He believes that "full employment" (less than 3 percent) could be achieved with government participation in the economy. The "consumption function" and the "multiplier" are central to his theory. The multiplier states that every dollar injected by the government into the economy

---

377 Skousen, *Big Three in Economics*, 108.

378 Skousen, *Big Three in Economics*, 82–92.

379 G. A. Cohen, *Why Not Socialism?* (Princeton, NJ: Princeton University Press, 2009), 1–10.

380 Adam Smith. The Wealth of Nations. Munich GmbH: Bookrix. pg. 21.

381 Jason Brennan, *Why Not Capitalism?* (New York: Rutledge, 2014), 70–99.

creates multiple dollars. In principle, this means the government can be a producer.

Keynes's theory has been challenged, but it is still popular.[382] Even if one accepts the existence of the multiplier, it must be greater than one, or it actually shrinks the economy.[383] Unfortunately, multipliers greater than one are like unicorns—they've never been seen. As an example, Christina Romer and Jared Bernstein projected a Keynesian multiplier of 1.54 for the stimulus in 2009.[384] A newer calculation on the multiplier from economists at Stanford and Frankfurt shows that it started at 0.96 in 2009. It then fell to 0.67 by the end of 2009 and fell even further to 0.46 by 2010.[385] That means that the stimulus hurt the economy because it actually destroyed wealth.

The Unholy Trinity

Three big players affect the US economy. In truth, the economy would probably be better off without all three. They are

1. The Federal Reserve,
2. The Department of the Treasury, and
3. Wall Street.

Congress has the power to borrow and coin money, but it delegates these powers to the Federal Reserve (Fed). The Fed is actually not a part of the government. It is the third incarnation of a bank of the United States. Unlike the first two, there is no sunset provision on the Fed. The first two banks were both allowed to sunset, and that is exactly what happened—without negative impact. Without a sunset provision, the Fed is burrowed in like a hedgehog. The Fed was formed as the result of the Panic of 1907. The Panic was the result of a *liquidity* problem

382 Skousen, *Big Three in Economics*, 206, 225–226.

383 Rickards, *Currency Wars*, 121.

384 Ibid., 120.

385 John F. Cogan et al., "New Keynesian versus Old Keynesian Government Spending Multipliers" (working paper, National Bureau of Economic Research, March 2009), http://www.nber.org/papers/w14782.

caused by the failure of the Knickerbocker Trust. J. P. Morgan led a team of bankers that organized a private financial rescue.[386] The Fed was formed by the Federal Reserve Act of 1913 to provide financial and monetary stability. Four more competing objectives were added in 1946 and 1978.[387] Simply looking at the decline in the value of the dollar shows how poorly the Fed has performed, but, worse, it even causes the very panics it was designed to stop.[388]

The Treasury and the Fed use treasury bonds and interest rates to either print money or take it out of circulation.[389] The theory behind it is called *monetarism*. Putting too many dollars in circulation for the size of the economy causes an *inflation* of the money supply that *devalues* the dollar. Having too few dollars in circulation increases the value of the dollar but can create a liquidity problem.

The idea behind a stock market is to provide capital investments for private business to start, thrive, and grow. As Peter Schiff points out, it is speculation, not investment.[390] Prior to 1978, when 401(k)s were enacted, speculation on Wall Street was for rich folks. Speculators among the middle class grew from 1978 to 2006, when almost all pension plans in the United States stopped. Now 401(k)s are about the only retirement plan anyone has—if that. This has had a direct impact on employee loyalty. It also has increased the financial risk of everyone in society because retirement is now dependent upon the stock market.

---

386 Rickards, *Currency Wars*, 38.

387 "The Goals of the Federal Reserve," Learning Markets, http://www.learningmarkets.com/the-goals-of-the-federal-reserve/.

388 David John Marotta, "The Purpose of the Federal Reserve," *Forbes*, May 10, 2014, http://www.forbes.com/sites/davidmarotta/2014/05/10/the-purpose-of-the-federal-reserve/#6a0e1f9642ff.

389 "How the Federal Reserve Manages Money Supply," Richard Cloutier, Investopedia, updated March 18, 2016, http://www.investopedia.com/articles/08/fight-recession.asp.

390 Peter Schiff, *Crash Proof* (Hoboken, NJ: John Wiley & Sons, 2012), 98,106.

Currency War

James Rickards has written an outstanding book about twentieth-century economics called *Currency Wars*. The book describes the currency war between the United States and China. The unhappy state in which the United States finds itself is a *solvency* crisis. In short, the government has borrowed so much money that it can never pay it off. Figure 8[391] shows the problem.[392] The upper line on the graph is spending. The bottom blue line shows tax revenues. Notice that tax revenues have been higher than ever, but the spending is outpacing it.

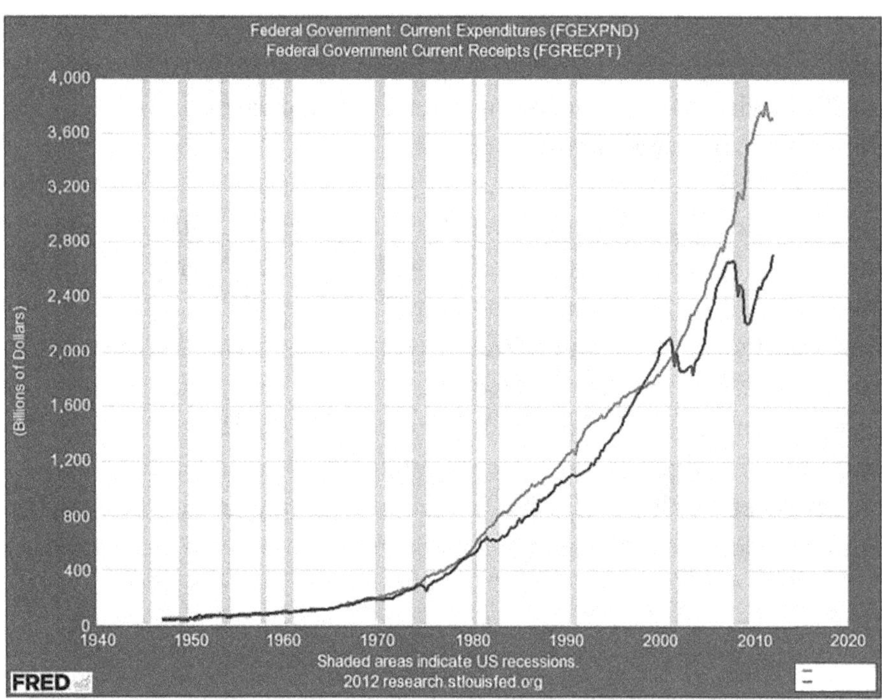

Figure 8 Government Spending versus Revenue

Henry Blodget from *Business Insider* has an article that summarizes the "federal" spending data from a number of "federal" agencies to show

391 Henry Blodget, "And Now for the Truth About the Size of Our Government," *Business Insider*, July 24, 2012, http://www.businessinsider.com/how-big-is-our-government-2012-7?op=1.

392 Rickards, *Currency Wars*, 113–114.

the overall picture of government.[393] Blodget points out some hard realities:

- The actual size of the federal government almost doubled between 1965 and 1970. This is a result of the Great Society. State and local governments have grown with the population (and federal laws), but the federal government has not grown disproportionately since.
- Federal spending has increased radically as a percentage of the economy.
- Spending on social programs is the big problem.
- Social programs consume almost all tax revenues.
- Spending on everything other than social programs has dropped.
- Social Security, Medicare, and Medicaid are the driving factors behind our nation's debt.

The bottom line is that quantitative easing has been a weapon that the Fed has used in the currency war. It is debasing the currency so that it pays debt with devalued dollars.[394] Devaluing the dollar is different from inflation, which is when there are more dollars in circulation than the size of the economy. The United States could devalue the dollar without incurring an inflation problem because it had a *slack* economy.[395] However, by flooding the market with dollars, the Fed forced China to move its peg of yuan to the dollar. They also exported the inflation to the rest of the world. Collateral damage included South Korea, Brazil, Indonesia, Thailand, Vietnam, and many others. You might say that the US government effectively pissed off the rest of the world.

China and Russia are actively trying to undermine the dollar as a reserve currency. China has been reallocating its holding into

---

393 Henry Blodget, "And Now for the Truth About the Size of Our Government," *Business Insider*, July 24, 2012, http://www.businessinsider.com/how-big-is-our-government-2012-7?op=1.

394 Rickards, *Currency Wars*, 9.

395 Note that your grocery bill has gone up a lot, but "there isn't any inflation."

commodities, especially gold. As a result, Japan now holds as much US debt as any other nation. Theories abound as to where the currency war will go next. The United States is not in a particularly strong position.

What It Means to You

Let's review the bidding. Figure 5 shows us that the US dollar has rapidly lost value in the last thirty years. Quantitative easing devalued it even more. This means that you will be paying more for essentials in the future. CPI does not include food or energy, so the increased costs are purposely masked.[396] Rents and mortgages are baked into the CPI cake so that they cancel each other out, which makes inflation look low.[397] Check your grocery bill from a couple of years ago, and compare it to today's.

Figure 8 shows that the government has a huge debt problem that it is trying to solve by devaluing the dollar. A devalued dollar works for the government's interests because it's a debtor. It works against your interests because you have to pay more—for everything. If for no other reason, this shows that the US government is incongruent with society.

Ultimately the government cannot devalue its way out of the debt crisis. At some point, it is going to have to reduce spending. How or if that is done remains to be seen.

Addiction

Drug addiction is not the biggest addiction in the United States. The biggest addiction is to social programs, and the national government is the pusher. De Tocqueville foresaw the modern welfare state in the 1830s. It's not clear that he could have seen the collapse of Western

---

396 Schiff, *Crash Proof*, 33.
397 Ibid.

society that the welfare state is currently threatening, but it upset him deeply.[398] The United States is in a critical state, just waiting for a trivial event to trigger disaster. The United States' way out of its problems would require sound mathematics that don't rely on value at risk.[399] Analysts need to replace normal distributions with the power law before that trivial event inevitably happens.

---

398 de Tocqueville, *Democracy in America*,. 304–308.

399 James Rickards, *Currency Wars: The Making of the Next Global Crisis* (New York: Penguin Group, 2012), 124-125.

15

Elections

I never wanted to delve into this subject, but I now realize that as a mathematician and a computer scientist, I have a moral obligation to present this chapter. The depth to which I have delved into this subject is well outside of the scope of this book; however, some of the high-level findings are of an urgent nature for every American to understand.

Elections are the process by which the people "rule." They are of no importance in systems that are ruled by a monarch or an oligarchy. Out of necessity, they must have integrity for either a republic or democracy. Once again, public virtue is key. In a true republic where a virtuous middle class rules, elections have integrity by definition. No such assumption can be made for a democracy. As the cornerstone of self-governance, the more an election is questioned, the more it injects Madison's mortal diseases of instability and confusion into the system. The more *real* fraud there is, the more injustice is injected into the system. It is a foundational problem that will lead to collapse if it is not fixed.

That is the theory. In practice, it's likely there has never been an election completely devoid of fraud in the history of mankind. The question is whether the amount of fraud overcomes the real difference in the election results. For this reason, close elections almost always lead to the loser crying foul. This has always been true, and it always will. It is just human nature. This leads most of us who are nonpartisan to do a shoulder shrug after each election.

Shrugging our shoulders is dangerous. Each and every one of us need to pay close attention to this issue. As the world's superpower, US elections are the prime target for any bad actor. It is imperative that we understand that ignoring security could lead to election fraud that could trap us all in tyranny.

Integrity

The integrity of an election depends upon its security. The results should be determined solely by legitimate voters. In a perfect world, only legitimate votes would count. In an honest system, the noise of illegitimate voting has no influence on the results.

Election systems are like a chain. They are no stronger than their weakest link. An "attack surface" is a cybersecurity term used to describe all the possible points at which a system can be attacked. It is a term that can be applied in a wider context, such as a military defense—or an election system. The larger the attack surface, the greater the security threat, so the primary defensive focus needs to be on reducing and hardening all the potential attack points. Shortening the chain reduces the attack surface and the number of weak links. As an example of what not to do, unattended ballot drop-off boxes both increase the attack surface and present soft targets for fraud.

Time is another consideration for security. The longer a target is exposed, the greater the odds of it being compromised. That is just as true with elections as it is a Naval ship, an Army unit, or an Air Force jet. Therefore, voting hours should be limited to only the necessary hours to allow all legitimate voters to cast their ballots. Extending an election more than a single day increases the risk of compromising the results.

Ease of Voting

Every qualified voter who wants to vote should be able to vote. For the last couple of decades, voting convenience has been the priority. Every step in this direction has been at the expense of security. The attack surface has grown significantly with electronic voting and mail-in voting. The exposure has likewise been increased by extending voting to multiple days.

There is no question that the conventional Tuesday election day poses challenges to working-class voters. Poll closing times can create problems for voting after work; however, state laws that require employers to let workers go vote are not uncommon. There is also nothing wrong with the proposals that have existed for making election day a holiday.[400]

Activists have been pushing for increasing voter turnout for decades, but consider the realities of this effort. When the Republic was young, voters would travel up to three days to get to a polling station to cast their vote. That is why Tuesday became election day. If a voter took that much time just to get to the polling station, that voter probably had a good idea what he/she was voting for. As voting becomes easier, the probability that a voter is concerned enough to make an informed decision goes down. At a tipping point, uninformed voters determine the election outcome. This can have catastrophic results.

So, where is the tipping point? As a rule of thumb, when the election comes to the unimpeded voter instead of the voter going to the election, things have gone too far. This litmus test alone should eliminate mail-in voting as a practical means of an election with any integrity at all. Of course, there will always be some potential voters who cannot go to the election, but those cases should be the exception, and the process should be initiated by the voter.

Recent Elections

In 2016, the Democratic party screamed bloody murder and subjected the country to a four-year temper tantrum while Donald Trump was in office. In 2020, the shoe wound up on the other foot with the Republicans.

In all honesty, I never had much interest in how elections were managed because I figured competent, honest people were involved. So,

400 Sutter, John D. "Election Day Should Be a Federal Holiday." CNN. Cable News Network, November 12, 2012. https://www.cnn.com/2012/11/12/opinion/ctl-election-holiday/.

I didn't need to be concerned. No one brought forward any damning mathematics as a result of the 2016 election. I figured if there were any, the media would have certainly published it. So, I did the shoulder shrug.

After the 2020 election, several mathematicians did come forward with interesting results that did appear to suggest voting fraud. They were pretty quickly censored by the media and big tech. Then accusations of corruption within voting system vendors appeared. This got my attention.

In 2000, the "hanging chads" in Florida led to efforts to improve voting systems. Two questionable components of these improvements were electronic voting machines (EVMs) and vote by mail (VBM).

EVM Engineering

Rather than retracing the ground that mathematicians had tread, I figured I should take the position of a senior computer scientist. So, I started looking for review artifacts for the electronic voting systems. After being called on to be an expert witness at the Colorado Legislative Audit Committee, I published my report on my blog (dhaugh.com).

Computer system engineering can be divided into two general categories:

1. Commercial
2. Mission-critical

The key difference is how flaws and weaknesses are assessed and handled. Both consider the severity and probability of occurrences. The difference is that commercial systems can accept a low probability of some pretty severe flaws. On the other hand, people can die when a mission-critical system fails. Therefore, a mission critical system cannot accept the occurrence of any severe flaws.

The engineering of our current computerized voting systems leaves a lot to be desired. The software is obviously bloated and does not comply to rudimentary standards of most commercial software systems.

Mission-critical systems, like human flight, have to meet rigorous standards because hundreds of people could potentially die. The results of an election can adversely affect the lives of every citizen (millions). As a result, election systems should be engineered with at least the same care that goes into creating human flight systems like the 787. But they are not even close.

Our election systems are prime targets for anyone wanting to influence election outcomes. Nothing is more tantalizing than a presidential election. Potential bad actors include nation-states with big resources, as well as the internal political parties themselves. Even worse, in a society where public virtue has lost its currency, the likelihood of a bad internal actor within the voting system manufacturer is high. One of the checks on an internal bad actor is to publish thorough review findings. If the inadequacy of the reviews were not dispiriting enough, there is clear evidence that EVMs have been certified despite failing to pass the requirements.[401]

EVM "security"

There is no faster way to perpetuate more fraud than to use an electronic voting system.

In 1999, GNU.FREE set out to create an open-source internet voting system. In 2002, the project was canceled when they realized that it was impossible to build a secure voting system on the Internet.[402] To quote the cybersecurity expert, Bruce Schneier, "a secure Internet voting system is theoretically possible, but it would be the first secure networked application **ever created** in the history of computers."[403]

401 "Source Code Review Dominion Democracy Suite 4.14-A Voting System." verifiedvoting.org. @Sec, n.d. https://verifiedvoting.org/wp-content/uploads/2020/08/democracy-suite.pdf.

402 GNU.FREE - GNU Project - Free Software Foundation (FSF). Accessed April 18, 2021. https://www.gnu.org/software/free/gnufree.html.

403 *Ibid.*

The 2004 presidential election in Ohio led to the *King Lincoln Bronzeville Neighborhood Association v. Blackwell.* The case was brought against the state Secretary of State, Kenneth Blackwell—a Republican. Stephen Spoonamore ran a credit card security company at the time and actually found the "man-in-the-middle" that exploited the voting system. As he points out at 38:30 in his YouTube video, *EVMs pose a problem that is impossible to solve for election integrity—the requirement that votes are anonymous.*[404] The only reason that credit cards can be used as they are is because the credit card company can detect likely fraud when it occurs. They know who has the credit card, where you are, and key habits that you exhibit. There is no such association for an anonymous ballot.

A secure Internet voting system may be theoretically possible, but not when votes need to be anonymous. The assumption that EVMs are not connected to the Internet is faulty. Simple "wardriving" has exposed that many EVMs thought to be off the Net were, in fact, connected. One problem is that the computer systems on which the EVMs are based are configured by default for Internet-friendly ease-of-use.

Then there's the notion that the reporting machines are safe to connect to the Internet. The man-in-the-middle machine that Spoonamore found was between the reporting machine and the destination of the report. It is child's play for a hacker to change the reported results.

These systems require frequent security updates that are not always applied. Thumb drives are the normal way that EVMs are updated, under the assumption that there is no Internet access. There is a reason that thumb drives are forbidden on DoD systems. They are a prime media for malware insertion.

---

404 eon3. "BUSTING the 'Man-in-the-Middle' of Ohio Vote Rigging." YouTube. YouTube, December 17, 2008. https://www.youtube.com/watch?v=BRW3Bh8HQic.

Vote by Mail (VBM)

Even before EVMs get in on the act, there is a question of how a voter submits his/her ballot. This process involves more links in the chain and presents an expanded attack surface that never existed when voters went to polling stations.

With full VBM like in Colorado, ballots are mailed to everyone on the voter roll. The integrity of the voter roll is the main question mark. Any ballot not received by a valid voter is potential fuel for fraud. There are three main ways this happens:

1. A voter moves, but the voter roll is not updated.
2. People die and are not removed.
3. The ballot is intercepted before delivery.

The problem is that VBM suffers a similar anonymity problem to EVMs. There is no way to verify with certainty that the person who returned the ballot is a registered voter. Because we are such a mobile society, it is not unusual for the change of addresses alone to exceed the margin of an election. Likewise, the aging and unhealthiness of the population make it possible for deaths and incapacity to provide sufficient fraud fuel to change an election. Of course, illegally intercepting ballots has unbounded potential for fraud.

It would be possible to reduce the problem by clearing the voter roll at a set date and requiring all voters to register for each election, but this only reduces the exposure. It doesn't fix it.

The only way to fix the problem of VBM is to reduce it to a manageable number of voters who use it. Certainly, deployed military personnel have earned the right to vote absentee. Likewise, we should accommodate the disabled in a reasonable fashion.

Everyone else should vote in person.

Summary

There is no juicier target on earth than US elections. They should be viewed as mission-critical beyond even that of human flight engineering. But current systems don't even deserve a good rating for commercial engineering.

There is no faster way to perpetuate more fraud than to use an electronic voting system.

A voting system is like a chain. It is no stronger than its weakest link. The more links, the larger the attack surface, and the more likely there will be a link that fails. This chapter has only presented a few innovations to the election system that increase the attack surface.

Anything on the Internet is subject to exploitation, and EVMs are no different. Exploitation cannot be prevented; it can only be detected and defused. But it is impossible to detect all forms of fraud when ballots must remain anonymous.

EVMs are the engines that run the voting system, but the ballots are the fuel they use. VBM can produce fraud potential on a scale that can easily overwhelm the typical margin of victory in any election.

Both VBM and EVM have been promoted by county clerks throughout the United States for two main reasons:

1. Cost reductions (fewer polling stations and workers).
2. Faster and more accurate results than hand-counting ballots.

Having an election for multiple days may be convenient, but it elongates the exposure to the attack surface. Additional convenience just invites more "lazy" voters. If a person doesn't see voting as a priority, what are the odds that that person knows what he/she is voting for?

Ignoring the fact that a person with an abacus could probably have resolved the vote counts for the 2020 elections faster, none of these reasons override the biggest requirement of an election—*it needs to reflect the voice of the people accurately.* That will never happen with VBM, EVMs, and multi-day elections.

Conclusion

Anyone can see one aspect of a problem. Our ability to solve a problem is limited only by our ability to gain the appropriate perspective to devise a solution. The best problem solvers have the ability to view a problem from multiple perspectives. It is necessary to differentiate between the cause and the effects. It is not about winning; it is about succeeding. Each of the modern tools presented in this book provides a perspective that can be used to see the problems confronting the United States.

Myers-Briggs testing shows that a supermajority of the population is composed of natural *sensors*. They do not naturally abstract problems or take multiple viewpoints. Sensors must *learn* such behavior. Likewise, more than half the population has a tendency to make decisions based on feeling rather than on thinking. These folks must *learn* to make decisions based on thought. These are two essential ingredients to problem-solving. Since human beings' best tool for survival has always been problem-solving, not physical prowess, nature itself is an excellent behavioral teacher. When the United States was an agrarian society, it was closer to nature, and the people naturally learned these behaviors. As we have become more urbanized, we have become more insulated from nature and more dependent on our educational system in order to learn these behaviors. National test results suggest that the educational system is not doing too well in teaching problem-solving skills. Successful self-governance requires this toolset.

Many recognize the threat to sovereignty posed by the economic problems in our nation. The US Department of Defense has stated that the biggest threat to national security is the national debt.[405] But the debt is an effect, not the cause of our "heaviest misfortunes." Ultimately

405 Tyrone Marshall, "Debt Is Biggest Threat to National Security, Chairman Says," Department of Defense News, September 22, 2011, archive.defense.gov/news/newsarticle.aspx?id=65432.

it is caused by deeper problems. The deeper problem of *cognitive traps* perpetuates spending by the national government well beyond its authority. James Payne's *Six Political Illusions* captures the problem well. Early American generations did not suffer any of these illusions. These illusions were the creation of the progressive movement. Their influence has grown through generational turns where the educational system has failed to teach beneficial behavior, including patience.

The most important tool presented is the simple overview of complex systems. Key to managing these systems is restricting their size in order to limit the effects of collapse. The founders knew that large republics throughout history had failed. They did not have our understanding of modern systems theory; however, they knew the lessons of history. Society must be cohesive, or it will naturally dissolve. Separate societies can be *coupled* into alliances. If the societies are too tightly coupled, however, they can be detrimental to one another rather than beneficial. The founders created a complex system from naturally cohesive states that were loosely coupled by the Articles of Confederation. The Constitution made this coupling tighter between the governments of the states, but the founders had the innate wisdom to keep the coupling loose. The Constitution clearly defines the boundaries of this dual sovereignty. Over the generations, we have unwisely tightened the coupling by ignoring the Constitution, thereby creating more interdependent risk.

James Rickards calls for *descaling* to mitigate the economic dangers to which the nation is exposed.[406] Descaling is reducing the size of a complex system to lessen risk. He also refers to managing risk by not letting any component grow too large.[407] This is advocating loose coupling of smaller complex systems as opposed to a system that is tightly coupled. This is fundamentally what the founders' solution of federalism did with the states. We have increased risk by abandoning federalism.

406 Rickards, *Currency Wars*, 137.
407 Ibid.

Society

Society is a complex system formed by people for the mutual benefits of 1) security, 2) justice, and 3) economy. It creates institutions to support these dynamic elements and to provide stability. American society should be viewed as a complex system that is regularly exposed to phase transitions, which are generational turns.[408] By far the most important institution for stability for any society is its educational system. Its primary role is to keep society from entering a critical state (and subsequent collapse) as the result of a generational turn.

The Educational System

The educational system can be divided into three sections: 1) family upbringing, 2) academic institutional learning, and 3) the press or the media. The family is the only institution created by nature and integral to society. It is a natural responsibility for parents to teach children how to survive and thrive in society. As the cornerstone of learning, the family is the most important educational institution. The media is also a part of the educational system in that its role is to keep a society informed about important events throughout the world.

There appears to be fairly wide agreement that family cohesion has suffered severely in the last quarter of a century. Since it is the cornerstone for society, it must be restored. Far too many children grow up without two parents—which usually starts their education out badly. To a degree, technology presents a number of struggles to parenting, but it can be managed through self-discipline—as all previous generations have done. On the other hand, the national government itself adds to the temptations for bad or absent parenting by its welfare rules. Again, it is personal virtue on the part of parents that leads to public virtue.

Instead of providing a stabilizing influence for generational turns, academic institutions have been doing the opposite for a couple of

408 Strauss and Howe, *Fourth Turning*, 64.

generations now. It is not clear if the damage can be repaired, but these institutions need serious reform.

There are two problems with getting information on current events. First, the information needs to be accurate. Competition among outlets leads to incorrect initial reporting that can end up as persistent misinformation. This reflects the failure of journalism schools to teach proper reporting. Second, there is so much information that the outlets must prioritize the stories. This is where media bias runs rampant. Bias is the result of inadequate education with respect to cause and effect. It is a disservice to everyone (including those reporting) when a report (or lack thereof) masks the dire consequences of corruption or bad decision-making.

The Middle Class

It is common knowledge that the middle class is important to the United States, but why that is proves lesser-known. Aristotle correctly identifies the middle class as being the best because it is prone to neither greed nor envy. As a result, it prevents either the rich (by power) or the poor (by numbers) from overwhelming the other. He concludes that the middle class would rule better than would either of the others.

It is important to take note of Aristotle's definition of the middle class. Today, the government provides statistics and figures to demark the middle class. All of these statistics are meaningless, because what matters is the percentage of people who are greedy or envious, not how much money they make. Debacles like Enron and the 2008 collapse demonstrate that there are many greedy folks among us. The incessant calls for the rich to pay their fair share are even more alarming because they demonstrate a large amount of envy. It isn't one's net worth that matters. It's one's attitude. This attitude can be viewed as personal virtue, which leads to stability, just dealings, and clarity of thought. The people who exhibit these virtues are the true middle class. When their numbers are greater than the greedy and the envious, the people can govern themselves.

Progressivism

The Progressive Era started with good intentions, but we all know what the road to hell is paved with.[409] Progressivism is the belief in using government (force) to effect social change. Every American alive today was inculcated into progressivism by the educational system. This is the antithesis of the goal of liberty. One of the more damaging aspects of progressivism is impatience. Progressives want what they want now—and they don't care whose liberty is abridged to make it happen. Early Americans valued liberty and were patient. One easy metric for seeing the distinction is savings versus spending. Previous generations of Americans saved for a rainy day. Today's Americans are into the instant gratification of spending. The government reflects society.

Institutions

Because of Pournelle's iron law, all institutions change from benefiting society to benefiting themselves. The corollary to Pournelle's iron law is that if society does not manage the institution, the institution will manage society.[410] This is especially true in the case of government. Contrary to Payne's voluntary illusion, government is built upon force.

The progressive movement has addressed institutional reform in its own way. Unfortunately, progressive solutions are always top-down and involve consolidation, centralization, and insertion of the (national) government into issues that should not be under its sovereignty. These are the results of the watchful-eye illusion and the illusion of government preeminence. Consolidation and centralization compound existing problems by creating larger and larger complex systems that risk larger collapse.

---

409 "The Road to Hell Is Paved with Good Intentions," *Wikipedia*, accessed July 08, 2016, https://en.wikipedia.org/wiki/The_road_to_hell_is_paved_with_good_intentions.

410 Fukuyama, "America in Decay."

Government

"We the People" have failed to properly maintain our system of government. The corollary to Pournelle's iron law is that instead of *serving* the people, government *rules* the people. There are a limited number of ways to correct the situation, but society itself is the problem. Traditional voting alone will not fix the national government. Too many citizens want the government to continue on its current path of an ever-growing, complex system. This is a huge problem given that the founders view the people as the *ultimate arbiter*, and the *last remedy* was to be removal of unconstitutional actors by election.

Technological improvements have shifted some of the bedrock on which the Constitution is based. We have not properly examined and derived solutions for this. In this manuscript, I have proposed just a couple of modifications that could improve the situation. First, it should be a felony to move money across state lines for any political reason. Second, the damage that can be done by officials who act outside of their constitutional boundaries has been accelerated by technology. Even if the public were aware that it is their responsibility as the *ultimate arbiter* to remove bad actors via election, waiting two, four, or six years to remove such officials is not effective. More frequent state conventions under a revised Article V might provide a remedy, whether the conventions are periodic or aperiodic. State recalls of national officials is another mechanism to consider.

The failure of the educational system loosens social cohesion. By refusing to enforce borders, the national government is further loosening the cohesion of society. As with the young, immigration can cause mood eras that lead to phase transitions that can put society in a critical state. Therefore, immigrants need to be properly educated to ensure the continuation of social cohesion. Desire of immigrants to bond with society enabled the melting pot to create a cohesive society. The cohesive elements that bind a society are the opposites of Madison's mortal diseases of instability, injustice, and confusion. The national government itself has disabled the melting pot by encouraging the immigration of those who seek to change society to their ways rather than to bond with the existing society.

The national government itself is divided between elected officials and lifetime bureaucrats. No matter who wins public office in an election, that individual has to deal with unelected bureaucrats who know they will outlast the elected official. This is simply why voting will never fix the national government. As things function today, the people have no control over the unelected bureaucracy. The elected officials have less motivation to gut the bureaucracy than they do to coexist with it. The people can change that, but again too many citizens want it to continue on its current path of an ever-growing, complex system. The fundamental problem with reaching these people is that they are prone to decision-making based on feeling rather than thought. Unfortunately, this means they need to experience the realities of an actual collapse like the Great Depression before the risk is internalized.

Political Parties

The national government today is really a reflection of the two dominant political-party agendas rather than of the will of the people. Again, the corollary to Pournelle's iron law applies. Whereas the people have not properly kept the government's power limited, the government has not properly maintained the political parties' boundaries. The interests of the two dominant political parties are overwhelming the interests of the people. Both of these parties have been near collapse in the last couple of decades. The best outcome would be if they both collapsed at once.

Taxation

The confusion during the ratification process of the Sixteenth Amendment was only the start of the confusion created by the current tax code. In addition to the tax code fomenting confusion, it is arguable that it is unjust. If we accept that argument, we have the national government spreading two out of three of Madison's mortal diseases via the tax code. At best, society suffers one out of the three every year in April when taxes are filed.

The Future

For now, the people of the United States can determine the future for generations to come. Alexander Hamilton expounded on his tightly coupled vision of the United States on 18 Jun 1787. The rest of the convention would have none of it. Today's national government is much closer to Hamilton's vision. Even worse, it supports globalization, where organizations like the G20 and the United Nations push for tighter coupling of the world of nations. They are acting in accordance with Pournelle's iron law, for their own benefit rather than for a practical application of complexity theory to benefit the people of the world.

It is possible that the American public may choose a path similar to that of the ancient Romans. The Romans chose to abandon the republic in favor of an empire. By abandoning the Constitution, the United States has headed down a similar path. Unfortunately, the debasement of the dollar is close to the debasement of the denarius at the end of the empire.

The other choice for the American public is to reengage the Constitution and take back control of the national government. In so doing, they would capitalize on the knowledge gained by the experience of all recorded history. Our modern understanding of systems theory clearly reaffirms the wisdom of the founders in loosely coupling the states. Honest assessments of technology's impacts, like the discussion on locality of faction, are worthy of consideration, but the core principles behind the Constitution stand up well against modern theory.

The question is simple. Do you want to be ruled or served? Either path is painful because all the economic and social problems must be addressed regardless. The pursuit of happiness only lies on one of the paths. The other path? Not so much.

Epilogue: Covid-19

Since the first edition of this book, the world has been hit with the Covid-19 pandemic. The pandemic itself did nothing to invalidate any of the content of this book, but it has raised some real concerns about the American society that require scrutiny.

Liberty vs. Security

There is always a tradeoff between liberty and security. How a society responds to security threats is telling about its ability to rule itself. Did the American people accept the risks associated with the pandemic like a free people? There are many reasons for concern that the independent spirit of the American people has been broken. Furthermore, there is reason for grave concern about those in power.

First, consider the people in power. In particular, consider the state governors. Virtually all ordered mask mandates and business closures. All these orders were an affront to individual liberty and did tremendous damage to individuals, families, and the economy at large. Theoretically, the Bill of Rights should have protected the people from the worst of these edicts; however, various "emergency powers" have been written into laws. Governors sent business owners to jail for refusing to close their businesses. People have been detained or removed for not wearing a mask. These events should bring certain constitutional issues that have long been festering to the surface:

- The Constitution is a *limiting, written Constitution.* That means that regular legislation cannot override the Constitution. Since the Bill of Rights is a part of the US Constitution to be enforced down to the local level, many emergency powers written into laws throughout the country are not constitutional and should be removed.

- The power of health departments is oppressive. Health departments are beneficial for advice about health risks, but they should not have the power to shut down businesses by pulling their licenses. This has been the big hammer the governors have used to shut down their states' businesses, and it is more dangerous than the average American knows.

In a republic, it is government's place to advise and assist the people during times of emergency. State health departments have adopted county-level color codes to alert the public to the intensity of the pandemic.[411] This information is appropriate and beneficial, but the government's role is not to dictate behavior beyond guarding against injustice and criminality. The actions of many in government have highlighted that they are enamored with power. They are less concerned with the liberty and pursuit of happiness of the people than their own power. With rare exception, our governments are what Aristotle would call *divergent* (to the interests of the people).

Now, consider the response of the people to the lockdowns, etc. The initial "two weeks to slow the spread" was a sensible goal to keep the hospitals from being overwhelmed. The people were lulled to sleep when the "slow the spread" became suspect, but it still remained policy. This is how tyranny proliferates. Initially, the policy was introduced as a cooperative agreement; then, it became a mandate. A public who understood the history of mankind would have rebelled immediately.

The Past: Distant and Recent

Not learning from history is deadly.

---

411 KRQE News 13 Albuquerque - Santa Fe. "Red, Yellow, Green, Turquoise Dashboard." KRQE News 13 Albuquerque - Santa Fe. KRQE News 13 Albuquerque - Santa Fe, April 14, 2021. https://www.krqe.com/health/coronavirus-resources/map-new-mexico-coronavirus-cases-by-county-zip-code/.

Vera Sharav is a holocaust survivor. She heads an organization called the Alliance for Human Research Protection.[412] She understands that the Nazis were able to commit the atrocities they did because the medical establishment forgot the Hippocratic Oath to "do no harm." As she explains, the Greeks well understood that the power to heal implies the power to kill.[413] Furthermore, she explains how the Nazi system destroyed social norms, divided people, and produced doctors who would kill as well as heal. They could not have achieved it without "the Big Lie." She sees a haunting reenactment of her childhood in the United States today.

There has been so much dishonesty in recording deaths due to Covid-19, it is impossible to know what the real statistics have been. The fact that the government paid hospitals more for Covid-19 deaths alone institutionalized dishonesty.[414] When the CDC stopped tracking regular flu deaths on 4 Apr 2020, how were those deaths attributed? You probably know the answer. Determining cause of death is not as cut and dried as we might think, but it appears in the final analysis that Covid-19 may be little deadlier than a regular flu.

We should have realized that the situation had to stop. At the point where we gained the upper hand on capacity and treatment, guidance to "speed the spread so this disease burns itself out" (while protecting the most vulnerable) would have been wise. There is nothing that can be done forever to keep a virus from spreading, and viruses will kill people. We can't change that, but we can change how we react to it. We chose perceived security over liberty.

---

412 Sharav, Vera, and Government Consigned Israeli Population to be Human Subjects in a Massive Experiment by Vera Sharav | February 1. "Homepage." Alliance for Human Research Protection, April 7, 2021. https://ahrp.org/.

413 "Apr 13 2021 - Vera Sharav & Reiner Fuellmich Webinar." BitChute. Accessed April 30, 2021. https://www.bitchute.com/video/H71mdRDCOQaY/.

414 Morse, Susan. "CMS Adds 20% to Inpatient Medicare Payment for COVID-19 Patients ." Healthcare Finance News. Accessed April 23, 2021. https://www.healthcarefinancenews.com/news/cms-adds-20-inpatient-medicare-payment-covid-19-patients.

What Now?

After more than a year, we still have lockdowns, and we still wear masks. Whether we admit it or not, we are being confronted by a fundamental question: "Are we going to assert our liberty, or are we going to submit to tyranny?" If we are going to assert our liberty, we need to address emergency powers head-on.

Despite the overloading of attribution to Covid-19, there are some reasonable deductions that can be made. This disease is not like the Spanish Flu that targeted people in the prime of life. There are rare exceptions (as there always are), but it targets the elderly and those with chronic diseases (especially diabetes). Although it is a horrible disease, we should consider that it has taught us that a lot of our assumptions about the common cold (also a coronavirus) and regular flus are wrong. Perhaps these diseases *are* communicable *before* we have symptoms. We already know that the regular flu kills between twenty and sixty thousand people in the United States each year. Perhaps our bookkeeping is skewed and the range is narrower or wider. Every characteristic of what we thought we knew about diseases should be reassessed. Regardless, we have always lived with deadly diseases, and we will always have to.

Understanding that disease will always be with us and that pandemics will happen is essential to prevent a total loss of liberty. Americans have lost some of the liberties in past times of crises. As is always the case, much of that liberty never returns. The key is to not give it up in the first place. We should always be on guard against the Big Lie and its ability to empower bad actors in positions of power. The balance between liberty and security is as old as civil society itself. There will always be people among us who will readily choose security over liberty. Those societies who let the fearful choose live in tyranny. Those who don't live free.

Our faith in "experts" has almost become a religion. A large part of this is because we don't have time to research every aspect of our complex system of life. To date, the American public has submitted to the will of "experts." Although health officials are perhaps the prime example in this situation, we need to learn that groupthink tends to dominate any field. "Experts" are those who get the most people to shake their heads in agreement. Consensus is not science, but it is necessary for a religion. We need to break the *tyranny of the experts*.

Since the pandemic, we have seen the abnormal become normal. That is the hallmark of Marxist takeovers like Mao's cultural revolution.[415] Hume's observation that "Seldom is liberty of any kind lost all at once" is being tested.[416]

---

415 "Lily Tang Williams: A Chinese Immigrant's Warning on Critical Race Theory." UnionLeader.com, April 15, 2021. https://www.unionleader.com/opinion/op-eds/lily-tang-williams-a-chinese-immigrant-s-warning-on-critical-race-theory/article_88cc1f5c-a3ae-5c63-b16d-059e34f67d83.html?utm_medium=social&fbclid=IwAR2aT5ayP9v_P_9WjHbXZZB6tuMdXXSQMoUzpWZDICrlngNy2zvWFTezqTw.

416 "David Hume, Of the Liberty of the Press," Founders' Constitution, http://press-pubs.uchicago.edu/founders/documents/amendI_speechs2.html.

Appendix (Franklin's Closing Speech)

As the Constitutional Convention was closing on 17 Sep 1787, Ben Franklin had a prepared speech read by fellow Pennsylvania James Wilson. Franklin was too weak to give the speech himself. It contains a great deal of wisdom and some ominous warnings for us today. The text follows.

Mr. President

I confess that there are several parts of this constitution which I do not at present approve, but I am not sure I shall never approve them: For having lived long, I have experienced many instances of being obliged by better information, or fuller consideration, to change opinions even on important subjects, which I once thought right, but found to be otherwise. It is therefore that the older I grow, the more apt I am to doubt my own judgment, and to pay more respect to the judgment of others. Most men indeed as well as most sects in Religion, think themselves in possession of all truth, and that wherever others differ from them it is so far error. Steele a Protestant in a Dedication tells the Pope, that the only difference between our Churches in their opinions of the certainty of their doctrines is, the Church of Rome is infallible and the Church of England is never in the wrong. But though many private persons think almost as highly of their own infallibility as of that of their sect, few express it so naturally as a certain french lady, who in a dispute with her sister, said "I don't know how it happens, Sister but I meet with no body but myself, that's always in the right — *Il n'y a que moi qui a toujours raison.*"

In these sentiments, Sir, I agree to this Constitution with all its faults, if they are such; because I think a general Government necessary for us, and there is no form of Government but what may be a blessing to the people if well administered, **and believe farther that this is likely to be well administered for a course of years, and can only end in Despotism, as other forms have done before it,**

when the people shall become so corrupted as to need despotic Government, being incapable of any other. I doubt too whether any other Convention we can obtain, may be able to make a better Constitution. For when you assemble a number of men to have the advantage of their joint wisdom, you inevitably assemble with those men, all their prejudices, their passions, their errors of opinion, their local interests, and their selfish views. From such an assembly can a perfect production be expected? It therefore astonishes me, Sir, to find this system approaching so near to perfection as it does; and I think it will astonish our enemies, who are waiting with confidence to hear that our councils are confounded like those of the Builders of Babel; and that our States are on the point of separation, only to meet hereafter for the purpose of cutting one another's throats. Thus I consent, Sir, to this Constitution because I expect no better, and because I am not sure, that it is not the best. The opinions I have had of its errors, I sacrifice to the public good. I have never whispered a syllable of them abroad. Within these walls they were born, and here they shall die. If every one of us in returning to our Constituents were to report the objections he has had to it, and endeavor to gain partizans in support of them, we might prevent its being generally received, and thereby lose all the salutary effects & great advantages resulting naturally in our favor among foreign Nations as well as among ourselves, from our real or apparent unanimity. Much of the strength & efficiency of any Government in procuring and securing happiness to the people, depends, on opinion, on the general opinion of the goodness of the Government, as well as of the wisdom and integrity of its Governors. I hope therefore that for our own sakes as a part of the people, and for the sake of posterity, we shall act heartily and unanimously in recommending this Constitution (if approved by Congress & confirmed by the Conventions) wherever our influence may extend, and turn our future thoughts & endeavors to the means of having it well administred.[417] (bold added)

417 "Speech of Benjamin Franklin - The U.S. Constitution Online - USConstitution.net." Speech of Benjamin Franklin - The U.S. Constitution Online - USConstitution.net. Accessed July 31, 2016. http://www.usconstitution.net/franklin.html.

Glossary

Attack surface	The composite of all points where a defense can be attacked
Cohesion	A bottom-up process whereby like entities bind.
Constructively limited	Limited by inference
Coupling	A top-down process whereby unlike systems are joined
Critical period	John Fiske identified the period between the Revolution and the first constitutional administration (1783-1789) as critical to survival.
Democracy	Direct rule by the people. Rage is unfettered. Aristotle and Polybius used the term differently. The founders used Aristotle's meaning, which is similar to Polybius' ochlocracy.
Dichotomy	A model of two opposing entities, like a tug of war or a teeter totter
ENFJ	The *Teacher.* Warm, empathetic, responsive, and responsible. Highly attuned to the emotions, needs, and motivations of others. Find potential in everyone, want to help others fulfill their potential. May act as catalysts for individual and group growth. Loyal, responsive to praise and criticism. Sociable, facilitate others in a group, and provide inspiring leadership.

ENTJ	The *Field Marshall.* Frank, decisive, assume leadership readily. Quickly see illogical and inefficient procedures and policies, develop and implement comprehensive systems to solve organizational problems. Enjoy long-term planning and goal setting. Usually well informed, well read, enjoy expanding their knowledge and passing it on to others. Forceful in presenting their ideas.
ESTJ	The *Supervisor.* Practical, realistic, matter-of-fact. Decisive, quickly move to implement decisions. Organize projects and people to get things done, focus on getting results in the most efficient way possible. Take care of routine details. Have a clear set of logical standards, systematically follow them and want others to also. Forceful in implementing their plans.
Extraconstitutional forces	All social forces that attempt to remove the limitations in the Constitution. These forces defy Book 5 of Aristotle and promote injustice, instability, and confusion.
Faction	"citizens united and actuated by some common impulse of passion or interest, adverse to the interests of the community" —James Madison
Federalism	Government based upon distribution of power. The true meaning of *federal* is *distributed—not* centralized. Human flight systems are called *federated because* they distribute control to avoid failures of centralized control.

First responder	The term "first responder" refers to those individuals who in the early stages of an incident are responsible for the protection and preservation of life, property, evidence, and the environment, including emergency response providers as defined in section 2 of the Homeland Security Act of 2002 (6 U.S.C. 101), as well as emergency management, public health, clinical care, public works, and other skilled support personnel (such as equipment operators) that provide immediate support services during prevention, response, and recovery operations.
Golden mean	A quantitative measure of virtue. "Nothing too much." "Everything in moderation."
Golden rule	A qualitative measure of virtue. "Do unto others as you would have them do unto you."
Hoplite	ancient Greek heavy infantry man, named after his shield, the *hoplon*
INTP	The *Architect.* Seek to develop logical explanations for everything that interests them. Theoretical and abstract, interested more in ideas than in social interaction. Quiet, contained, flexible, and adaptable. Have unusual ability to focus in depth to solve problems in their area of interest. Skeptical, sometimes critical, always analytical.
Intraconstitutional tensions	The structure and behaviors designed into the Constitution to limit the national government and maintain a stable society.
Judiciary nature	According to John C. Marshall, "A controversy between parties which had taken a shape for judicial decision."[418]

418 " 'Of a Judiciary Nature': Observations on Chief Justice's First Opinions." Review. *Pepperdine Law Review* 34, no. 4 (May 15, 2007): 1032.

Justice	A theoretic condition where there is no injustice. In the course of human events, such a condition is impossible. The best that can be done is to *strive* for eradicating injustice.
Linear	When a functional result produces a straight line. *Nonlinear* is a functional result that produces any but a straight line. Examples of *nonlinear* functions are geometric and exponential functions. Compounded interest is a classic example.
Malinvestments	Ludwig Von Mises term for badly allocated business funds
Manumission	Legal freeing of slaves
MBTI	Myers-Briggs Testing Indicator. The individual personality types referenced in this book are listed independently in this glossary.
Middle class	The segment of society that is neither greedy nor envious. It is not properly defined by income.
Mood era	The timeframe in which a dominant mood holds society.
Mortal diseases	Injustice, instability, and confusion.
Ochlocracy	"Mob rule." A degeneration of democracy, which can always be the result of direct rule.
Phalanx	The tight formation of heavy infantry. In particular, it is a tight rectangular arrangement of ancient Greek hoplites.
Phase transition	A state transition in a complex system. The concern is a transition from stable to unstable.
Pursuit of happiness	"that feeling of self-worth and dignity you acquire by contributing to your community and to its civic life"—Justice Anthony Kennedy
Republic	Indirect rule by the people. The principle is to dampen rage to let reason prevail.
Tall poppy syndrome	a social phenomenon driven by envy whereby the best and brightest of a community are cut down in stature, ostrisized, or killed

The Long Blue Line	The virtual line created by all of the graduating classes of the US Air Force Academy. West Point has *The Long Gray Line.*
The Third Way	A center-left movement attempting to reconcile the left-right political divide.
Turning	The state resulting from the natural turnover of the population due to births and deaths.
Ultimate arbiter	The entity with the power to determine what is and is not constitutional. The framers considered this to be the people of the United States.
Vertigo	A nauseous feeling due to spin.
W3C	World Wide Web Consortium is the main international standards organization for the World Wide Web.

Index

D

E

F

G

H

I

J

K

L

M

N

O

P

R

ἀ

Κ

ὀ

Π

www.ingramcontent.com/pod-product-compliance
Lightning Source LLC
Chambersburg PA
CBHW062208270326
41930CB00009B/1684
9781737252238